Lives in Progress

This book is printed on recycled paper. ♻

Lives in Progress

Case Stories in Early Intervention

by

P.J. McWilliam, Ph.D.
Frank Porter Graham Child Development Center
University of North Carolina at Chapel Hill

with invited contributors

·P A U L·H·
BROOKES
PUBLISHING Cᵒ

Baltimore • London • Toronto • Sydney

Paul H. Brookes Publishing Co.
Post Office Box 10624
Baltimore, Maryland 21285-0624

www.brookespublishing.com

Typeset by Barton Matheson Willse and Worthington, Baltimore, Maryland.
Manufactured in the United States of America by
The Maple Press Company, York, Pennsylvania.

The case stories in this book are based on actual experiences of professionals
working in early intervention. Names, places, and certain aspects of the
situations have been altered to mask the true identities of those whose lives
are described. In some instances, the cases are composites of numerous
real-life situations.

An accompanying manual, *Instructor's Guide for **Lives in Progress***, is available. For
information, contact Paul H. Brookes Publishing Co., P.O. Box 10624, Baltimore,
Maryland, 21285-0624 (1-800-638-3775; www.brookespublishing.com).

Library of Congress Cataloging-in-Publication Data

Lives in progress : case stories in early intervention/ by P.J. McWilliam,
   with contributions from Miki Kersgard . . . et al.
      p.   cm.
   Includes bibliographical references.
   ISBN 1-55766-365-3
   1. Social work with children—United States case studies. 2. Social
case work—United States case studies. I. McWilliam, P.J., 1953– .
II. Kersgard, Miki. III. Title: Case stories in early intervention.
HV741.L56 1999
362.7'0973—dc21   99-31077
                                                              CIP

British Library Cataloguing-in-Publication data are available from the British
Library

Contents

Chapter 1   **Leaving Wisconsin**
P.J. McWilliam 1

Fresh from graduate school, a special education teacher newly transplanted to the South must decide how much to push when the school's speech and occupational therapists resist her ideas for applying recommended practices.

Chapter 2   **A Change of Plans**
Miki Kersgard 9

After a series of misunderstandings, an angry administrator wants to know why an agitated mother has pulled her out of a meeting to discuss an unexpected change in her daughter's school placement—and why no one has answered her questions before this point.

Chapter 3   **Money Matters**
P.J. McWilliam 17

Family finances may force a stay-at-home mom— whose daughter with severe physical disabilities has progressed wonderfully under her care—to return to work, and now the interventionist must develop a new strategy for working with and locating resources for this family.

Chapter 4   **Mother of Two**
Miki Kersgard 25

An interventionist tries to help a young mother and her two small children secure housing in a safe neighborhood while she struggles with her promise to keep the mother's secret about who the children's father is.

positive, to a pediatric clinic and is caught off guard when staff members take her aside to divulge their own concerns about the pair.

An interventionist has suspected for weeks that a young child she visits has autism, but she is afraid that sharing her suspicions will further burden the child's mother, a likely victim of domestic violence.

As a result of a feud with her ex–mother-in-law, a mother enrolls her son in a distant—and less inclusive—preschool, and the interventionist must decide whether to mediate the argument in order to secure a better environment for the child.

When a grandfather permanently removes his grandson from a preschool classroom after he witnesses him cry during a physical therapy session, the teacher tries to find a way to ensure that the boy will receive the intervention he needs.

When money is missing from her desk, a preschool teacher strongly suspects it was taken by the mother of a child in her classroom—a mother who is perpetually late and provides a home life of questionable quality for her daughter.

At the order of the mother, a preschool teacher attempts, usually unsuccessfully, to control the food intake of a child in her classroom with Prader-Willi syndrome; however, the child's resulting temper tantrums make her question the mother's approach.

In planning a young boy's transition from an infant
program to a preschool program, several unexpected
problems cause the child's service coordinator to
question the child's future and the support that his
grandparents will receive after the transition.

During a home visit, an interventionist begins to
question what percentage of a young child's delays
can be attributed to her premature birth and vision
impairment; at the same time, she tries to determine
what to say to the child's mother, who is obviously
expecting some answers.

At a school placement committee meeting, a 5-year-
old's service coordinator encourages the parents to
stand up to the chairperson of the committee—who is
not recommending an inclusive placement—and finds
herself in hot water with her supervisor.

An interventionist who has been providing services to
a family of illegal Mexican immigrants feels
overwhelmed by the family's reliance on her and
wonders why she seems to be the only one trying to
hold the family together.

An interventionist receives a referral from a local
pediatrician for a 9-month-old who has anencephaly;
after working with the family for 3 months, the
interventionist is shocked to discover that the boy's
parents have accepted an institutional placement for
the child.

About the Authors

P.J. McWilliam, Ph.D., is a research investigator at the Frank Porter Graham Child Development Center at the University of North Carolina at Chapel Hill and also directs its child care program. She has served as the director or investigator for a number of grant-funded personnel preparation, model demonstration, and research projects, and she has conducted numerous training events across the United States and Canada. Her recent work has focused primarily on early intervention personnel preparation, with a particular emphasis on the development and evaluation of training strategies to assist others in implementing a family-centered approach to services. Since 1990, much of her effort has been devoted to developing case stories and related instructional materials for use in the case method of instruction and promoting the case method as an alternative or supplement to more traditional methods of personnel preparation. Dr. McWilliam is co-author of two previously published books: *Working Together with Children and Families: Case Studies in Early Intervention* (Brookes Publishing, 1993) and *Practical Strategies for Family-Centered Intervention* (Singular Publishing Group, 1996).

Miki Kersgard was a case writer for the Case Method of Instruction (CMI) Project at the Frank Porter Graham Child Development Center at the University of North Carolina at Chapel Hill. Still working at the Frank Porter Graham Child Development Center, Ms. Kersgard now serves as a graphic designer and writer in the Publications and Dissemination Unit. She is involved in designing training materials and producing a nationally distributed magazine about early childhood development, *Early Developments*, which is sponsored by the National Center for Early Development and Learning. Prior to working at Chapel Hill, she served as an assistant editor for *San Francisco Focus Magazine*.

Wanda B. Hedrick, Ph.D., is currently an assistant professor in the Department of Education at the University of Texas at San Antonio (UTSA), where she teaches undergraduate and graduate courses designed to help practitioners teach children with reading difficulties. Prior to her position at UTSA, Dr. Hedrick worked on the Case Method of Instruction (CMI) Project at the Frank Porter Graham Child Development Center at the University of North Carolina at Chapel Hill, where she gathered case information through field investigation and wrote stories for use in early intervention personnel preparation.

Kathryn Matthews is the mother of three children, including 8-year-old Elizabeth who has Prader-Willi syndrome (PWS). In addition to her full-time responsibilities at home in Doyline, Louisiana, Ms. Matthews is actively involved in Partners in Policymaking in an effort to work with Louisiana state legislators on policies related to people with disabilities. She also provides individual support and assistance to other families in her community who are attempting to advocate on behalf of their young children with disabilities. Ms. Matthews is currently preparing to conduct public awareness activities related to PWS in hope of increasing understanding of the syndrome and reaching out to other families who have children with PWS.

Nancy Frame, B.A., is the teacher for the Parent–Infant Program for Deaf and Hard of Hearing Infants/Toddlers at the Hearing & Speech Center in Yakima, Washington. She has had a rich experience of more than 40 years of teaching and tutoring children and adults who are deaf or hard of hearing. Ms. Frame was also instrumental in establishing the Hearing & Speech Center where she has worked since shortly after it opened in 1971. A burgeoning population of Hispanic families in her community and on her caseload has made her increasingly aware of the need for cultural sensitivity and a family-centered approach to services for infants and toddlers. In addition to her professional credentials, Ms. Frame has four adult children and seven grandchildren.

Introduction

The field of early intervention has undergone tremendous change since the early 1980s. Accumulating research on child development and intervention efficacy, along with changing perspectives about the role of families, the goals of service provision, and the rights of young children with disabilities, has resulted in recommended practices that differ significantly from those of earlier times. These changes should help early interventionists to provide services that are meaningful, effective, and sensitive to the unique characteristics of each child and family that receives the services. The realization of improved services, however, will rely on the ability of individual practitioners to apply recommended practices on a case-by-case and situation-by-situation basis.

The work of an early interventionist can be extremely rewarding, but it is not without its challenges. Every day, home interventionists, therapists, teachers, social workers, health care professionals, and program administrators face situations for which there are no easy answers. Knowledge of recommended practices and specific skill competencies, although important for interventionists, is seldom sufficient for effectively handling the varied and complex situations that these professionals face in their daily work. Interventionists must be able to thoughtfully analyze the unique aspects of each situation that they encounter and arrive at a well-reasoned course of action to follow. Even then, there is rarely a sense of certainty that the decision the interventionist has reached will be the best method for resolving the situation in question.

The Case Method of Instruction

The teaching of problem-solving and decision-making skills is at the very heart of the case method of instruction (CMI). The method was adopted and refined by the Harvard Business School in the mid-1900s, and numerous professions have since incorporated the method into their training agendas to help bridge the gap between theory and practice. In CMI, the instructor or facilitator presents students or trainees with narrative descriptions of situations that practitioners in the students' chosen profession are likely to encounter in their work. These narratives, or case stories, present a dilemma from the point of view of a practitioner or group of practitioners, and, in the end, the situation is left unresolved. As in real life, the situations that are described are complex, with multiple factors. In addition, there is no single obvious solu-

he problem but rather several possible solutions. After the instructor presents each case to the participants, the students or trainees engage in a group discussion of the case situation. A skilled instructor leads the group through the decision-making process, which includes the following:

1. Identifying the problem
2. Analyzing the factors that are contributing to the problem
3. Identifying alternative solutions
4. Choosing among the various options that the participants have identified
5. Developing a course of action to follow in implementing the chosen solution

As instructors who use CMI will affirm, it is the *process* of arriving at a solution rather than the actual solution itself that is of primary importance and benefit to the trainees. In addition to mastering the basic steps of effective problem solving and decision making that students or trainees can then apply to any situation, participation in the *process* teaches them how to listen to the perspectives of others, how to effectively communicate their own views, how to deal with uncertainty, and how their personal values and beliefs contribute to their perspectives of a situation and the decisions that they make.

About the Case Stories

An interventionist who provides home-based services arrives at an inner-city apartment only to discover that the young mother that she was supposed to visit isn't home. Even worse, the mother has left her baby in the charge of a 6-year-old girl. Another interventionist provides home-based services to a family living in a rural trailer park. On one visit, the mother answers the door, and the deep purple bruising on her face suggests that her domineering husband has battered her again. She tells the interventionist that she has fallen; however, the interventionist doesn't believe her and must decide whether to do anything about it. A third interventionist spends the day in an HIV hospital clinic with a teenage mother and her 17-month-old son, both of whom are infected with the virus. The interventionist has tried for months to foster a relationship with the young mother, but the teenager's persistent anger and sullen attitude make it impossible for the interventionist to get through to her. Meanwhile, the clinic staff at the hospital is threatening to have protective services remove the baby from his home. Another case story is about an interventionist who is a teacher in an inclusive preschool. She has been trying very hard to understand and honor the requests of a mother whose 3-year-old daughter has Prader-Willi syndrome, but it isn't always easy. The parents of the other children in the classroom are complaining, other staff members are critical of the mother, and the teacher herself is beginning to question whether the mother's requests are *really* in the best interest of the child. These are a few of the people and situations that you will read about in this collection of case stories that are based on the real-life experiences of early interventionists across the United States. Names, places, and specific circumstances have been altered to preserve confidentiality and to make the stories more suitable for teaching certain content areas. Some of the stories are actually composites of multiple children, families, and professionals who have had similar experiences or from whose stories common themes have emerged.

The stories in this collection address a broad sampling of the types of situations that early interventionists face every day in their work with young children and their families. The children featured in these stories vary in terms of age, gender, type of disability, severity of disability, and the length of time that they have been receiving early intervention services. The characteristics of the childrens' families are also diverse in terms of their ages, socioeconomic status, family structure, and concerns and priorities, as well as in terms of how they respond to professionals. Finally, the stories vary with respect to the type of services that are offered to the families (e.g., classroom-based, home-based, inclusive preschools, clinic) and the types of communities in which these services take place (e.g., urban versus rural, service rich versus service poor, fragmented versus coordinated services). Within these contexts, the case stories address a variety of topics including family-centered practices, service coordination, inclusion, transition, assessment, intervention planning, supervision, and interdisciplinary teaming. As in real life, each case addresses more than one topic or issue. Furthermore, idiosyncratic complications that are described in each story make it virtually impossible to apply "cookbook" solutions to resolve the situations. Rather, each situation challenges readers to sort carefully through the facts of the case and to apply their knowledge from a variety of content areas to arrive at a well–thought-out solution that addresses the unique aspects of the described situation.

Case instructors and facilitators have used the stories in this collection successfully with both students and veteran practitioners across a variety of professional disciplines. Some audiences also have included paraprofessionals and families of young children with disabilities. In fact, many of the stories in this book may best be used with audiences that are composed of individuals from diverse backgrounds in order to obtain a greater variety of perspectives on the situations that are described in the cases. Therefore, many of the case stories are well-suited to interdisciplinary training endeavors. For students, the cases offer up a slice of reality: an opportunity to view real life in early intervention and to grapple with the decisions that interventionists must make and the possible consequences of those decisions within the relatively safe and supportive environment of the classroom. For more seasoned professionals, the case stories provide an opportunity to practice applying new knowledge and skills to the types of situations that they encounter in their daily work and, consequently, to help bridge the gap between theory and practice.

Although individuals may benefit from reading the case stories on their own and contemplating how they might approach each situation, the case stories in this collection are designed primarily for use in CMI, in which a skilled instructor leads the trainees through the process of problem solving and decision making. The case method may also be used in individual mentoring or supervisory situations; however, some of the benefits of group training may be sacrificed, such as the opportunity to hear divergent perspectives on the same situation, to practice communicating one's own viewpoint, and to engage in the type of group decision making that is required for effective teaming in early intervention.

A companion instructor's guide to *Lives in Progress: Case Stories in Early Intervention* is available through Paul H. Brookes Publishing Co. The instructor's guide contains general directions for implementing CMI, guidelines for matching case stories to teaching objectives, specific teaching tips for each case story in this collection, and supplemental case materials for conducting team simulations, role plays, and student assignments.

For the Reader

In order to reap the greatest benefit from the case method, you must fully prepare yourself for the case discussion. This preparation includes carefully reading each case story in advance of the discussion, thoughtfully considering the various factors that may have contributed to the situation and developing potential solutions to the problem. I have provided discussion questions at the end of each case story to help you think through the various issues surrounding the situation prior to the group discussion. In preparing for discussion of a case, I recommend that you first read through the story quickly, then read the discussion questions, and finally read through the story a second time, making notes for yourself related to the issues raised by the questions. While attempting to answer the questions, you might also want to seek out information to help guide your responses or to verify an approach that you have developed for resolving the situation. You may obtain this information through course textbooks or through independent searches at the library or via the Internet.

Active participation in case discussions is important for developing competencies through the case method of instruction (CMI). This may be more challenging for some participants than for others and especially challenging for those participants whose natural tendency is to listen and observe rather than to talk. If you happen to be among those who are by nature more quiet or reserved, use the case discussions as an opportunity to practice communicating your ideas to others. After all, these skills are important in working with both families and other professionals in early intervention. Keep in mind, too, that there are rarely absolute right or wrong answers to the case stories, just as there are rarely absolutes in solving the dilemmas of real life. Your perspective on a case situation may be one that other members of the group have not considered; therefore, the other participants may benefit from what you have to say. If, however, you are among those who are natural born "talkers," sharing your ideas during case discussions may not be a problem at all. Consider yourself lucky. At the same time, consider using group discussions as an opportunity to practice *listening* to the perspectives of others. This may require conscientious self-monitoring to ensure that you don't dominate the discussion as well as use of your people skills to encourage those who are less outspoken to contribute to the discussion. These skills are also important in team work.

If you have not participated in CMI before, you will probably find it very different from your previous learning experiences, perhaps even a little frustrating at the beginning. The role of the instructor in CMI is different from the instructor's role in more conventional approaches to teaching. Instead of feeding information to the audience to ensure that participants come up with the "right" answers to questions, the case method instructor acts as a facilitator. He or she is responsible for assisting the group in finding their *own* answers to the questions that the case stories raise. Therefore, if you are accustomed to looking to the instructor for verification, you may be surprised by the instructor's nonjudgmental stance during case discussions. But hang in there. As you develop more confidence in your own ideas, you will become less dependent on the instructor's approval.

There may also be times when you feel confident about your solution to a situation that is described in a case story. You present your idea to the group, and the other participants wholeheartedly endorse your point of view; however, the instructor continues to ask a seemingly endless number of questions. At such times, the discussion may seem tedious and pointless. But again, hang in there. Remember that the *process* of arriving at a solution is more important in CMI than the actual solution itself. It may seem as though the instructor is fishing for the "right" answer, but in actuality, the instructor is exploring the reasoning that you and the other participants used to arrive at your solution. An exploration of your reasoning may involve going back through any number of steps in the problem-solving process, from the identification of the problem itself, to the assumptions that were made while analyzing the factors that contributed to the problem, to exploring alternative solutions and their relative merits. In order to gain the greatest benefit from the case discussions, it is important that you avoid becoming defensive about your initial solution. Try to be open-minded as you explore the reasoning by which you arrived at your solution, and, at least temporarily, entertain alternative perspectives on the situation. You may be surprised by what happens. Even if you decide to stick with your initial solution, your willingness to back up and take a second look at the situation may result in a new perspective on the situation that you had not previously considered. You may also come away with a better understanding of how your personal values and past experiences can distort your perceptions of a situation and influence the decisions that you make.

Finally, as you read the case stories and struggle to resolve the dilemmas, keep in mind that the situations that are described in the stories are merely snapshots of the lives of these children and their families. Numerous events preceded the situations that are described in each story, and entire lives remain to be lived afterwards. Hence, the collection is entitled *Lives in Progress*. Rarely do early intervention professionals have available to them all of the information that they might need to make fully informed decisions. Interventionists may not know why one parent is so angry all of the time or why another parent resists implementing interventions that a child so desperately needs. Similarly, interventionists may not understand why a professional from another agency is so critical of a particular family or why another professional won't cooperate in joint intervention planning. Even without access to such information, decisions must be made. In doing so, however, professionals need to be fully aware that they don't know all of the factors that may be influencing a situation and, therefore, need to guard against making unverified assumptions.

Just as past events affect current situations, so too will today's decisions affect the future. I, therefore, recommend that, as you select among the various options for resolving the situations, you give ample consideration to the futures of the children and families that are depicted in the case stories. What information, skills, or competencies are these families likely to need, not only to cope with future events but also to feel truly successful and fulfilled? Would any of the options that you have considered be better than others in terms of preparing these children and their families for the future? In making your final decision, however, the needs of the future may have to be balanced against the oftentimes more pressing needs of today. Nevertheless, both are worthy of consideration.

Acknowledgments

The case stories in this collection were developed by the Case Method of Instruction (CMI) Project, a special project grant (No. H024P50015) sponsored by the U.S. Department of Education, Office of Special Education Programs. Numerous preservice and inservice instructors from across the United States served as field-test reviewers for the project. These instructors provided feedback about various aspects of each of the case stories as they were completed and made suggestions about topics that might be addressed by future case stories. Their guidance was invaluable to the success of the project. Special recognition goes to Dr. Patricia Snyder at Louisiana State University Medical Center who, in addition to serving as a field-test reviewer, also assisted the project in training instructors on how to use CMI and collaborated with the project in her research documenting the effectiveness of CMI in early intervention personnel preparation. The project is also indebted to numerous early intervention professionals and programs who told their stories to project staff and allowed us to "ride along" and observe them in action in their daily work with children, families, and other professionals. Further thanks is extended to the families who permitted us brief but poignant exposures to early intervention from another viewpoint. And finally, I personally appreciate the skill, sensitivity, and insight with which my project co-workers, Miki Kersgard and Wanda B. Hedrick, went about their work of gathering case information and translating it into stories.

In loving gratitude to
the Geschwendt sisters who provided
my first lessons about
the power and endurance of stories:
Frieda, Louise, Dorothy, Helen, and Lillian

Lives in Progress

chapter 1

Leaving Wisconsin

P.J. McWilliam

iz sat at her desk in the small office that adjoined the classroom. She slowly leafed through the pages of a child's file while making occasional notes on a pad of paper. Although she appeared to be engrossed in her work, the letters on the pages blurred before her eyes. She couldn't get her mind off the meeting she'd had with Helen Rohe earlier in the afternoon. Her emotions oscillated between anger and depression as she mentally re-enacted their conversation.

Bernice Lewis, known by all as "Bernie," was cleaning the classroom in preparation for the long Labor Day weekend. Bernie hummed a tune as she whisked the last toys off the floor, wiped the tot-sized tables with a damp cloth, and stacked the colorful cube chairs in the corner of the room. She worked like an automaton and was extremely agile for a woman of her size. With the last chair in place, she reached for her big black purse and her *Cosmopolitan* magazine on the shelf above the children's cubbies. Liz had thought the magazine to be most unlikely reading material for Bernie when they first met, and it bothered Liz that Bernie read it in the classroom while the children napped. But it came with her to work every day, as did the green Tupperware tumbler and the vintage Wonder Woman lunchbox she now pulled off the shelf.

Bernie, nearly as wide as she was tall, approached Liz's open door. "Y'all have a nice evening now," she said in her usual cheerful voice. "And don't be wasting your time frettin' over anything that Helen might have said. She's a little scratchy sometimes, but she's good folk deep down." Bernie flashed a smile at Liz, hoisted her black bag onto her shoulder, and started toward the door before Liz had a chance to respond. Then Bernie retraced her steps to Liz's office and added, "Now, I meant it about comin' on over for barbecue on Sunday. I'd like to show off my new boss lady to the family." She smiled again. "And don't be pretendin' that you have a dinner invitation with the governor, 'cause you haven't been here long enough for me to believe a story like that." With a final grin, Bernie turned and left the building. Again, Liz was left speechless.

Liz couldn't get used to Bernie's familiarity. It bothered her that Bernie, a classroom assistant and someone she was supposed to be supervising, acted like her mother. All of Bernie's interactions with Liz seemed to start with "Now honey, . . ." or "Let me tell you, sugar. . . ." Sometimes it was nerve-racking. Liz tried to tell herself that Bernie's way was just a part of the southern culture that she would have to get used to. After all, Bernie seemed to mean no harm by it. Then again, there were times when Bernie seemed to be almost laughing at her or chiding her for taking her job seriously.

What bothered Liz most about Bernie was her ability to read her like a book. What had just transpired was a case in point. Liz had said nothing at all to Bernie about the conversation she'd had with Helen earlier in the afternoon. And, afterward, Liz had calmly gone into her office and busied herself with the children's files. How could Bernie have possibly known she was upset?

Realizing she was getting nowhere on the files, Liz prepared to go home. She filed the folders in the cabinet, put stray papers in the drawer, and straightened the photograph above her desk. The photo was a pastoral scene of Wisconsin in its autumnal splendor. Her fellow graduate students had given it to her as a going-away present last month, saying they hoped it would comfort her whenever she felt homesick for Wisconsin and the change of seasons. She felt homesick now as the long weekend yawned before her without plans. Maybe she would buy curtains for the apartment. She should do something to celebrate her first paycheck.

Liz left the classroom and headed toward the front lobby. Her footsteps echoed through the now-empty hallways. She passed Helen's closed door, and, once again, her mind flooded with the words that had passed between them.

Helen was Liz's immediate supervisor and the principal of the elementary school in which Liz's classroom was located. Helen had, in fact, been one of the people who had interviewed Liz for the position she now held. Liz remembered that, at that time, Helen had seemed particularly excited about her ideas for incorporating the principles of developmentally appropriate practice in the preschool classroom and for providing more opportunities for parent involvement. Liz assumed that Helen had played a significant role in choosing her for the teaching position.

Although Liz had been in her new job for nearly 3 weeks, she had only spoken briefly to Helen when they passed in the hallways. This was understandable—the start of the school year was a busy time for everyone. Besides, Liz rather liked being left on her own. Over time, however, Liz had become increasingly dissatisfied with the lack of cooperation she was getting from Tanya, the speech-language pathologist, and Allen, the occupational therapist, so she'd asked to have a meeting with Helen to clear things up.

Helen had begun the meeting by asking Liz if she was settled in her new apartment, what she thought about the school, whether she had all of the supplies she needed, how she was getting along with her class of six preschoolers, and whether there was anything she could do to help out. Liz took advantage of this last question to open the topic she had come to discuss.

"There is one thing I could use your help with," began Liz.

"And what is that?" asked Helen.

"I'm confused about what to expect from Tanya and Allen. I mean, they're supposed to provide services to the children in my class, aren't they?"

"Haven't they been?" There was a concerned look on Helen's face.

"Yes, but what they are willing to do seems quite limited."

"Limited. . . . What do you mean, limited?"

"Well, you know I've been trying to develop the children's IEPs and. . . ."

"By the way," interrupted Helen, "do you know that they all have to be completed by September 30th?"

"Yes. I found that out last week," said Liz. She immediately regretted the hint of disgruntlement in her voice and hoped that Helen had missed it. "Anyway," she continued, "I've been visiting some of the parents at home to find out if they have any specific concerns or priorities that should be addressed in their children's intervention plans."

"That's an interesting idea," mused Helen aloud.

"Yes. It's part of a family-centered approach to the IEP process," explained Liz. "But Tanya and Allen don't seem to agree with it."

"How's that?"

"The idea, you see, is to use the information provided by the parents to write the goals for the IEP," explained Liz. "Actually, the parents and I go through their child's home and school routines and identify skills they would like to see their child develop in each routine."

"That's certainly an unusual approach."

"Yes. It's quite different from traditional IEP development, but we used it at the university preschool in Wisconsin, and the families loved it."

"So, what about Tanya and Allen?" asked Helen.

"I explained to both of them how I wanted to develop IEPs for the children, and I gave each of them an article that described how a routine-based approach operates. But, when I held our first IEP meeting, I realized that they weren't going to go along with it."

"Why? What happened?"

"Well, the parents and I started off talking about what their goals were for each routine and asking Tanya and Allen for any suggestions they might have on how to accomplish each goal. They went along with the process for the first goal or two, but then they took up their own agendas."

"Their own agendas? What do you mean?"

"They started telling the parents what Sonya—it was her IEP—what Sonya needed to work on and what they were doing with her in therapy sessions," said Liz, scowling.

"Is that so inappropriate?" asked Helen.

"It's just that they wouldn't follow the routine-based goals. Instead of providing functional interventions—practical suggestions for the classroom and the home—they were talking about their individual therapy with Sonya." Liz realized that she was talking louder and faster and tried to regain her composure. She took a deep breath and continued, "Perhaps the thing I found most troubling is that Tanya and Allen were talking about their own goals for Sonya and not addressing the goals that her parents had identified."

Before Helen could respond, Liz handed her the papers she had been holding on her lap. "Tanya even brought this to Sonya's IEP meeting and showed it to her parents." The papers were IEP forms on which Tanya had written out five pages of goals, objectives, and criteria for completion. The first goal read, *Sonya will demonstrate lip closure on initial consonant sounds /p/ and /b/.* The criterion was, *Will demonstrate complete lip closure on 4 out of 5 attempts.*

Helen leafed through the papers, glancing briefly at each page. Then she handed the papers back to Liz, sat back in her chair, and placed her hands in a position of prayer under her chin. "Tanya and Allen are good therapists," she began. "They are well qualified, and they're great with the kids . . . especially the little ones."

"I know they are," said Liz. "I didn't mean to—"

"Liz, I appreciate your wanting to make changes in the preschool program. You have some good ideas. That's why I recommended you for the position, and that's why I'll try to support you. We can really benefit from the specific knowledge and skills you have in early childhood special education. I know we can."

"It's just that in order to—"

"Wait a minute, Liz," interrupted Helen. "You need to understand that you're not in Wisconsin now. This is not a university-based model preschool." She sat forward and leaned her elbows on the desk. "Right or wrong, we have to comply with a lot of bureaucratic regulations that you may never have had to deal with before. For starters, the IEP forms that Tanya completed are in line with the requirements imposed on us by the state auditors. We have to outline well-defined behavioral goals with objective measures of accomplishment. In addition, Tanya may feel a professional obligation to write down what she sees as appropriate goals for Sonya. After all, it is her reputation that's on the line."

"I'm also a little concerned about how far we can go with your family-centered approach," Helen continued. "I believe in the principles, but we have to be careful not to promise parents services we can't offer. You mentioned something about identifying families' goals for their children at home. Well, we're a classroom-based program, and, because we serve 3- to 5-year-olds, the school system is not under the mandates of Part C."

Liz was stunned by Helen's comments. She didn't know what to say. She just stared at Helen in disbelief.

"Liz, please try to understand me," said Helen. "I like your ideas and think you're doing a great job. I wish all of the teachers here were as committed as you are. I'll try to give you as much leeway to implement your ideas as I can. But I also have a responsibility to support Tanya and Allen, and I need to make sure that we're operating within the guidelines of the public school system. Can you understand that?"

"I suppose so," replied Liz in a soft voice.

"I hope so," said Helen. "We can make changes, but we'll have to take it slowly. And I think you'll find that Tanya and Allen are skilled and dedicated professionals. They're really good people when you get to know them. They're also familiar with the singles scene in this town, so perhaps they could show you around."

"You mean they might know something that Bernie doesn't?" Liz joked half-heartedly.

"She's a real hoot, isn't she?" replied Helen with a smile. "But the children love her."

"Yeah, she is quite good with them."

"Now then," said Helen, "let's see if we can't get you your first paycheck. Did you by any chance bring along your time sheet?"

"Yes, here it is," said Liz, handing it over.

Helen looked at it, signed the bottom line, and handed it back to Liz. "I hate to quibble about this," she said, "but I see that your home visits have resulted in quite a few hours of compensatory time. We need to watch out for that. After all, I don't have someone to take over your class when you want to use your comp time."

"Oh, okay," said Liz.

Helen rose from her chair, signifying the end of the meeting. "I hope you enjoy the long weekend. If you don't have plans, there's a music festival and craft fair downtown that you might want to check out."

"Thanks, I might do that," said Liz. Then she left Helen's office and headed across the hall to turn in her time sheet and get her paycheck.

As she left the school building, Liz tried to make herself stop thinking about her meeting with Helen. She tried to focus her thoughts on what she would do this weekend. Maybe she should go to the festival and craft fair. She might find something to dress up her apartment.

The front door of the elementary school locked behind her, and she headed across the circular drive toward the teachers' parking lot. As always, her eyes were drawn to the gnarled cypress tree in the center of the circle. Its webs of Spanish moss swayed in the light breeze coming off the gulf. Although she was usually entranced by the tree, today it held no magic. Instead, Liz longed for the reds and golds that painted the Wisconsin countryside this time of year.

What was she going to do now? Maybe she could work around the obstacles she faced in developing the IEPs, but was there any possibility of integrating speech-language and occupational therapy into the classroom routines? Liz had even hoped that she could eventually talk Helen into including typically developing children in the preschool classroom, but now that seemed most unlikely.

Discussion Questions

1. What factors have or may have contributed to the situation Liz now faces?

2. Aside from staying in Wisconsin, could Liz have done anything differently to avoid or reduce the resistance she has encountered from Tanya, Allen, and Helen? If so, what?

3. Given the present situation, to what extent is the quality of services in the preschool likely to be compromised? How might the children be affected? Their parents?

4. Identify at least three options that Liz has for handling the situation she faces? What strategies could she use to implement her ideas and improve the quality of services to preschoolers?

5. If you were in Liz's position, which of the three options or combination of options would you choose? Why?

6. Based on the option(s) you have selected, what should Liz do on the day she returns to work? What should she do over the next few weeks? The next 6 months?

7. Let's suppose for a moment that Helen Rohe really does agree with Liz's ideas about how to write IEPs. What strategies might Helen use to facilitate their use in the preschool program?

8. Should Liz be concerned about Bernie's style of interacting with her or about Bernie's behavior in the classroom? What, if anything, should Liz do to address the discomfort she sometimes feels around Bernie?

9. To what extent are the issues raised in *Leaving Wisconsin* a function of southern culture? Are there, in fact, regional differences in the quality of services across the United States?

chapter 2

A Change of Plans

Miki Kersgard

Linda Malcolm felt like a walking time bomb. According to her calculations earlier that morning, she was 9 months, 11 days, and 3 hours pregnant. Of course, all this was based on Linda's estimate of when she had conceived, but that was good enough for her. Besides, it gave her something to do in the idle moments she had between appointments. Linda sighed, looked at her watch, and checked her calendar. She decided that she had just enough time before Elvie Bishop and her mother Valerie showed up to sneak away to the mall for another look at that stroller she had her eye on.

Linda pushed back her chair and hoisted herself up from behind her desk. *No sense in rushing,* she thought, fighting the feeling that she would tip over as she got to her feet. For the year and a half that Linda had been providing speech-language therapy to Elvie, Valerie had been late more often than not—that is, when she showed up at all. Linda was thankful for the few times that Valerie had bothered to call to cancel Elvie's appointment. At least then she knew they weren't coming.

At first Linda had tried to include Valerie in her sessions with Elvie, but Valerie seemed to hinder the process more than help it by scolding Elvie and scaring her into what Linda thought at first was just shyness. "Go on!" Valerie would yell. "Tell the lady what that is. Don't pretend you don't know the answer when you do. You do as you're told!" Finally, Linda had asked Valerie to wait with her infant, Mitchell, in the lounge during therapy sessions. Elvie was more responsive to Linda in her mother's absence, but her improved responsiveness only made her other delays more evident. Elvie was sweet and friendly but still spoke very little. Linda wondered whether Elvie was ready for kindergarten and had asked Valerie to think about waiting another year to send her, especially since Elvie's birthday was in the summer and close to the cutoff date. Valerie, however, wouldn't consider it. She insisted that Elvie start school like all the other kids she knew. Elvie's cousin Bethany was going to kindergarten in the fall, and Valerie thought Elvie would feel left out if the cousins couldn't go together.

If only Valerie had enrolled Elvie in the preschool classroom this past year, Linda thought, *she might be better prepared for kindergarten.* Maybe she should have tried harder to convince Valerie that Elvie would benefit from being in the classroom. Linda couldn't help feeling that there must have been *something* more she could have done for Elvie. Then again, why should she blame herself? Elvie hadn't seemed that far behind in anything other than her speech at the time. And it was Valerie who had decided not to enroll Elvie in the preschool class, not her. Regardless of who was to blame, the fact remained that Elvie was making the transition to kindergarten, and the only service she had received during the past year was speech-language therapy from Linda. Unfortunately, even the speech-language therapy had been limited because Valerie and Elvie frequently failed to show up for scheduled appointments.

The options for kindergarten that Linda had discussed with Valerie seemed reasonable enough to Linda. Elvie could go to the school in her neighborhood, Riverside Elementary, but she would probably need some special resource help. Or, she could go to a county-sponsored, self-contained classroom in another elementary school a few miles away. Linda didn't really know much about this classroom but had heard the preschool teachers talk about it in several meetings concerning other children. Valerie had said that she wanted Elvie to go to Riverside, though, because that was where Bethany would be going. The two girls could walk to school together in the mornings.

Linda's growing concerns about Elvie's overall delays had prompted her to suggest that Valerie have Elvie evaluated by the child development clinic at the hospital in Fairmont before school started.

She knew that schools would require more complete assessment information before they could offer Elvie any special services. Linda had tried to make an appointment for Elvie in February, hoping that the assessment information would be helpful in developing some intervention strategies for Elvie this spring and summer. But Linda hadn't known about the clinic's 4-month waiting list. It was already the middle of June, and Elvie's appointment hadn't been scheduled until this week. Linda straightened the calendar pad on her desk, recapped her pen, and picked up her purse from its place on the bookshelf. As she locked the door to her office, Linda wondered if Valerie had ever made it to Elvie's appointment in Fairmont.

Getting to the Bottom of Things

Valerie Bishop slammed on the brakes and managed to keep her daughter Elvie, her infant son Mitchell, and the telephone books she was sitting on from sliding off the front seat of the car.

"Elvie! I told you not to bang on the window! If we break Gramp's car he won't let us borrow it no more." Valerie lifted herself slightly to straighten the telephone books and shifted the car into first gear when the light turned green. "We're going to get this settled once and for all, Elvie, and then you can go to kindergarten. But first we have to find out where."

As the car lurched forward, Elvie looked out of the window and soundlessly smacked her lips open and closed while she watched the wavy reflection of the car in the storefront windows.

When they got to the Center, Valerie looked for Linda Malcolm because she wanted to tell her what the man at the clinic in Fairmont had said. Linda's office was empty, and so was the lounge where Linda sometimes waited for Valerie to show up with Elvie for their appointments.

"Have you seen Mrs. Malcolm?" Valerie asked a woman who was pouring herself a cup of coffee from the pot in the lounge.

"Why, no, I haven't," the woman answered. "For all I know, she could be having that baby of hers this very minute." The woman edged between Elvie and Valerie, who—carrying both her son and a large canvas bag filled with diapers and baby bottles—was taking up most of the doorway. "Why don't you check with Karen at the front desk. Maybe she knows," suggested the woman before she headed down the hall.

Valerie stormed into the reception area and, after depositing Elvie on the floor, slammed her stained canvas bag and a huge ring of keys on the counter in front of Karen.

"I want to see that director lady, Mrs. Anston," said Valerie.

"I'm sorry," said Karen. "Mrs. Anston is in a meeting with the Board of Directors. She really can't be disturbed."

"Elvie! Don't touch that. Leave those things alone!" Elvie swung around to face her mother, knocking the toy she was reaching for, and several others, off the shelf.

"It's okay, Mrs. Bishop. Those toys are there for the children to play with. Do you want me to make an appointment for you with Mrs. Anston for next week?"

"No, I have to see her today. I only have the car today, and I came early so I could find out where to send Elvie to school. The doctor at the hospital said she wasn't ready to go to Riverside and to see about changing schools."

"Did he say why he thought Elvie shouldn't go to Riverside?" asked Karen.

Elvie had picked up one of the puzzle boxes and was trying to push a piece back into the hole it had come out of, but she couldn't figure out that she had to turn the piece around in order to do it. She patiently struggled to fit the wrong end of the block into the hole over and over again.

"He said Elvie's speech wasn't good enough and that she couldn't play with the other children. If I don't find out where she's going, how do I find out how to get her there? The doctor said she has to go to a special school and that I had to come here to make arrangements for her to get taken there."

"Well, I'm sure Mrs. Malcolm will be able to straighten all of this out for you at your appointment later."

Valerie switched Mitchell from one hip to the other and gave him a set of plastic keys to replace the real ones he'd been playing with. She glared at Karen as though she were about to lose the last ounce of patience she had. "No she can't! She's not here. The lady upstairs told me she was having her baby."

Karen looked at the sign-out sheet to see if Linda had indicated that she had left for the hospital. "She's not here on the sign-out sheet. Maybe she was in too much of a hurry. I'll check with her husband." Karen flipped through the Rolodex and dialed the number. "Mr. Malcolm, please." Karen looked up and gave a tug at Mitchell's leg while she was put on hold. The baby giggled, but Valerie just sighed and straightened out her blouse, which had gotten twisted from holding the squirming infant. "Mr. Malcolm? This is Karen at the Center. Has Linda checked into the hospital to have her baby?" She paused for an answer. "Oh, okay. Would you call back and let me know?"

Karen looked up to tell Valerie that Mr. Malcolm was going to call Linda's obstetrician and that he would call back to let them know if Linda had checked into the hospital. But instead of waiting, Valerie had gathered up the keys, the canvas bag, and her two children and was on her way out of the reception area.

"Mrs. Bishop!" Karen called out, but Valerie kept moving through the double doors that swung out into the hallway. The woman working at the photocopier behind Karen's desk looked at Karen, fanned the air in front of herself, and wrinkled her nose. The smell of stale cigarette smoke and body odor lingered in the office.

Going Straight to the Top

"Excuse me," said Valerie. "Could you tell me which way the conference room is?"

Mr. Gillwray, the janitor, looked up from the blocked vent he was working on and waved his wrench to the left. "Down this hall 'bout a hundred feet . . . can't miss it. It's the one with the fancy glass doors."

Valerie walked down the hallway and peered through the glass doors that spanned half the length of the conference room. She spotted Mrs. Anston just as the people sitting around the table got up and started walking toward a large buffet set up at one end of the room. Valerie tapped on the glass door with one of the keys from the huge ring, which Mitchell had resumed chewing on. When a man came to the door, she asked, "Please, could you send out Mrs. Anston? It's an emergency."

Mrs. Anston stepped up to the doorway to meet a disheveled and frustrated Valerie. "Mrs. Bishop. I'm sorry I don't have much time to talk. As you can see, I'm in a meeting," said Mrs. Anston as she led Valerie over to the couch across the hall from the conference room.

"I know. Karen told me."

Valerie proceeded to explain that Linda Malcolm was having her baby and that no one had been there to see Elvie for her appointment. Her words tumbled out in a torrent, barely leaving her enough time to take a breath, her face reddening with each problem she presented. She told Mrs. Anston about Elvie's evaluation earlier in the week and the unexpected change in Elvie's school placement. She then told Mrs. Anston that she wanted to know which school Elvie would be going to when she started kindergarten, and she wanted to know today.

With each explanation, Mrs. Anston's jaws clenched a little tighter. "Mrs. Bishop," she said when Valerie had finished, "why don't you take Elvie and the baby down to the children's playroom, and I'll see what I can do about all of this."

Hot Water

Karen knew she was in trouble the minute Mrs. Anston came through the door to the reception area. "Yes, Mr. Malcolm," she said into the telephone. "I'm really sorry you had to go to all that trouble. . . . No, I had no idea you had to go all the way to the hospital. . . . Yes, I'll tell her to call you the minute I see her." Karen put down the phone and braced herself.

"Now what?" asked Mrs. Anston.

"I was looking for Linda. . . . Valerie Bishop said she was in labor and . . ."

"And?"

"So I called Mr. Malcolm to see if he knew where Linda was. He couldn't get through to the obstetrician's office—the answering machine said they had gone to lunch and wouldn't be back until 1 o'clock."

"And?"

"He drove over to the hospital to see if Linda was in labor and having the baby."

"And?"

"She wasn't there."

Barely controlling her anger, Mrs. Anston carefully put the notebook she was holding down on the reception counter, opened it to a blank page, wrote *Bishop, Valerie* at the top, and looked up at Karen.

"I want to know how this mess got started and why I was pulled out of a meeting with the Board of Directors by a woman whose questions could, or rather *should*, have been answered by any number of other people."

Discussion Questions

1. What factors may have contributed to Valerie Bishop's outburst at the Center?

2. Could anyone have prevented this unpleasant situation?

3. Linda Malcolm regrets that Elvie didn't attend preschool this past year. Should she have tried harder to convince Valerie to enroll Elvie?

4. As Elvie's sole service provider, Linda Malcolm was responsible for planning her transition to kindergarten. Could she have managed the transition process better than she did? Should others have been involved?

5. Did Mrs. Anston handle her encounter with Valerie Bishop appropriately?

6. When Linda Malcolm returns to the Center for Elvie's appointment and learns what has just transpired, what course of action should she take?

7. What role, if any, should Mrs. Anston play in resolving the situation with the Bishop family?

8. What courses of action can be taken over the next 2 months to ensure an appropriate placement for Elvie in the fall and a successful year in kindergarten?

9. Given that Linda Malcolm will soon be out on maternity leave, what should she, or other Center staff, do to help Valerie make decisions about Elvie's school placement and to ensure that Elvie obtains the services she will need in the coming year?

10. What implications does this situation have for the appropriate management of services for children who receive single therapies (e.g., speech-language therapy, occupational therapy)?

Money Matters

P.J. McWilliam

construction paper turkey on the front door gave a welcoming grin to Anne-Marie when she arrived at the Seagroveses' home for her customary Friday morning visit. Each holiday and season was heralded by new decorations on the door—all homemade artwork by Judy Seagroves and her two children, Blair and Nick. The grinning Thanksgiving turkey reminded Anne-Marie that this month marked the 1-year anniversary of her relationship with the Seagroves family.

Judy answered her knock on the door. "Hi, Anne-Marie! Come on in. The place is a real wreck, but we're here."

Anne-Marie returned Judy's greeting and followed her to the living room. With half-folded laundry on the sofa and toys strewn all over the floor, the place was in a bit of an upheaval; but, Anne-Marie always felt comfortable in the Seagroveses' home. A real family atmosphere permeated every room of the house.

Anne-Marie had been assigned as Blair's primary service provider shortly after the Seagroves family moved to Forest Hills from Minne-

sota. Blair's father, Randy, was a store manager for a large chain, and
he had been relocated to take over the management of a newly opened
store. At the time of the move, Blair had been a little older than 3 years,
and her brother Nick had been a kindergartner. In addition to the
stresses of relocating with two young children, Randy and Judy also
had to take Blair to the hospital twice during their first winter in Forest Hills, once for pneumonia and a second time for dehydration as the
result of the flu.

"Have a seat, won't you?" offered Judy. "If you'll excuse me for
just a minute, I have to tend to the washing machine. I'll be right back."
Judy disappeared through the kitchen door.

Anne-Marie quickly glanced around the room. *Sesame Street* characters paraded across the television screen to the amusement of Blair,
who was in her usual place, propped up by pillows in the overstuffed
armchair. "Hi, Blair!" said Anne-Marie. "How are you this morning?
It's good to see you."

Blair had made great progress during the past year. Randy's and
Judy's doubts and worries about Blair's cognitive abilities had all but
vanished, and Anne-Marie had come to agree that Blair was an extremely bright little girl. The fact remained, however, that Blair had
severe physical disabilities and did not speak. Blair's age and the realization of her intelligence increased the probability that these two con-
ditions were permanent. No one knew for sure, but her parents' suspicions were beginning to find voice.

Blair lifted her drooping head and smiled at Anne-Marie. Drool
spilled out of one corner of her mouth.

"That a girl!" she told Blair. "The old head bone gets kind of heavy
after a while, doesn't it? Too many brains, I suppose. Is that the problem? Just too smart?"

Blair's face brightened further, and she laughed.

"Watching *Sesame Street* again?" asked Anne-Marie.

Blair tried to nod her head but lost control, and her chin fell down
to her chest. With much effort, she righted her head and gave another
little smile.

"My favorite is Cookie Monster because I love cookies, too. Who's
your favorite? Is it Ernie . . . ?" Anne-Marie paused for a moment, and
Blair pursed her lips. "Is it Bert . . . ?" Again, Blair closed her lips
tightly and wrinkled her nose. "Is it Grover . . . ?" Blair's face burst into
a smile. "Ah ha! It's Grover!" exclaimed Anne-Marie.

"Sorry for being so rude," said Judy, returning from the kitchen.

"No problem," said Anne-Marie. "Blair and I have been discussing
the relative virtues of Cookie Monster and Grover . . . some pretty
heavy stuff, you know."

"Above my head, I'm afraid." Judy smiled and sat down on the sofa. "Would you like a cup of coffee?"

"No, thanks, I just had some before I left the office." Anne-Marie stroked Blair's blonde curls, then moved to sit in the rocking chair near Judy. "So, how has the picture board been working out for Blair?"

"Pretty good. . . except when we try to get her to touch the pictures herself. Then it just doesn't work very well."

"Why is that?"

"Once there are more than four cards on the board, it's too difficult for her to show us which one she wants. She just doesn't have enough control of her arms. And with just four choices, it's easier to play the 'yes-or-no' game we've been playing all along."

"I'm sorry it didn't work out. I wonder if—"

"We have done something different, though," interrupted Judy. "Instead of trying to make Blair touch the card she wants, we touch the cards ourselves, and she lets us know when we touch the one she wants. It's not exactly what we talked about doing, but it seems to be better than restricting her choices or having all of us get confused and frustrated."

"It sounds good to me," said Anne-Marie. "Have you given any more thought to the idea of an electronic communication board with a voice synthesizer?"

"Yes. Randy and I talked about that a lot this week." Judy paused to take a deep breath. "Actually, we talked a lot about everything that Blair will need as she grows up. Of course, we still hope that Blair will be able to speak one day, but we're beginning to realize that she may need other ways to communicate before that happens . . . if it ever does."

Anne-Marie didn't know what Judy was leading up to, but the look of concern on Judy's face told her that the conversation was about to get serious. "I don't think that any of us have given up on Blair's speaking, but I think you're right to consider alternative communication methods . . . at least for now."

"Anne-Marie, our real problem right now is money. Randy and I just don't have enough to—"

Anne-Marie interrupted, "Maybe we could find a place that would loan you an electronic communication board. It would actually be better because you could try it out and see if it's right for Blair before you purchase it, and—"

Judy held up a hand to stop Anne-Marie. "It's not just the communication board," explained Judy. "Randy and I have decided that I need to find a job . . . at least part-time work and maybe even full-time. It's been far more expensive living in Forest Hills than we thought it would be before we moved."

"Oh, I see. . . ." Anne-Marie was at a loss for words. She was aware that the family was on a tight budget, and she remembered that Judy had taken temporary work during the Christmas shopping season last winter. But she had never imagined that Judy would need to go to work permanently. What would her working mean for Blair? Anne-Marie nervously fiddled with her watch clasp.

"In addition to regular living expenses, we have Blair's hospital and doctor bills from this past winter. Randy's medical insurance is pretty good, but it certainly didn't cover everything."

"I had no idea that was—"

"There's the future to think of, too," continued Judy. "You know, we've talked about getting a wheelchair for Blair before she goes to school. And if she uses a wheelchair, we'll probably need to buy a van with a ramp." Judy looked down at her hand on her lap and centered her diamond ring on her finger.

Anne-Marie wanted to respond but couldn't find the right words.

Then Judy clasped her hands together and looked up at Anne-Marie. Her eyes were moist with tears. "I hate the thought of it, but maybe Randy's right. Maybe we can't continue to ignore the possibility that she may never walk. We don't want the future to catch us off guard."

"I can understand planning for the future, but—"

"And at the rate we're going," said Judy, "we'll never own our own home. . . ." The sound of the back door slamming distracted her.

"MOMMY! Can I have a drink? . . . MOM!" It was 6-year-old Nick.

Judy stood up immediately, wiped her eyes with the back of her hand, and went into the kitchen to tend to his needs. Anne-Marie wondered why Nick was home from school, but she really didn't care right now. His intrusion came as a relief.

Money problems . . . work . . . wheelchairs . . . vans . . . ramps? Where was all of this coming from? She thought today's visit was going to be about communication boards for Blair. How was she supposed to respond to everything that Judy had just said?

Before Anne-Marie could come up with a plan, Judy returned from the kitchen. The back door slammed again. Nick must have gone back outside.

"Sorry about the interruption," said Judy.

"No problem. Is this a school holiday?"

"No. It's a teacher workday. I can't believe that they scheduled a teacher workday a week before Thanksgiving vacation."

"That does seem a little strange," agreed Anne-Marie. "How's Nick doing in first grade?" She was hoping to buy herself time to think by getting Judy to talk about Nick for a few minutes.

"I don't think he's ever really adjusted to our move from Minnesota."

"What do you mean?"

"Well, he had some problems in kindergarten last year after we moved here. You know . . . not staying in his seat, not getting his work done, talking or horsing around when he wasn't supposed to. I thought it was just because the schools here were more conservative and structured than his school in Minnesota. But the same problems are coming up again this year."

"That's a shame. What does his teacher have to say about all this? Has she been very helpful?"

"I've tried to talk with her, but she's young, and all she can see are the problems—not the solutions." Judy glanced over at Blair in the armchair, then walked toward her. Blair had gradually slipped down farther and farther into the nest of pillows.

"What do you think might be going on?" asked Anne-Marie. So much for buying herself time to think. She realized that financial worries and Blair's future weren't the only things bothering Judy. Nick was obviously having some problems at school. But what Anne-Marie really wanted to talk about now was Judy's announcement that she needed to look for a job. How could she steer Judy back to that topic? Or maybe Judy didn't want to talk about it any more today.

"I don't know what's going on," answered Judy. She lifted Blair out of the armchair and carried her to the sofa. Blair's long, thin legs were a testimony to the fact that she was indeed growing up. "His teacher seems to think he's hyperactive, but I wonder if she knows what should be expected of a new first grader. Six-year-old little boys aren't built to sit still in chairs for long periods of time."

"No, I don't suppose they are. Have you had any problems with him at home?"

"He's always been a bit of a pistol. All boy, as Randy likes to put it." Judy struggled to position Blair in her arms as she spoke. "But, no, he's not all that difficult to manage. As long as you make the rules clear, he's usually pretty good about toeing the mark." Judy lifted Blair's dangling legs and laid them across her own lap. "I don't know, maybe we should have him seen by someone. . . . But first we need to get Blair's hospital bills paid off."

Again, the issue of money had come up. Maybe this was Anne-Marie's chance to get back to Judy's working. "Judy, you mentioned before that you were considering going back to work. How definite are you about that?"

"I don't think I really have a choice. You know I love being a stay-at-home mom, but I suppose that's going to have to change for now. We'll all have to make some compromises."

"Is there anything I can do to help out?"

"To be honest, I don't know where to start. I'll need to find a place for Blair—all of our family is back in Minnesota. I don't suppose you could talk them into moving here for me, could you?" Judy grinned at Anne-Marie then looked into Blair's face. "How about that, Blair? You'd like having Grandmom come to take care of you, wouldn't you?" Blair's excited arms and flashing smile indicated her approval.

Anne-Marie smiled back at the two on the sofa. On the inside, however, she wasn't smiling. Had Judy considered anything other than getting a job as a way to solve their money problems?

What alternatives were there, if any? If Judy did start working, where would Blair stay during the day? What type of program could offer her the kind of attention that Judy had been giving and help her to continue her current progress? Could Blair still see the private physical therapist in Concord, the one Judy was so pleased with? Could a parent support group help Judy during the transition? What types of information and support systems were out there, anyway? And then there was Nick. What could Anne-Marie suggest or offer to Judy to ease her concerns about him?

Discussion Questions

1. What are the Seagroves family's concerns and priorities? Make a list.

2. What additional concerns, if any, would you have if you were a service provider for the Seagroves family?

3. What possible strategies might Anne-Marie use to address the Seagroves family's concerns and priorities?

4. What types of resources, services, or assistance might Anne-Marie need to implement each of the strategies you identified above (Question #3)?

5. Do you think Anne-Marie responded appropriately when Judy announced that her family's financial difficulties were forcing her to return to work? Did she respond appropriately to the news about Nick's problems in school?

6. If you were Anne-Marie, what would you do or say before the end of this particular home visit? What would you want to accomplish during the next few weeks or months?

7. If the Seagroves family lived in your community, what resources or services would be available to help them address the concerns and priorities you identified in your answers to Questions #1 and #2?

chapter 4

Mother of Two

Miki Kersgard

Rhonda packed her tote bag and gave Eunice Parker's son Martin a pat on the head. "Have a nice night, Eunice. I'll see you next week."

"You drive safe goin' home, honey. It looks a little slick out there. Nasty weather we're havin'."

"Oh, I don't get to go home just yet," replied Rhonda. "I still have one more stop at Harrison Street before I'm done."

"Harrison Street! What you doin' goin' to Harrison Street after dark? When it gets dark this early, I don't even think 'bout goin' there after 3 o'clock." Eunice studied Rhonda for a moment, seemed to be about to say something, then stopped.

"What is it, Eunice?" Rhonda asked.

Eunice crossed her arms and shook her head slowly. "You have no idea what you're dealin' with here, do you, child?"

Rhonda stared blankly at Eunice.

"There's drug dealers and criminals. . . . Those gang members don't care if you get in the way of one of their bullets. And some strung-out junkie doesn't give two hoots 'bout your life compared to how much they want your money, do they? You carry protection with you?"

"Protection?"

"You got some kind of handgun with you?"

"No," replied Rhonda, "I wouldn't dream of it! I wouldn't know what to do with a gun if I owned one."

"Not even a can of Mace?" asked Eunice.

"Eunice, it's only two blocks away. Do you carry a gun when you go out around here?"

"Honey, two blocks 'round here can mean the difference between life and death. And, yes, my sister Amanda lives on Harrison Street, and when I have to go over there at night, I *do* carry a gun."

"I'll keep that in mind," Rhonda said, laughing nervously. "Thanks for the advice."

"It's advice you'd better think of takin' seriously, child. My boy and I would miss you if you came out of there on a stretcher one night."

Sorting Things Out

Rhonda drove slowly down Harrison Street looking for a parking space and breathed a sigh of relief when she found one right in front of her destination. After 4 months of working with Corey Matthews, Rhonda thought she'd gotten used to the housing project. But after Eunice's warning, she felt more apprehensive than ever. Locking up the car, she thought that it wasn't so much the street itself that worried her but the thought of Corey and his mother Crystal living on it. Every time Rhonda thought about how young and frail 19-year-old Crystal looked, she couldn't imagine her surviving in such a dangerous environment.

Crystal could easily pass for a 13-year-old, and, with her close-cropped hair, she looked more like a young boy than the mother of two children. Whenever Rhonda saw Crystal's 4-year-old daughter Pepper, she couldn't help wondering what Crystal must have looked like when Pepper was born. The thought of it always made Rhonda's heart ache.

Broken glass crunched under her feet as Rhonda walked around her car and stepped over a torn plastic garbage bag spilling its rotting contents over the curb. An image of a child picking through the trash and finding a used syringe flashed through her mind, but Rhonda quickly shook it out of her head. She scanned the street, and Eunice's words of caution echoed as Rhonda hurried into the building where Crystal and her children lived.

When she opened the door of the apartment building, a thousand smells assaulted her nose—the combined odors of strong disinfectant and old urine, the stench of the overflowing garbage cans wafting in from the open door at the other end of the building, and the aromas of a dozen dinners being cooked. Rhonda turned the corner and looked down the hall at her choices. The elevator or the stairs? One's as bad as the other, she thought. Eunice's warnings echoed again as Rhonda hurried down the dark hallway and ran up the stairs. When she reached Crystal's door, she leaned against the cold wall and stood there for a minute while she calmed down. As she took a deep breath, a few chips of mottled beige paint fell from the wall.

When Crystal opened the door, Rhonda could tell that things weren't going well. Chairs were tipped over, unfolded laundry was scattered all over the couch, Pepper was clinging to Crystal's leg, and Corey was screeching so loudly that his face was turning purple.

"I don't understand," said Crystal, holding the crying infant. "Nothin' I usually do for him seems to be workin' today. I can't get anything done with him cryin' all the time. He won't eat anything I give him, either. I can't get Pepper to let go of my leg long enough to get any housework done at all." Pepper peered up at Rhonda from behind her mother's leg and then quickly ducked back with a shy giggle.

Rhonda stepped inside and looked around the apartment, her gaze landing on the kitchen counter covered with half-empty bottles of formula and plates of something mashed that she couldn't identify. Pots and pans filled the sink. It looked like this had been going on for more than just a day.

"Maybe if you try to give him some, he'll take his formula, Miz Spelling." Rhonda had given up on getting Crystal to call her by her first name. Crystal handed Rhonda the bottle, and Rhonda tried to feed Corey the formula, but he didn't seem at all interested. Corey's feeding difficulties worried Rhonda.

"Crystal, he feels a little warm. Have you taken his temperature?"

"No, ma'am," answered Crystal.

"Why don't you get the thermometer, and I'll help you."

"I'm sorry, Miz Spelling, but the one you got me broke."

"It broke?"

"I left it on the floor one day, and then I stepped on it by mistake."

On the floor, thought Rhonda. She decided not to push the issue by lecturing Crystal on the sanitary upkeep of thermometers and made a mental note to pick up a new one the next chance she got.

"Well, I think we'd better be on the safe side and see if we can make this little guy more comfortable. Do you have the Tylenol drops we got at the clinic?"

With a little clucking and some rattling of toys, the two women got Corey settled into the infant carrier that was propped up on the coffee table in front of the couch. Meanwhile, Pepper was easily entertained by a new coloring book that Rhonda had in her bag. We give so much of our attention to Corey, thought Rhonda, I wonder if Pepper is getting short-changed. Pepper had never been identified as having any substantial delays, but her speech seemed immature for a child getting ready to enter kindergarten. Well, Rhonda thought, that will have to wait for another day.

Rhonda heaped the laundry onto the center of the couch and plopped down next to the pile with a breathy sigh. She absently started folding little T-shirts, placing them on the coffee table in front of her.

"Please, Miz Spelling," said Crystal, "I'll do that folding. You shouldn't be havin' to do stuff like that."

"Really, Crystal, I like to. Besides, it's one of those activities that helps me think. My thoughts seem to fall into place, just like the clothes. Maybe you can help me with something, though. Could you get a pen and a piece of paper out of my tote bag over there? The pad of paper is in the middle pocket. . . . Yes, right there. And the pen is clipped to the little pouch in the front."

Crystal brought the pad and pen to Rhonda and held them out to her.

"Hold on to them for a minute. Why don't you help me make a list while we talk? I'll show you how to do it."

Crystal hesitated, looked down at the blank page, then looked up at Rhonda. "Sure, Miz Spelling," she said as she sat down on the other end of the couch, her shoulders just barely visible over the mound of laundry.

"We'll make a list of the things that you and Corey need or want. Let's see," said Rhonda, straightening the legs of a terrycloth jumper. "At the top, let's put Corey's name with a line under it." Crystal wrote slowly and deliberately. The letters occupied the entire space between the lines, but they were well formed and neat. "Now, we can't ask Corey what he wants, so we'll just have to guess. First, I think he'd want us to do something about this fever we think he might have. We should call the Health Department to see if they can move his appointment from next Wednesday to one day this week."

Crystal wrote *Health department* on the next line then looked up at Rhonda. "Good lists," continued Rhonda, "leave nothing to be remembered. Why don't you put a dash after that and write *call for new date.*"

Corey

Health department—call for new date

"Is this Corey's regular formula?" asked Rhonda, picking up the bottle on the coffee table while Crystal wrote. "It looks a little strange."

"Yes, ma'am. . . . Well, it is, but I had to add a little water to it. My food stamps don't come 'til tomorrow. There was just a little formula left, so I thought I'd just stretch it out for this one day. That sure didn't work, though, did it? No sense stretching somethin' out if he won't have anything to do with it, is there?"

"No," answered Rhonda. "Not really." Rhonda was beginning to think that Crystal was hopeless; every time Rhonda thought Crystal was getting the hang of things, she came up with a foolish idea like this.

Rhonda and Crystal continued to organize Crystal's clothes and the things in her life that needed attention. They made lists of agency names and numbers, calls that Crystal needed to make, and appointments that she needed to meet or reschedule.

"Miz Spelling?"

"Yes . . . what is it?"

"Shouldn't I wait 'til after the appointment at the Health Department before I go buyin' a lotta formula? I mean, maybe the doctor will tell me to do somethin' different or get some other kind, or somethin'."

"Good thinking!" said Rhonda. "Perhaps you should only buy what Corey will need between now and when the doctor can see him."

Crystal looked down at the page, smiling shyly. Beside *Buy formula* she wrote *wait for doctor.*

Corey

Health department—call for new date
Make appointment at clinic—Thursday
Call agency—today before 4:30
Change doctor's appointment to Wednesday—
     call today
Get food stamps
Buy formula—wait for doctor

The sound of a door slamming startled Rhonda, and she lost her train of thought. Eunice's warning popped into her mind again. "I want to ask you about something," said Rhonda.

Crystal, who was having trouble squeezing what she wanted to write into the page's small margins, took a moment to look up.

"Do you ever feel like you or the children are in danger here? Has anything ever happened to you?"

"Happened?" Crystal looked down at Pepper. For a minute, Rhonda thought she had offended Crystal.

"I mean with the gangs I've been hearing about . . . or anything like that."

"I try to avoid the corners they hang out on. Besides, if you think too much about it. . . ." Crystal's voice trailed off.

"Do you feel safe here at night?"

"Safe?" Crystal looked uncertain about what she was being asked. "I don't go out at night, ma'am," she finally said.

"Never?"

"No, ma'am. I try not to go out at all if I can help it."

"Don't you feel trapped by that?" asked Rhonda. Fumbling to move on from what she realized was a poorly worded question, she said quickly, "I mean, what if you had an emergency?"

"I try not to think about that."

"Do you ever think about moving out of here? Trying to live in a safer neighborhood?"

"Do I ever think about gettin' out of this pit? Sure I do. Takes money, though, don't it, Miz Spelling? Rich people don't have crack dealers livin' in their neighborhoods, do they?"

The strength of Crystal's question took Rhonda's breath away. "Well," said Rhonda when she had gathered herself back together, "next on the list, then, is to look for better housing for you and the kids. Celine Garner at Social Services can probably help us out with that one. She's who you see about your monthly checks, isn't she?" Crystal nodded. "I'll see if I can get you an appointment to see her sometime this week."

"Do you really think there's a chance of me and my kids gettin' a new place?" asked Crystal.

"It might take some work," replied Rhonda, "but I don't see why not."

Jumping Hurdles

For 2 days, Rhonda spent every available moment on the telephone. She scheduled and rescheduled appointments and arranged transportation to and from agencies for Crystal and Corey—all while trying to keep her appointments with the other families on her caseload.

At 10 o'clock on Thursday, Rhonda figured that Crystal must have gotten home from her visit to the Health Department and her meeting with Celine Garner. She dialed Crystal's number and, after 10 rings, was just about to hang up when she heard Crystal's breathless voice.

"Hello?"

"Hi, Crystal. It's Rhonda Spelling. Are you okay? You sound out of breath."

"Oh . . . yeah . . . I'm just . . . I just came in. I had to drop everything and run to get the phone."

"I'm so sorry to make you run like that. I thought you would have gotten home a while ago. Was the van from Social Services late?"

"Not at all. In fact, I had to make him wait. My appointment with Miz Garner started a little late."

"Would you like me to call you back in a few minutes?"

"No," replied Crystal. "I'll get my breath in a second. It's fine, really."

"I was just calling to see how everything was going." Rhonda waited a moment for a reply and then realized that Crystal might not have understood that her last phrase was a question. "So," she rephrased, "is everything going okay?"

Crystal hesitated for another moment and then said, "Well, to tell you the truth, Miz Spelling, things aren't so great."

"Oh, Crystal. . . . I knew we were trying to do too much this week. I feel just terrible about pushing you like that. Do you want me to cancel Pepper's appointment for kindergarten registration?"

"No. Really, that's okay. That's not what I mean. All that's going fine, except. . . ."

"Except what?"

"Well, things didn't go so good with Miz Garner today."

Hmmm, thought Rhonda, what's Celine up to now? "I'll tell you what," she said to Crystal. "Why don't I stop by after my lunch meeting? I'm on my way out there now, and I could come over afterward. We can talk about it then," she said, flipping through her calendar quickly to make sure she hadn't already scheduled anything for the afternoon. "Would that be all right?"

"I have to go pick up Pepper. She and my sister, Neecy, are down at my friend Shana's place, but I'll be back after that. How soon will you be here?"

"Oh, I won't be there until after 1:30. Can you be back by then?"

"Sure. I'll be back before that. Shana just lives downstairs."

"Great. See you then."

A Secret Revealed

When Rhonda rang Crystal's doorbell, she could hear the sounds of dishes rattling, a faucet being turned off, and then someone running across the floor. "I thought I asked you to straighten up that stuff, Neecy," she heard Crystal yell. "Can't you do things the first time I ask?" Crystal flung open the door, towel in her hand and suds up to her elbows. "Come in, Miz Spelling. You got here sooner than I thought."

"Bad food can really speed up those lunch meetings," quipped Rhonda with a quick laugh. She entered the apartment and noticed a teenage girl lying on the couch, her head bobbing up and down to music coming through the tiny headphones stuck in her ears. Mounds of blankets and pillows surrounded her. Rhonda could hear a rhythm that sounded like raspy static and munchkin tambourines blaring through the headphones. Must be Neecy, thought Rhonda, surveying the room. Looks like someone's been camping out. It's no wonder the food money runs out if there's a teenager staying here on a regular basis.

Crystal walked over to the couch and pulled one of the plugs out of the girl's ear. "You gonna go deaf from that stuff, Neecy. Turn that off, and fold up those things like I asked you to twice already."

Neecy glared up at her older sister. "You didn't ask me nothin'," she said.

"If you'd get those things out of your ears once in a while, you'd hear what people were sayin' to you. Now hurry up. I've got somethin' I need you to go do for me." Crystal looked over at Rhonda and then turned and headed off toward the kitchenette. "Can we talk in here? I got to keep workin' on these dishes, Miz Spelling. I'm tryin' to get better at keepin' up with this stuff. It sure has a habit of gettin' away from you, don't it?"

"Sure. No problem." Rhonda followed Crystal and pulled out a chair at the little round table that was shoved into a corner of the small room. She sat down and plopped her overstuffed tote bag on the floor beside her. "Is there anything I can help you with?"

"No, that's fine. I'd really rather do it myself." Crystal was scraping what looked like 3-day-old dried-up chili off of a plate, but she wasn't having much success.

"Why don't you tell me what happened with Celine Garner?"

Crystal looked nervously over her shoulder toward the living room. "Neecy!" she yelled. Neecy appeared in the doorway, and Crystal shut off the faucet. "Go downstairs to Shana's for me and bring Pepper back up. She's been playin' down there with Jonathan long enough. And ask Shana to write out that chicken recipe she was talkin' about for me. Would you?"

"Now?"

"Yes, now. Don't you want some chicken for dinner?" Neecy slouched off toward the door, mumbling to herself while sticking her earphones back in.

As soon as Neecy was gone, Crystal dried her hands and sat down at the table with Rhonda.

"So what happened with Celine Garner?" asked Rhonda.

"She kept asking me all these questions I didn't think was none of her business. At the hospital, when I had Pepper, they didn't make me tell. Or when I had Corey, either. They asked me . . . but they didn't say I had to tell. Why should I have to tell *her* now?"

"Tell what?" asked Rhonda, but she thought she already knew.

"Who the father was. She wanted to know who Pepper's father was . . . and for Corey, too. Then she said maybe I should move back in with my parents."

"I suppose," said Rhonda, "that she needs to establish what kind of support is available for the children before she can determine what the government should pay for. Sometimes we have to follow rules that don't seem to make sense, even to us. I'm sure Celine wouldn't be prying into your personal matters just because she wants to."

Crystal rolled her eyes in exasperation. Rhonda decided to try a different approach. "Maybe I could help you out a little. I'll try to talk to Celine for you," she offered. "But tell me something. Would moving back in with your parents be all that bad? I'd think things would be easier for you if you had other people to help you look after your children. Couldn't that be one of your options?"

"No, it couldn't." Crystal took on a look that Rhonda had never seen before. The girl's face seemed to turn into a mask of stone.

"Crystal?" Rhonda said softly, "I'm not trying to pressure you, but, under the circumstances, I think including the father could help you out a great deal. He's as responsible for these children as you are, and it might mean the difference between you living in public housing and getting a place in a better neighborhood. We both know you and the children would be better off somewhere else."

"It won't matter," said Crystal. "Even if he wanted to, he don't have no money to be handin' out." Crystal's eyes lost their stony look for a moment and glowed with impending tears.

Rhonda reached out for Crystal's arm. "If you want to talk about it, you know you can trust me."

"I have your word you won't tell no one?" asked Crystal softly.

"You have my word." Rhonda leaned forward to hear Crystal's voice, which was now barely louder than a whisper.

"It's why you just got to help me," pleaded the young girl. "It's my daddy. He done it before when I got Pepper, and then he done it again. He promised he was finished last time . . . after Pepper. He swore. . . ." The tears that had been welling up in her eyes now slid down Crystal's cheeks.

"Does your mother know?" asked Rhonda, trying her best to hide how shocked she was by this revelation.

"She knows," said Crystal, "but she don't believe it. She says it's not true, but I think she knows it is. She knows in her heart I'd never lie about somethin' like that."

Either that, thought Rhonda, or she just doesn't want to have to choose between her daughter and her husband.

"She made me swear, though. She said she'd help me out whenever she could if I didn't tell no one else these stories about him. So you can't tell no one about this. Not no one. She'll never help me with nothin' again if you do."

Rhonda put her hand on Crystal's shoulder and then wiped the last remaining tear off the girl's cheek. "Don't worry, Crystal. I won't tell anyone if you don't want me to. If you want, I'll go have a talk with Celine as soon as I can."

"That'd be fine. Thank you."

Keeping a Promise

Rhonda sat across from Celine the following day and was growing more and more frustrated as Celine spoke.

"But maybe she can't cope with life on her own," continued Celine. "Especially in that neighborhood. Frankly, Rhonda, I don't see too many choices. She's asking for better housing but can't manage the money that she's getting now. I've tried to go over budgeting with her, but I don't seem to be getting anywhere. I'm running out of ideas. The parents haven't refused to let her move back in, have they?"

Rhonda tried desperately to think of something other than the truth. She finally decided to just skip the explanation and settle for the simplest answer she could find. "No," was all she said. "No, I don't think so."

Celine shook her head and looked down at her hands. "I'm afraid there's not much I can do. It looks like a simple case of teenage rebellion, if you ask me, and those two children are paying the price for it. Why don't you talk to Crystal about moving back in with her parents? Maybe she'd be more responsive to the suggestion if it came from you."

Celine put the papers that were scattered around her desk back into their folders and began to file them. There was a finality to her motions that Rhonda interpreted to mean the meeting was over.

Out in the hallway, Rhonda paced back and forth in front of the elevator doors as she waited to go downstairs to her car. What could she possibly say to Celine to get her to change her mind without revealing Crystal's secret? If only Celine knew the truth! Could she ever convince Crystal to tell Celine herself?

Discussion Questions

1. What do you think about the manner in which Rhonda Spelling conducted the first home visit described in the story? What did you like about her overall approach to working with Crystal? Do you think that she should have done anything differently?

2. Rhonda obviously has some concerns about her own safety in Crystal's neighborhood. What can she do or should she do to protect herself?

3. Should Rhonda have mentioned housing and safety issues to Crystal? Is the safety of Crystal and her children a legitimate concern? If so, what course of action should she take to help Crystal secure safe housing?

4. What responsibilities, if any, does Rhonda have regarding the welfare of Crystal's daughter Pepper and her sister Neecy?

5. Should Rhonda have promised to keep Crystal's secret? Should she honor the promise? If not, who should she tell, and how should she go about it?

6. What legal issues regarding the reporting of sexual abuse would Rhonda face in your state? How would these laws influence the decisions Rhonda makes?

7. Is there anything Rhonda could do to help change Celine Garner's perception of Crystal and convince her to provide more support for this family?

8. Based on the information available in the story, what do you think Crystal's priorities are for herself and her family? Make a list.

9. If you were Rhonda, what concerns or priorities would you have for working with Crystal and her two children? Are these compatible with Crystal's priorities?

10. If you were in Rhonda's position and had to develop an IFSP for Corey and his family, how might you proceed?

11. If Rhonda was the service coordinator for Corey and his family, what should she do during the next few weeks or months to ensure that appropriate services and resources are being provided?

12. If someone other than Rhonda (e.g., Celine Garner) was the service coordinator for Corey and his family, would Rhonda's responsibilities be different? If so, how?

13. In your community, which agency would be responsible for providing service coordination for this family?

14. What services and resources would be available to the Matthews family in your community? Make a list.

chapter 5

Absent Mother

Wanda B. Hedrick

Lynne's cheeks flushed with anger when her repeated knocks were met with silence from within the second floor apartment. This made the third "no-show" for Angela in less than a month. Now what was she supposed to do? It didn't take Lynne long to decide. She pulled a slip of paper out of her purse and began to write a note. As usual, the note would remind Angela that they had made an appointment and that it was important for Angela to be there with her son, Chauncey, so he could continue making progress. Lynne was signing the note when little Shantae, Chauncey's oldest sister, came running, breathless, up the two flights of stairs.

"Miss Lynne, Gramma says to come to her house," Shantae blurted out. "Chauncey, Monique, and me is there."

"Is your momma there, too?" Lynne asked.

"No, we don'ts know where Momma is, but you is to come to Gramma's house. She sents me here to get you."

Lynne hesitated a moment then folded the note and stuffed it in her purse. It was more likely that Angela would see it if she left it with Frances, the children's great-grandmother, anyway. "Okay, I'll come. Where is Gramma's apartment?"

"Not far, just over there at the next building, past the phone booth." Shantae turned and galloped down the stairs.

Lynne's bag of toys bumped rhythmically against her legs as she trotted to keep up with Shantae. Once on the street, Shantae turned right and skipped down the busy sidewalk. They wove their way through children at play on Hot Wheels and in-line skates. Three girls jumping rope called for Shantae to join them, but she told them that she was busy and would come out later.

As they approached the steps to Frances's house, Lynne saw a man standing on the street hand money to two men through the open window of their red Miata. The two men in the car wore white shirts and stylish silk ties. Much to her disgust, Lynne recognized the transaction as a drug deal. Her heart beat faster. She couldn't imagine living in this kind of neighborhood and wondered what chance these children had of escaping the influence of drugs. One of the men looked straight at Lynne, making her realize that she had been staring at them. She quickly averted her eyes. "Let's hurry up and get inside," she whispered to Shantae. "I'm sure Gramma is worried about us taking so long." She gave the men one last look and then climbed the stairs to Apartment 2B.

Shantae plopped down on a big pillow in front of the television and, after one click of the remote control, immersed herself in a popular talk show. The apartment was filled with the smells of supper cooking. Lynne had missed lunch and wondered what southern dishes Frances was making. Fried yellow squash, black-eyed peas, and candied yams had become Lynne's personal favorites since she moved to this area. When her mother visited last spring, Lynne had served a southern meal of these dishes, and it was amusing to see the look on her mother's face as she tasted the food. Throughout the entire meal, her mother had talked to her about moving back home to New York, settling down, and getting married to some "nice Jewish boy."

"Come on back to the kitchen—I can't leave it right now." Frances's friendly voice jerked Lynne back to the present. She followed the sound of Frances's voice to the kitchen at the back of the apartment.

Monique, Chauncey's 5-year-old sister, sat at the kitchen table with Chauncey on her lap. Although she was a kindergartner with lots of energy, she looked quite content entertaining Chauncey while Frances cooked. Her maturity was not surprising, though, considering how often Monique and Shantae were left to watch Chauncey while

Angela ran to the corner store. Lynne felt a smile creep across her face as she watched Monique and Chauncey playing and laughing loudly together. On two of her home visits today she'd faced crying children, so this one was a treat.

"Well, I'm glad you came over here," said Frances. "I was afraid Shantae might have missed you." She stirred a pot of steaming beans on the stove as she spoke.

"No. Shantae caught me as I was leaving Angela a note. Do you know where Angela is?" asked Lynne.

Frances shook her head. Then she told Monique to carry the baby into the living room and play with him on the blanket on the floor. Monique picked up Chauncey and placed him in the crook of her right arm. Carrying him past Lynne, Monique looked up and said, "See how I carry the baby, Miss Lynne?"

"Very good! I'm happy to see you carrying Chauncey that way," complimented Lynne.

Monique grinned broadly. "I 'membered what Momma told me 'bout carryin' the baby this way 'stead of my old way."

Lynne recalled her conversation with Angela about carrying Chauncey in the crook of her arm facing forward instead of carrying him on her hip. Angela must have taught Monique how to hold Chauncey that way, too. Indeed, Angela had incorporated many of Lynne's suggestions into her daily care of Chauncey. Lynne felt especially proud that Angela had faithfully kept her appointments at the clinic for the baby's checkups and immunizations.

When Chauncey was born, he tested positive for cocaine, and Angela had told the hospital staff she wanted help for her drug addiction. A hospital social worker had included Angela's exact words in her report: *I don't want to do drugs no more. Will you help me so I can be a better momma to my kids?* The social worker had helped Angela gain entry into the detoxification unit for a few days and then referred her to a substance abuse counselor. Chauncey had gone home from the hospital with Frances, who cared for him and the two girls until Angela returned home 3 weeks later. Lynne made her first visit to the family 2 weeks after Angela's return, and, until recently, she had been impressed with the care Angela provided for all three of her children.

As Monique bounced proudly out of the room, Lynne noticed tears welling up in Frances's eyes. Frances dropped into the chair that Monique had left vacant, and crying replaced the laughter that had filled the room only seconds before. Frances covered her face with her rough hands, put her elbows on the table, and began to sob. Lynne stood there feeling helpless, not knowing what had provoked such a sudden display of sadness. She wanted to ease Frances's pain with some comforting words, but her mind was blank. She opted instead for a supportive touch on Frances's shoulder.

"I don't know what's happened to Angela," Frances said when she regained control of her voice. "I'm so afraid she will turn up dead with one of those riffraff she hangs around with." The tone of her voice suddenly reverberated with anger; the look on her face grew determined; and a coldness hardened her soft, brown eyes.

"She won't raised to be this way," Frances continued. "She was saved, sanctified, and filled with the Holy Spirit in my church when she was Shantae's age. She sang in the choir and everything. She was fine 'til she got mixed up with that drug-addict convict of a boyfriend of hers." Frances gathered steam as she accented each point with a slap of her hand on the table. "I went over to her place yesterday, and these kids was by theirselves, so I just brung 'em over here and left a note on Angela's 'frigerator that they was here. Course the 'frigerator was empty as usual. I ain't heard from her yet. I'm gonna try and just keep these young'uns with me. That Angela ain't doin' right by 'em, anyway. She shore won't raised to be this way."

Frances's whole body seemed full of anger as she continued her tirade. "She brings those no-good friends into her apartment, and they be doin' dope right in the livin' room 'cause I smelt it the other day when I was there." Frances paused, took a deep breath, and then loudly exhaled through her tightened lips.

"Are you sure about this?" was all that Lynne could think to say. She was embarrassed that she had been unaware of Angela's drug use. Now that Frances was saying these things, however, the pieces started to fall into place. Maybe that was the reason for the missed appointments. Maybe Angela appeared so keyed up during recent visits because she had been using cocaine. Maybe . . . maybe . . . maybe. . . . But what good did it do to rehash the past? Lynne needed to help Frances at this moment, but she wasn't sure what her role could or should be. Nor did she know what Frances wanted from her. She was well aware that if Frances's fears for Angela came true, the effect on the children could be great. She opened her mouth to speak, but Frances began talking again.

"Yeah, she's doin' drugs again," began Frances. "I tell you what was the final straw—Monique had on the same clothes yesterday when I got there that she was wearin' the day before. Shantae told me she got Chauncey to sleep the night before by singin' to him—said her Momma had gone out and left them by theirselves. I reckon Angela got home before morning, 'cause the young'uns told me she was asleep when they woke up. Shantae said she barely got to school on time." Frances's voice grew louder as she continued to describe Angela's poor supervision of the children. "That Shantae didn't even have no cereal before she left. God only knows what Monique had to eat all day. At least the baby got a bottle, 'cause Monique's been feedin' him anyway. That Angela left again just as soon as Shantae got home from school. Can you believe it? I had to do something, so I brung 'em all over here and left Angela a note, like I said. No tellin' when she'll get home."

Lynne felt the urge to defend Angela a little. All of Frances's accusations were probably true if drugs were once again ruling Angela's life, but Lynne also knew that Angela was a good mother when she wasn't on drugs. Lynne had spoken to Angela's counselor at the First Steps program only a month ago, and he reported that Angela had been attending group meetings regularly.

"Frances, when drugs aren't controlling her, Angela is a good mother."

"I suppose so, but. . . . "

"You see," said Lynne, "she wants those drugs now more than she wants anything, but, when she's herself, she does right by the children. You know that."

"Well, maybe that's true. Those kids sure do mind their momma when she's home. Angela don't put up with no sassin' or backtalkin', and those kids behave theirselves."

"They sure do," agreed Lynne. "Angela has done a fine job of teaching them what's right."

"Lots of kids today be backtalkin' their mommas . . . but not these young'uns." Frances's voice was softening now.

Lynne reassured her, "You know, if Angela wasn't doing those drugs right now, she'd be looking after the children better."

"I know Angela's been down about her boyfriend gettin' arrested for writin' those bad checks. She's had a lot on her, and three kids ain't easy to look after. . . . I know how hard it is. I had four myself—the first three just like stair steps." Frances paused for a moment to think and then continued, "Angela's momma was my first one. A piece of me died when she got killed in that car wreck. I always prayed to God I'd never live to see one of my children in the grave, but God didn't see fit to answer that one. I wonder if that's what might be causin' Angela to do wrong. I tried to be just like a momma to her growin' up, but maybe. . . ." Frances's voice faded, and she never finished what she'd started to say.

Lynne quickly encouraged her, "Frances, you can't blame yourself for Angela's drug problem. She had a weakness, and, when she was exposed to drugs, she couldn't resist them. She was hooked. You can't stop it—she'll have to do that. I thought she had succeeded, but apparently she's had a setback."

"My friend Mattie Cole—her boy done quit them drugs. He won't even come around Angela. You know, his momma turned him in to the police. She told him she was gonna get him help even if he didn't want it. He's been out of prison since just after Chauncey was born, and he don't do those drugs no more. Do you think I could do something like that for Angela?"

"Well, I don't know if—"

Frances didn't wait for Lynne to respond. She pressed on. "Could I have her committed to one of them drug places again or turn her into the police for doin' drugs? You know, I think she's helpin' sell it, too. No tellin' who she's helped to hook on those drugs. The devil's weapons on the young today is what they are. This world needs to look to the Lord. Have you ever called upon the Lord, Miss Lynne?"

Lynne was speechless, but Frances silently waited for a reply to her last question. Lynne attempted to form an answer, but her thoughts were interrupted by the sound of the front door opening. It was Angela.

Lynne drove home feeling completely overwhelmed by what she had learned about Angela from Frances. She felt foolish for not having suspected that Angela was using drugs again. Worse than that, she had no idea what she should do next. Were the children in any kind of immediate danger? Would Frances call the police and ask them to arrest the granddaughter she had raised as her own child? Lynne also began to question what she had done when Angela had shown up at the apartment—or what she *hadn't* done.

Angela had breezed into Frances's kitchen and announced that she was taking her children home. Frances and Lynne stood there, speechless, as Angela quickly gathered the children and walked back out the front door. Gathering her senses, Lynne had raced down the stairs after Angela and asked if she could come out to see her and Chauncey the next afternoon. Angela had just shrugged her shoulders and mumbled, "Do as you please." And she continued down the sidewalk with the three children.

Lynne stopped by a shopping center to use a pay phone. She tried to reach her supervisor, but her supervisor had already gone home for the day. Fortunately, her secretary was still in the office, and Lynne succeeded in arranging an appointment with her supervisor for the following morning.

Lynne returned to her car and headed home. She needed to step away from the situation and forget about it for a little while. Lynne desperately hoped that her friend Cathy would be able to take a walk with her that night. Walking with Cathy always helped clear her mind of work—it was hard to be around Cathy without talking of diets and the newest low-fat recipe. Lynne longed for the relaxation she would get from their walk. She chanted quietly to herself, "Cathy, please be home tonight." Then she turned her car radio up to its full volume.

Discussion Questions

1. Was it appropriate for Lynne to have entertained Frances's discussion of Angela's shortcomings as a mother and of her suspicions of Angela's drug use? If so, did Lynne handle the conversation appropriately?

2. If you had been in Lynne's position, would you have done anything differently while you were in Frances's apartment?

3. Lynne felt foolish for not suspecting that Angela had resumed using drugs. Should she have picked up on it earlier? If so, how would she have confirmed her suspicions? What could she have done to help Angela if she *had* known about her drug use earlier?

4. On the way home, Lynne wonders about the safety of the children. Is there any immediate threat to their welfare? If so, what action should Lynne take to prevent the children from being harmed?

5. What role, if any, should Lynne take in helping Frances to get Angela off drugs? What responsibility, if any, does Lynne have in supporting Frances?

6. What options does Lynne have for resolving the situation described in this story? Make a list.

7. Of the options you identified in your answer to Question #6, which would you choose? Why?

8. Based on the option you chose in your answer to Question #7, what should Lynne do when she visits Angela and Chauncey tomorrow afternoon?

9. What should Lynne do if Angela is not at home when she arrives for their appointment tomorrow?

10. Was it necessary for Lynne to arrange to talk with her supervisor about this family's situation? What, if anything, can the supervisor do to help Lynne?

11. In general, what legal issues must be taken into consideration in dealing with this situation or other similar situations involving suspected child abuse or neglect?

chapter 6

Passing Time

Miki Kersgard

Rachel Thomas greeted Tonya, "How's our favorite little sister today?" Rachel stepped into the narrow hallway of Mavis Steele's apartment and bent down to give the beaming 6-year-old a pat on the head. "Are you home helping your big sister take care of her baby?"

"I'm not the little sister today. I'm the little mommie!" shrieked Tonya, clapping her hands together.

"That's nice, honey." Rachel absently played with Tonya's braids as they walked into the living room, where a commercial for a diet soft drink blared from the television. Rachel stood in the middle of the room, not really paying attention to what Tonya was saying.

"Look!" said Tonya. "Look what Jamille and I did. We got dressed up!" Jamille, Arora Steele's son, sat on the sofa in his infant carrier. Arora is Mavis's daughter and Tonya's older sister. She is 17 years old and gave birth to Jamille 7 months ago.

Rachel had taken an immediate liking to Arora despite her suspicions that the feeling was not mutual. Arora was a small, slender girl with a mysterious and slightly Asian look. She seemed both old and young at the same time, and her graceful movements reminded Rachel of a ballet dancer. Try as she might, though, Rachel could never get Arora to open up to her. Any knowledge Rachel had of Arora's life before she met her had come from Mavis.

The first 2 months after Jamille's discharge from the neonatal intensive care unit had been a bit shaky. He experienced numerous respiratory infections and was hospitalized twice for pneumonia and dehydration. After the first rough months, though, things had gone much more smoothly. Jamille was healthier, and Rachel's visits had become rather routine—until a few weeks ago, when Arora's attention to her son had seemed to wane. Maybe she'd lost interest because Mavis was out of the house more now that she had a part-time job, or maybe something had happened to Arora that she wouldn't talk to Rachel about. There was no telling.

"Look!" Tonya insisted again, tugging at Rachel's sleeve and interrupting her thoughts. Tonya's black patent-leather shoes were dangling from Jamille's feet, and her red felt beret rested jauntily on his head, covering one of his eyes. "Don't tell Mama—he's got on my new hat and the shoes that Mama got me for goin' to church!"

"My, he looks the dashing young man. . . . Don't worry, I won't tell anyone. Did you do that all yourself, or did Arora help you?"

" 'Rora went to the store. I dids it all by myself. Don't he look nice?"

Went to the store? "How did Arora like it when she saw it?" asked Rachel uneasily. She was beginning to think that she wasn't going to like the answer to her question.

"She don't see it. 'Rora's not back yet."

Rachel's feeling was right—she didn't like the answer. "Oh? How long has Arora been gone?"

"Um . . . well, she went out when . . . I think it was. . . . " The little girl looked up at Rachel with a shy smile on her face and an exaggerated shrug of her shoulders. "I don't know," she laughed, and turned her attention toward the television.

Rachel glanced up at the newscaster on the television and thought for a minute. "Well, let's see. . . . I'll bet we can solve this little mystery of ours. Was it just a few minutes before I came in?"

"No, longer than that," replied Tonya.

"Was it all day?" Rachel asked, tickling Tonya to diffuse the tension building up in both of them.

"No!" giggled Tonya, squirming to get away from Rachel. "Not that long."

"I know!" said Rachel, glancing at the television again. "Who was on the TV when she left?" She picked up the *TV Guide* that was laying on top of the old black-and-white television, glanced at the dial to see what channel it was set to, and began thumbing through the daytime listings. "Was it Oprah? Or was it Sally Jesse, the lady with the glasses?"

"Oprah! It was Oprah," yelled the little girl.

Rachel looked at the *TV Guide* again and checked her watch. *All My Children* had already begun, which meant that Arora had left at least an hour ago.

During the past two months, Arora had asked Rachel several times if she could work with Jamille alone for a few minutes while she ran to the store or down the hall to a neighbor's apartment. Rachel hadn't minded at first. The requests seemed reasonable to her, and she was glad to be able to help out. But the requests had become more frequent, and Arora's "few minutes" had stretched into 30, or sometimes 45, minutes.

Two weeks ago, Rachel talked with Arora about the importance of being present during her visits with Jamille. She pointed out that the hour or so she spent with Jamille each week wasn't very much and that the time Arora spent with him practicing what she had learned in that hour would make the biggest difference in his development. Arora seemed to understand and didn't ask to leave during last week's visit.

Even so, Arora didn't seem nearly as enthusiastic about Jamille as she once was. To make matters worse, Jamille's delays were becoming more obvious. He wasn't yet sitting up by himself, and the muscles in his legs were becoming increasingly tight. Rachel was concerned, too, about Jamille's subdued responses to social interactions. Even taking his prematurity into account, he should have been engaging in more social play than he was.

Rachel sat down on the edge of the sofa next to Jamille and looked at Tonya. She had to do something. But what?

"Where's your mama today?" Rachel asked, wondering if there might have been some confusion between Mavis and Arora as to who would watch the children.

"Mama's working today. She's helpin' Miz Page at the home, so I'm helpin' 'Rora take care of Jamille."

Mavis had often talked about her work at the nursing home, but Rachel had no idea which home it was.

Past Mistakes

Mavis had been a big help to Arora in caring for Jamille—especially during those first few months when he was sick so often. Together,

Mavis and Rachel had helped Arora learn the ropes of infant care. They taught her how to take Jamille's temperature, warm his bottle, bathe him, make his formula, and administer medicine. Rachel doubted that Arora would have been able to take care of Jamille without Mavis's help.

Now that Mavis was working, she often wasn't around when Rachel came to visit. Rachel found that she missed her and wondered if Mavis's contributions weren't even more important to Jamille's progress than she had originally thought. These thoughts brought back memories of Rachel's first visit to the family, shortly after Jamille had come home from the hospital.

During that visit, Mavis had been the one who answered all of Rachel's questions about Jamille and their living situation. At one point, Arora left the room, and Rachel asked Mavis whether she or Arora should be considered the primary caregiver for Jamille. "That girl didn't even knowed she was pregnant 'til she was 5 months along," replied Mavis. "How she gonna know what some primary caregiver is?"

Arora hadn't received prenatal care until Mavis discovered her daughter's condition. Mavis was now convinced that her daughter's ignorance and neglect during the first months of her pregnancy had caused Jamille's illness and delays, and she made no bones about stating her opinion to Rachel in front of Arora. Rachel had wondered about the effects of this criticism on Arora, and she wondered now if it contributed to Arora's declining interest in Jamille.

Rachel also wondered whether she, too, might be partly to blame. What could she have done differently to make Arora feel more responsible for—and closer to—Jamille? Had she relied too heavily on Mavis? Had she and Mavis made Arora feel incompetent to care for her own son? Somehow, Rachel felt responsible for Arora's absence. But how could she possibly have known that this was going to happen?

Searching for Answers

Rachel looked through her bag for a toy or two to occupy Tonya and Jamille while she did some quick thinking. She handed Tonya two dolls. Then she brought down some cups, saucers, and plates from the kitchen cupboard to set up a tea party on the carpet. Jamille waved the rattle she had given him and then banged it on the edge of his infant carrier. He does look tiny, she admitted to herself. But if you think about it, he was 2 months premature, and that would make him only 5 months old now if he had gone full term. For a 5-month-old, he's not so small. Rachel caught herself rationalizing and shook her head. The fact was, his weight was still below the fifth percentile for a 5-month-old. I have to stop protecting Arora, she thought, and start thinking more about protecting Jamille.

"Look," said Tonya, interrupting Rachel's thoughts, "this baby doll's almost big as Jamille. Can he come down and play tea party with us?"

"Jamille and I are going to do something together in a minute," answered Rachel. "Anyway, I think he wants to play with his rattle right now. Maybe you could show the dolls the rest of the house. You know . . . give them the grand tour." Tonya thought this was an excellent idea and marched off toward her sister's bedroom to show them around.

Rachel glanced at her watch for the fourth time since she arrived at the apartment. More than a half an hour had gone by, and there was still no sign of Arora. Rachel's next appointment was scheduled for an hour from now, and it took half an hour to get there. While she gently stretched Jamille's legs, she thought about her options. She couldn't call to cancel her appointment from the apartment because the Steeles didn't own a telephone. "Tonya?" she called into the bedroom. "Do you have a key to the apartment?"

"No, ma'am," Tonya answered. " 'Rora took it. She said I was to stay here and look after Jamille, and that I wouldn't need it 'cause I didn't have no bizness leavin' him by hisself."

"That's okay," said Rachel. "I was just wondering."

That leaves that out, thought Rachel. She hated to just take the children and leave without having a key to lock up. She couldn't leave the children, and she really couldn't take them with her to her next appointment. The number of options was quickly diminishing. The temptation to just pack up her things, leave the house, and call Protective Services from the nearest telephone booth nagged at the back of her mind with a disturbing forcefulness. Calm down, she thought. There's a solution here. I just haven't found it yet.

Decision Time

It was getting close to the time that she should leave. Rachel called Tonya in from the bathroom, where the dolls' tour had ended and their bath time had begun.

"I have to leave soon," she told Tonya, "and I was thinking that maybe you and Jamille could come for a ride in my car with me. Would you like that?"

"Really?" asked Tonya. "You don't think 'Rora would be mad?"

"I'm sure Arora won't mind," said Rachel as she quickly towel dried and packed up the dolls. "We're just going to go to a phone booth so I can make a couple of calls. We'll even take the dolls with us." Rachel gathered up her bag and slung it over her shoulder. She hoisted Jamille into his carrier and took hold of Tonya's hand, and the three of them headed out the door.

As they approached the end of the hallway, Rachel heard the elevator clank and whine as it began its ascent from one of the lower floors. Rachel's heart raced as she pushed the down button and stood in front of the metal door. Please, please, let this be Arora, she thought. If it wasn't Arora, she might have to call Protective Services. If it was, she would have to confront Arora about her absence. Neither of these prospects seemed very pleasant.

Discussion Questions

1. What factors may have contributed to Arora's waning interest in her son Jamille? Make a list.

2. Could Rachel have done anything differently on previous visits that may have prevented Arora from losing interest in Jamille or from leaving Jamille alone with Tonya?

3. Rachel questions whether she has been protecting Arora at Jamille's expense. Do you think that she has been?

4. According to the laws of your state, has Arora been unlawfully negligent in leaving the children alone? Is Rachel legally responsible for reporting this incident?

5. Do you think that Rachel's decision to take the children and leave the apartment was her best choice? If so, why? If not, what might have been a better alternative?

6. If Arora is on the approaching elevator, what should Rachel do or say when she gets off?

7. If Arora is not on the approaching elevator, what are Rachel's options for handling the situation? Make a list.

8. Of the options you identified in Question #7, what are the pros and cons of each? Which of these options would you choose if you were Rachel, and why?

9. After this immediate crisis is resolved, should Rachel alter her approach to working with this family? If so, how?

10. In general, what tips or precautions would you give to professionals who are: 1) working with teenage mothers and 2) working with extended families (e.g., grandmothers)?

Proceed with Caution

P.J. McWilliam

arrie Richards inched her car along the curb, closely inspecting the numbers on the mailboxes and storefronts. Fortunately, there was little traffic, and the road was wide enough for passing cars. After 2 years of working for the Preschool Inclusion Program (PIP), Carrie prided herself on knowing her way around the neighborhoods of Baxter, but this was new territory. She had followed Gloria's directions to the letter. This must be the right street, she thought; but so far nothing she saw suggested a child care center.

Connell Street was lined with single-family dwellings and semi-detached houses, about half of which had been converted into small commercial enterprises during the past several years. Through the driver's window, Carrie spotted a cluster of storefronts—410, Apex Hardware . . . 412, Lou's Sporting Goods . . . 414, Betty's Beauty Salon. Gloria had said that Violet's place was near a beauty shop, so she must be close. Carrie glanced at the clock on the dashboard—8:41 A.M.

Gloria had assigned Carrie to work with Nathan Hammond, a new referral to PIP. Nathan had been identified early in infancy as having developmental delays of unknown origin. He also had a seizure disorder that had proven to be somewhat difficult to control. The county's early intervention infant program had provided home-based services for Nathan during the past 2 years; but now that he was 3 years old, the program could no longer be reimbursed for its services. The woman who had made home visits to Nathan's family had informed PIP that Nathan's mother resumed full-time work about 6 months ago and had enrolled Nathan in child care at Violet's place.

According to Gloria, Violet Webster was considered to be a pillar of Baxter's African American community. She started a small child care operation in her home more than 15 years ago. When word spread of the excellent care she provided, her operation expanded into a separate building with two full-time and several part-time caregivers. Both African American and white children were presently enrolled in her center. In fact, Gloria's own child had been cared for at Violet's several years ago.

Gloria had told Carrie that Violet frequently invited one or more of the children to her home for the weekend and that Violet was known to take children home for supper if their parents needed to work late or had an emergency. Violet was also a strong advocate for the children she had cared for in the past and, on more than one occasion, had spoken to the school board on a child's behalf. This all sounded a bit like fantasy to Carrie, and she wanted to meet this pied piper of Baxter.

Two houses beyond the beauty shop, on the opposite side of the street, Carrie saw a yellow-shingled house. A chain-link fence spanned the width of the small front yard, and Carrie spotted an aging wooden sign posted on a mimosa tree to the right of the driveway gates. Carrie came to a stop by the curb to read the sign.

Although the paint was weathered, she could make out the letters that spelled "Smiling Faces Day Care." Maybe she had gone too far. Then Carrie noticed a blue van in the driveway. Above its rusting rear bumper, a personalized license plate spelled out *V-I-O-L-E-T*. This must be the place, Carrie thought, but Gloria had never referred to the center by anything other than "Violet's place." Carrie parked her car and walked toward the front door.

Meeting the Pied Piper

A slender, young African American woman answered Carrie's knock. She opened the door, greeted Carrie with a soft "Hi," and stood silently waiting for a reply. Two bashful toddlers peeked out from behind her and stared at Carrie.

"Hi, I'm Carrie Richards from PIP—the Preschool Inclusion Program. I'm supposed to see Nathan Hammond today." Carrie gave a little wave to one of the toddlers, who giggled in return.

The giggle attracted the attention of the young woman, who turned toward the children. "You two best get back in your chairs," she warned. They immediately scampered off into the room beyond, and the young woman again faced Carrie.

"This is Violet's place, isn't it?" asked Carrie.

"This is Violet's," she answered. "Wait a minute, and I'll go get her." She left Carrie standing in the doorway while she summoned Violet.

Within a few minutes, Carrie was greeted by Violet herself. "Good morning!" Violet's smile radiated a warm welcome. "We've been expecting you. You're the one who's supposed to be working with our Nathan, isn't that right?"

"Yes, that's right. I'm Carrie Richards from the Preschool Inclusion Program." Carrie extended her hand, and Violet accepted a handshake. "It's a pleasure to meet you," continued Carrie. "I've heard so much about your center from Gloria."

"Gloria Compton?"

"Yes. Gloria is my supervisor. She's the director of PIP."

"Well, you're real lucky to be working for her," said Violet. "She's a fine woman. She's got a fine young boy, too. You know, little Sammy used to stay here with us not too long ago."

"Yes," said Carrie, "Gloria mentioned that he had."

"Well, won't you come on through, and we'll see if we can't find young Nathan for you?" Violet led Carrie through an entryway lined with cubbies and coat hooks.

When they entered the classroom, Carrie was immediately struck by the smell of pine disinfectant, a scent that reminded her of the summers she had spent at her grandparents' rustic vacation home beside the river. Actually, much of what she saw reminded her of her grandparents' vacation home. The room was clean and neat, but there was nothing new about it. The walls, the shelves, and even the furniture had that secondhand, painted-over look. Oddly comforting but certainly not vibrant.

Six small tables formed a neat row along the windows that faced the front yard. In the center of each table was a cutout plastic milk jug filled with crayons. Children ranging in age from about 1 or 2 years to about 4 years were picking up crayons from the floor, putting away coloring papers, and moving chairs from the tables to the opposite side of the room. The young woman that Carrie had met at the door was helping a group of the youngest children to pick up crayons at the first table.

"This here is Leanne," said Violet, introducing Carrie to the young woman. "I believe you two have already met."

"Hi, Leanne," said Carrie, extending her hand.

Leanne ignored Carrie's extended hand, softly said "Hello," and returned her attention to the group of toddlers.

"Leanne works this room," explained Violet. "She has the older ones most of the day, but she and I usually keep all of the children in this room until Diana arrives at 9 o'clock. Then Diana takes the little ones into the other room until about 4 o'clock, when it's time for Leanne to go."

"Which room is Nathan in?" asked Carrie.

"Oh, yes. I almost forgot our Nathan." Violet scanned the room and pointed out a blond little boy who was pushing a chair aimlessly around in a circle. "He acts sort of lost sometimes. . . . Did you want to take him off by himself?"

"Actually, I'd like to spend some time just observing him today, if that would be all right with you."

"That would be fine by me. You just let me know if I can do anything else for you." Violet smiled again at Carrie and then walked to the far side of the room where she switched on a television that sat on a high shelf.

Bugs Bunny and Pals

The set crackled and flickered on, revealing a fuzzy image of Bugs Bunny outwitting Elmer Fudd in his usual slapstick fashion. The older children, who had already moved their chairs in front of the television, screeched them into place and sat down. Meanwhile, Leanne moved the younger children's chairs from the tables to the viewing area. The toddlers followed like little ducklings and were soon seated cross-legged on their chairs in the front row.

As Leanne stepped back to survey her charges, a noise from the other side of the room attracted her attention. It was Nathan. He had abandoned his chair in the middle of the room in favor of a plastic bucket of colored pegs. He had pulled the bucket off a low shelf, and several pegs clattered to the floor. His blue eyes stared blankly at Leanne as she approached him.

"Nathan, I told you to go sit down by the TV. It's not time for toys now." Leanne put the pegs back into the bucket, and then she took Nathan by the hand and led him toward the group. She grabbed his chair with her free hand and quickly situated him on the end of a row of viewers.

Nathan appeared unaffected by his change in location. He curled his legs under himself, put a thumb in his mouth, and twirled his hair with the index finger of his other hand. His blue eyes stared again, this time at the flickering images on the screen.

Leanne once again surveyed her charges, rubbed the back of her neck, and then, without saying a word, crossed in front of Carrie on her way to the sink. Leanne picked up a damp sponge and began to re-trace her steps when Carrie broke the silence by asking, "Would it be all right if I sat down with the children and watched?" Leanne looked at Carrie briefly, gave a quick nod, and shrugged her shoulders. Then she walked over to the abandoned tables and began to wipe them with the sponge.

Carrie decided that she would have to take care of herself. She qui-etly moved a tot-size chair to the back row and sat down between two little girls. She felt quite awkward in the little chair and pulled at her skirt to cover her raised knees. With her hands in her lap like a good schoolgirl, Carrie began to watch Bugs Bunny and Elmer Fudd.

After a minute or two, Carrie sensed the stare of a nearby viewer. She turned to her right to find two big, brown eyes accompanied by an ear-to-ear grin. Carrie returned the smile.

"Mama buy new shoes," the little girl whispered. She stuck out her foot to show Carrie a tiny pink sneaker.

"Very pretty!" said Carrie.

"They gots a Minnie Mouse!" The little girl lifted her foot on top of Carrie's raised knees and pointed to a Minnie Mouse emblem on the side of her shoe.

Carrie was bending forward to admire Minnie Mouse when she was startled by Leanne's voice: "Brittany! Keep your hands and feet to yourself." Brittany quickly removed her foot from Carrie's lap, sat up-right, and faced the television. Carrie felt a bit scolded herself, but what bothered her most was that she had contributed to Brittany's being reprimanded. Her guilt was somewhat relieved when Leanne resumed wiping the tables, and Brittany stole a moment to flash Carrie a sheep-ish grin.

Carrie's attention returned to Nathan, who sat two rows in front of her to the far right. Carrie could see that he was starting to squirm in his chair. As she watched, he turned to face the children in the row be-hind him, and soon after he was kneeling on the floor with his tummy on the seat of his chair. Carrie tried to catch Leanne's reaction, but Leanne was standing in the doorway talking to a woman who had just arrived. Carrie wondered if the woman might be Diana.

Meanwhile, Nathan had abandoned his chair altogether, and a 20-gallon aquarium that sat on a partition between Leanne's and Diana's rooms caught his eye. He was already pointing his index finger as he toddled toward the lighted display of goldfish. Carrie couldn't decide whether she should intervene or continue to sit and watch. Nathan was within inches of the fish tank; but, before Carrie could make up her mind, he stumbled and fell.

The sound brought Leanne scurrying into the room. She scooped Nathan off the floor and quickly inspected his forehead, elbows, and knees for damage. Nathan didn't cry or resist Leanne's inspection. Then Leanne pulled a highchair from the corner in front of the television, put Nathan in it, and snapped on the tray.

The last 5 minutes of *Bugs Bunny and Pals* were relatively quiet and uneventful. Nathan remained in the highchair, Carrie remained in her seat, and Brittany became engrossed in the cartoon. At one point, the little girl on the other side of Carrie became interested in Carrie's dangling star earrings and tried to touch them. Without making eye contact, Carrie gently nudged the child's hands away and made a mental note not to wear such things on future visits.

A, B, C and 1, 2, 3

After 20 minutes of cartoons, Leanne turned off the television, and the children rose from their seats. The woman who had entered was, in fact, Diana, and she took the children who were younger than 3 years of age into the next room with her. Leanne announced to the remaining 11 or 12 children that it was circle time and instructed them to move their chairs. The children scooted their chairs across the linoleum floor until they formed a semblance of a circle. As the children seated themselves, Leanne made some minor adjustments to the circle and placed Nathan between Brittany and another little girl, Elise, who was much larger than Nathan. Carrie sat on a chair behind the group.

"Quincy, can you say your ABCs?" asked Leanne.

Quincy stood up, took a big breath, and began, "A, B, C, D, E, F, G, H, I. . . ." He made it all the way to 'Z' without a hitch.

Thomas's turn was next. He got mixed up somewhere around "G, H, I, and J"; but Leanne got him back on track, and he made it to the end. The rest of the children took turns reciting the alphabet, and then Leanne moved on to counting from 1 to 20.

Somewhere around the shift from letters to numbers, Carrie noticed that Elise was holding her arm and leaning away from Nathan. Carrie continued to watch and saw that Nathan was grabbing and squeezing Elise's arm and pushing her leg. Carrie felt sorry for Elise and was surprised that she was not complaining out loud to Leanne. Part of the problem seemed to be that Elise's chair was too close to Nathan's, and her greater size put her right up against him. Carrie quietly moved Elise's chair a few inches away from Nathan's. The little girl glanced briefly at Carrie with a look of relief and gratitude.

A minute or two later, Nathan slipped between the two chairs and headed toward the toy shelf. Leanne immediately retrieved him, put him back in his chair, and pushed Elise's chair back against Nathan's.

Leanne never asked Nathan to recite the alphabet or to count to 20 by himself. Nevertheless, when they sang the alphabet song as a group, Nathan's little voice sang out "A, B, C," and he fumbled through the rest of it, making up sounds to go along with the tune.

The last activity during circle time was naming colors. Leanne had a stack of cardboard on her lap. Each piece of cardboard had a square of a different color pasted on its front. She went around the circle asking each child to name the color she was holding before them. After the second or third round, Quincy and Thomas became distracted by their own game.

The discreet nudging of one another's feet had rapidly escalated into a nonverbal competition: Whoever could stick his foot out farther while keeping his bottom on his chair would win. Being the shorter-legged of the two, Quincy fell off his chair during the heat of the competition. The circle erupted into laughter. Carrie looked up for Leanne's reaction only to find Violet standing in the doorway behind Leanne. The boys spotted Violet at the same time and were immediately sobered by her presence.

Violet displayed no emotion as she took two steps forward. "Quincy . . . Thomas . . . won't you two come with me? I think we need a little talking." She turned and walked back through the doorway.

Thomas reluctantly stood up, and Quincy pulled himself off the floor to stand beside his competitor. The two boys looked at each other briefly, then walked one behind the other, heads down, through the doorway and into the room that Violet had just entered.

Brittany named the next color correctly—purple. Now it was Nathan's turn. Leanne held up a green square. "Nathan, what color?"

"Pa-pa," Nathan said proudly.

"No, it's not purple." Leanne tapped the green square with her finger. "Look now. . . . What color?"

"Bwew."

"No, not blue. Look again, Nathan. You know this color."

"Pa-pa," he said softly.

"Not purple . . . not blue. What color?"

Nathan screwed up his face and rubbed his forehead with both hands. Elise leaned over and whispered, "Green."

Nathan removed his hands from his face. "Gween!"

"That's right, Nathan. This is green." Leanne tapped the square again for emphasis. "Green. . . . Green like the grass. You had a little help on that one, didn't you?"

"Gwass gween," repeated Nathan, his pride restored.

Elise was next. "Red," she said in a loud, clear voice. She beamed with pride when Leanne confirmed her response.

"Wed," echoed Nathan, smiling proudly himself.

Meanwhile, Carrie noticed that Quincy and Thomas had returned. They stood in the doorway with their heads back, looking up at Violet's face. Violet said something to them, and they nodded their little heads in unison. Then she spread her arms, and the two boys wrapped their arms around her ample thighs. Violet returned their hug, gave each of them a quick kiss on the top of the head, gently patted their bottoms, and sent them on their way. The boys hurried over to their chairs and sat down.

An Energizing Snack

Circle time was soon brought to a close, and the children moved their chairs into place at the tables for snacktime. While pushing his chair toward the tables, Nathan was accidently knocked over by the reckless driver of another chair. Elise witnessed Nathan's fall and came to his rescue. She reached around his middle and was struggling to get him upright when Leanne came by and scooped him off the floor. He stretched the palm of his hand toward Leanne's face. She gave his hand a quick kiss, wiped a tear from his eye, and put him in the highchair beside the table with Quincy, Thomas, and two other children.

Leanne passed out waxed paper cups of juice and selected a child to go around the tables offering graham crackers from a plastic basket. Each child took two crackers, except Nathan, who took one and was given a second, and Thomas, who took three and had one snatched back by Leanne.

Nathan handled his snack independently; however, he did make a sizable pile of crumbs on the highchair tray. About midway through snacktime, Quincy and Thomas started blowing bubbles in their juice, making enough noise to entertain each other but not enough to attract Leanne's attention. Nathan thought their antics were quite amusing, and he started to giggle, which only encouraged the boys to continue.

Then Nathan tried the trick himself, but something went wrong. Juice spewed across the tray in a shower, and Nathan sputtered and coughed in an attempt to clear his throat. Carrie started toward Nathan, but Leanne made it there ahead of her.

"Nathan! Nathan, what's wrong?" Leanne quickly removed the tray, leaned Nathan forward, and started patting his back. Nathan's red-rimmed eyes were as big as saucers as he continued to sputter, gag, and cough. When he regained his breath, Leanne released him, and he slouched against the back of the highchair looking stunned and exhausted.

"Nathan, what happened? Did you choke on a cracker?" asked Leanne. Nathan just stared. Then Leanne turned toward Quincy and Thomas. "What happened to Nathan?"

Guilt was written all over their faces, but the two boys just shrugged their shoulders and took a bite of their own crackers. Carrie felt sorry for Nathan, who still looked a bit dazed. She wanted to tell Leanne what had happened, but then she would have to admit that she had just stood by and watched. Something told Carrie that Leanne wouldn't be very pleased about that, so she decided to feign ignorance. Besides, Quincy and Thomas had been in enough trouble this morning already.

The Cleaning Crew

After snacktime, the children lined up in single file at the door to Diana's room. Then Leanne told them to "Walk—don't run!" out to the play yard. Diana's room was empty and dark as she had already taken her group outside. The children walked through Diana's room and then through the screened-in porch at the back of the building.

Nathan, fully recuperated by now, began to follow the group but was stopped at the door by Leanne. "Nathan, you stay in here with me while I sweep the floor." She reached into Diana's room and positioned a safety gate in the doorway between the two rooms. It was just the three of them now.

Leanne immediately busied herself with wiping the tables. Nathan made his way over to the toy shelf and pulled down the plastic bucket of pegs he had gotten out earlier. He sat on the floor and carefully took out one peg at a time, making a neat pile of pegs beside the bucket. Carrie walked over to Nathan and stooped beside him.

"Look at all the colors!" Carrie pointed to the pegs in his pile one by one. "Red, yellow, blue, green . . ."

Nathan looked up at her, then looked down and pointed to a red peg. "Pa-pa," he proudly announced.

Carrie quickly poked around in the bucket and found a purple peg. "Here's a purple peg. See . . . pur-ple. You want pur-ple?" She gave the peg to Nathan, who accepted it with a smile and placed it on the pile beside the bucket.

Then Nathan pulled a red peg from the bucket and extended it toward Carrie. "Want pa-pa?"

"Thank you," said Carrie, accepting the peg.

The sound of Leanne sweeping the floor caught Nathan's attention. He pushed himself up to a standing position and toddled over to her, leaving Carrie by herself.

"Bwoom . . . all dirdy?" Nathan inquired of Leanne.

"Yeah," said Leanne, "You guys made a mess in here."

"Dirdy?"

"It's dirty all right. You want to help clean it up?"

"Nate-Nate do?"

"Tell you what, Mr. Nate-Nate. How about you get the dust pan for Leanne?" Leanne pointed to the dust pan that was leaning against the side of the sink.

Nathan got the dust pan and was walking toward Leanne when he stumbled and fell. He picked himself up without a whimper and continued on. He squatted in front of her broom and held the dust pan an inch or two above the floor. Leanne pushed it down with her toe and swept up the graham cracker crumbs.

Carrie had returned the pegs to the shelf and was standing near the sweeping crew. "He's a pretty smart little fella, isn't he?"

"He does all right by hisself," said Leanne. She picked up the dust pan and emptied it into the wastebasket beside the sink. "He just needs lovin' like the rest of them."

"I suppose everyone can use that," said Carrie.

"Course, he can be a handful sometimes, too."

"I can see how that might be true."

Leanne put the broom and dust pan away and removed the safety gate. She reached for Nathan's hand and paused a moment to look at Carrie. "If only he wouldn't fall down so much. He's gonna break his neck one day." Then she and Nathan walked through Diana's darkened room. Carrie followed a few steps behind.

Safety First

The play yard had the same secondhand, mix-and-match look as the rooms Carrie had just left; although nothing looked new, there seemed to be plenty of old to go around. The entire yard was surrounded by a chain-link fence. The remains of boxwood hedging along the fence told of attempts to conceal its industrial look, but the fence maintained its prominence.

The interior of the yard was divided into three play spaces by additional fencing. In the far left-hand corner was a perfectly square play space with a swing set, an old log cabin playhouse, and a large home-made sandbox. Diana sat on top of a child-size picnic table, sipping from a plastic tumbler and monitoring the activities of the toddlers in this play area.

The right side of the yard boasted a bigger swing set, a slide, and a tire swing. Someone had also built a plywood structure resembling a tugboat cabin on top of a real rowboat. It must have been impressive at one time, but the yellow, red, and green paint had long since faded and peeled.

The porch door opened to a third play area, which sat between the other two. Although quite narrow where it adjoined the other play areas, it formed a crescent around the side of the building where a homemade tree house and an old shed stood. One wall of the shed had been removed so that the children could play inside.

Carrie squinted as she stepped into the bright sunshine. She spotted Thomas and Quincy sitting at a large picnic table in the center play area and approached them.

"Hi, fellas! What are you up to?"

The two boys grinned at one another and looked down at their swinging feet under the table.

"Don't tell me you've worn yourselves out already?" teased Carrie.

"They're being punished," said Diana from her perch in the toddler play area.

"Oh . . . I'm sorry," said Carrie. "I didn't know." Carrie realized she had committed yet another faux pas. But how was she supposed to know they were being punished? And for what? Probably just for having fun, she thought. This hard-nosed approach to discipline was beginning to get under her skin. She was also growing tired of trying to be friendly to Leanne and Diana when her efforts were not being reciprocated. They should show more respect for her. After all, she was a professional, and she was there to help them—not the other way around. The least they could do was try to be friendly.

Carrie walked away from the picnic table and headed toward the play yard around the side of the building. She wanted to get as far away from Diana's watch as she could. As she walked around the corner, pink-sneakered Brittany and another little girl called to her from the tree house and invited her to play. Carrie waved to them and smiled, but she declined the invitation. She was sure that Diana would not approve of her joining the girls in the tree house, and she didn't want to give Diana the opportunity to ridicule her.

At the far end of the side yard, a group of boys and girls were playing in the old shed. They were building a variety of structures with large wooden planks and plastic crates. Nathan was wandering along the fence at the far end of the play area, and Carrie walked over to greet him.

"Hi, Nathan! What are you doing over here?"

Nathan looked up at her but said nothing. Then he stooped beside the fence and began pulling bits of grass from the other side.

Carrie crouched beside him. "What are you doing, Nathan?"

"Nate-Nate do." Nathan grabbed a handful of grass and showed it to Carrie. "Look it!"

"Thank you, Nathan." Carrie held out her hand to accept the gift, but Nathan held on to it. "What is that, Nathan?" she asked.

"Fow-a," said Nathan proudly.

"A flower?"

Nathan nodded his head vigorously.

"That's a very nice flower." Carrie looked over her shoulder to see if Diana or Leanne was watching, then she reached though the fence and plucked three nearby buttercups. She offered them to Nathan. "Here are some more flowers—pretty, yellow flowers."

Nathan grabbed the flowers, smashed them against his nose, and sniffed loudly. Then he pushed them into Carrie's face and said, "Do!"

Before Carrie could respond, Nathan was distracted by a loud rumble. He dropped the buttercups and stood up as his eyes searched for the source of the noise. It was Quincy and Thomas, their time-out at the picnic table finished, speeding around the corner of the building in a squeaky, old wagon. Thomas sat inside holding the handle tightly with both hands, and Quincy was pushing from behind. They were headed straight toward the side of the shed, but Quincy stopped the wagon just inches short of catastrophe.

"Hi, lady!" Thomas said with a wave of his hand.

"Hi, boys!" said Carrie. "That's some fast wagon you've got there."

"Yeah, I gotta drive it. Don't wanna make a crash."

"Looks like you drive it pretty well."

"Yeah, I drive it real good," said Thomas, and he turned to follow Quincy into the old shed.

The boys began negotiating with the other children to get a few planks and a crate to fix up their wagon. Meanwhile, Nathan wandered over. He was trying to figure out how to move the wagon's up-turned handle so that he could pull it, too, when Quincy spied the interloper.

Quincy dropped his plank and ran toward the wagon screaming at Nathan, "Hey, that's our car! Go away! We had it first!" He yanked the handle out of Nathan's hand. Nathan was stunned. Confused, he stared at Quincy and rubbed his hand.

Carrie again quickly looked around for Diana and Leanne. Finding them absent, she decided to intervene. "Wait a minute, Quincy. How about if you guys take Nathan for a ride in your car? He'd really like it."

Quincy maintained a firm grip on the wagon handle. "Nah. He can't ride it. He's too little."

"He doesn't look too little to me. How about it? Maybe just a short ride, then you guys can have it all to yourselves?"

"Nah. . . . He'll fall down. He's a baby."

"Yeah," chimed in Thomas. "He's a baby. We had it first."

Carrie continued negotiating with the two boys, and they finally agreed to give Nathan a short ride—provided that Nathan held the planks and the crate in the wagon for them.

Nathan sat proudly amongst the planks and crate while Quincy pulled the handle and Thomas pushed. They informed Carrie that they were heading toward the boat, where they were going to fix up their "car." As they rounded the corner of the building and passed in front of the toddler yard, Carrie hoped that Diana would see how she had managed to include Nathan in the other children's play.

The boys were nearing their destination when a plank fell out of the wagon, and they stopped to make adjustments to the load. Nathan tried to help, but his foot got caught on the crate, and he toppled over the side of the wagon. His crying brought Leanne to the scene.

She stood him up and inspected the damage—only a scratched knee. Then she turned to Thomas and Quincy for an explanation. Before they could say anything, Carrie told Leanne that the boys were just giving Nathan a ride and that they did not cause him to fall. The boys looked relieved.

Leanne said nothing to Carrie but told Thomas and Quincy, "It's okay to play with Nathan, but you need to remember that he's little. You have to be careful that he doesn't fall." Thomas and Quincy nodded their heads and went off in their wagon, leaving Nathan behind. Leanne took Nathan inside to wash his knee.

When Leanne returned, she put Nathan in one of the baby swings in the toddler yard where she said he would be safe. It looked as though Nathan would be spending the rest of playtime in the toddler yard, so Carrie decided she would try to talk to Violet for a few minutes before the children came back indoors.

An Explanation

"What did you think about our Mr. Nathan?" asked Violet. She continued cutting bologna and cheese sandwiches and piling them onto the tray in front of her.

"He's a cute little guy," remarked Carrie. "He's doing some nice talking, too."

"Yes, he has started coming out lately. But he hasn't always been that way."

"You mean he's just started talking recently?"

"It's not just the talking," Violet wiped her hands on a towel and gave her full attention to Carrie. "When he first came here, he was like a little zombie. I told his momma—her name's Ruth—well, I told Ruth that she needed to tell those doctors to ease up on those drugs they were giving him. You know, children can't learn when they're walking around half asleep!"

"What drugs were those?"

"That medicine he was taking for his seizures. I'm always forgetting the name—never could pronounce it anyway." Violet smiled and continued, "Well, Ruth finally told them, and they did just that. Made all the difference in the world." She pulled an industrial-size can of pear halves from a shelf and began to open it.

"Does he have seizures often?"

"Every once in a while, but not very often. Let me tell you, though, the first time he did—well, it like to scared Leanne half to death!" Violet chuckled warmly as she scooped the pear halves one by one into small paper dishes.

"If you don't mind me asking, Mrs. Webster, why does Leanne put Nathan in the highchair? Does it have anything to do with his having seizures?"

"No. Not really. Leanne just can't be watching him all the time—not with all the other children she has. He's always wandering off on his own, and if he's not getting into one thing or another, he's falling down. She has to put him somewhere he won't get hurt."

"Oh, I see," said Carrie. Actually, she didn't understand at all. Maybe he was prone to wandering off, and maybe he did fall down a lot; but the use of restraints seemed a little excessive from what she had observed. What was the purpose of his inclusion if he was always being restrained? And what was he learning if every time he fell he was locked into the highchair or a baby swing?

"Actually," continued Violet, "I've been telling Leanne to try to keep him out of the highchair as much as she can. She's trying, but she hates to see him get hurt."

Violet picked up the tray of sandwiches. As she walked past Carrie she looked over her shoulder. "Sometimes I wonder if Leanne doesn't favor him a little over the other children." She smiled and walked through the doorway that led to Leanne's room.

Parting Thoughts

The children were washing their hands and seating themselves at the small tables by the windows. Leanne was locking Nathan into the high-chair. A funny way to show love, thought Carrie.

Carrie said good-bye to Violet and asked if next Tuesday morning would be a good time for her to visit again. Violet smiled her usual smile and informed her, "We'll be here. You just come whenever you want. We'll do whatever we can to help you out."

On her way out the front door, Carrie said good-bye to Leanne and thanked her for letting her observe. Leanne just said, "Uh-huh," and continued serving sandwiches to the children. She didn't look at Carrie.

On her way back to the office, Carrie wondered what she should do about Nathan. She had always been a firm believer in inclusion, but this situation left her with some doubts. Maybe she should recommend to Nathan's parents that they look for another child care center. Nathan was so cute, and, although he appeared to have definite limitations, he had a lot of potential. She hadn't met his parents yet, and she wondered if they were aware of what was going on at Smiling Faces Day Care.

Perhaps she should talk to Gloria about setting some policies on where PIP will provide consultation services. If not, maybe they could develop a list of child care centers that PIP recommends for children with disabilities and provide the list to parents. On second thought, hadn't Gloria raved about Violet's place? Gloria's own child had gone there. Maybe it was best to work around Gloria in this case. Then again, maybe Gloria knew something about Smiling Faces that she didn't. There was a lot to think about before next Tuesday.

Discussion Questions

1. Did Carrie conduct herself in an appropriate manner during her visit to Smiling Faces Day Care? What did you like about the way she handled the visit? What, if anything, would you have done differently if you had been in her position?

2. Carrie did not perceive Leanne and Diana as being very friendly toward her. Is Carrie's perception accurate? If so, what might have contributed to Leanne's and Diana's unfriendliness?

3. Could anyone have done anything prior to Carrie's first visit to Smiling Faces Day Care that might have improved relations between Carrie and the staff?

4. How would you rate the overall quality of child care that the staff of Smiling Faces Day Care provided? Make a list of the program's strengths. Make a second list of the concerns you have about its quality.

5. Make a list of specific recommendations that you would, if asked, offer to Violet as a means of improving the overall quality of her child care program.

6. Is Smiling Faces Day Care an appropriate environment for Nathan?

7. One of Carrie's major concerns was Leanne's use of the highchair to keep Nathan from wandering off or falling down. Is this a valid concern? How might Carrie address her concern with Leanne?

8. Carrie was thinking about recommending that Nathan's parents look for an alternative preschool placement. Is this Carrie's best option? Why or why not?

9. What should Carrie's role be with Nathan's parents?

10. What should Carrie's role be with the staff at Smiling Faces Day Care?

11. If you were Carrie and responsible for providing specialized services at Smiling Faces Day Care, what would your plan of action

be? What would you hope to accomplish, and what specific actions would you take during the next few weeks to attain your goals?

12. Inclusive preschool education is typically based on a consultation model. This model involves a three-way relationship between the specialist or therapist, the child's parents, and the staff of the program in which the child is placed. What should the role of each be in making decisions for a child? How can this team maintain effective communication and working relationships?

c h a p t e r   8

Beyond Duty

Miki Kersgard

Carrie Richards drove slowly down Connell Street in Baxter. She was early for her appointment with Violet Webster, the director of Smiling Faces Day Care, and had time to watch the neighborhood start its day. Her weekly appointments as a consultant for Nathan Hammond, one of the children at the center, were usually in the afternoon; however, Carrie had scheduled an important meeting about another child for this afternoon and so arranged to come to Smiling Faces in the morning. The street looked different in the early morning light, and Carrie was enjoying the new perspective.

The man sweeping the sidewalk in front of Apex Hardware stopped for a moment and waved good morning as Carrie drove by. Carrie had become familiar with the neighborhood and with Smiling Faces. All of the things that troubled her when she had first been assigned to work with Nathan—in particular, the center's tough-love discipline and her fear that the staff members wouldn't welcome her suggestions— seemed silly to her now. Carrie was laughing at herself as she parked her car in front of the yellow-shingled building and saw Violet talking to a short woman who looked to be in her sixties. The woman was standing with her hands on her hips, and she was shaking her head in frustration. Too old to be a parent, thought Carrie as she walked past the fenced-in yard. I wonder what's going on?

A Curious Situation

"And when he told me that Davin was suspended," Carrie heard the woman saying to Violet, "I didn't know who else to come to but you. Can I bring him back here after I go to pick him up at school?"

"Suspended! Since when do they suspend children from kindergarten? I never!" Violet bent down to help 2-year-old Jenny put a pail of sand back into the homemade sandbox where it belonged. "Did they say why they were suspending him?" she asked.

"Not yet. Something must have happened as soon as he got to school this morning. Mr. Roberts wants to talk when I come to pick Davin up." A look of worry crossed the woman's face. "Violet, he said that if I didn't come get Davin right away, he was going to call Social Services and have me charged with child neglect. He made me feel like it was my fault, like I wasn't taking care of Davin like I should be."

"We all know that's not true, Sondra." Violet's arm encircled the woman's shoulders. "You do what you can—I know you do. You take off from that job more than you should already, taking him to his appointments at mental health and all that."

"What more am I supposed to do?"

"Well, honey," Violet said, "you just go pick that child up and bring him on over here. You know how much I care about him. I'll take him any time you need me to. We love him here."

"But Violet, I can't afford to pay any more money."

"Don't worry about that. We'll work something out. Now you just go get that boy out of there."

Carrie watched as the woman got into an old white pick-up truck with "Guilford Electronics" painted on its side, and she drove off down the street. Carrie had momentarily forgotten about Nathan Hammond and was filled with questions about the woman and the little boy she would be bringing to Violet's. "How old is her little boy?" Carrie asked as she and Violet watched Sondra drive away.

"It's her grandson, Davin. He's 5. He used to stay here with me, but he started kindergarten this year. It's his first year at a new school, and he's not adjusting as well as he might be. He has a temper, that one, but you just have to show him some love, and he'll mind you."

"Can they really suspend a kindergartner?" asked Carrie.

"Oh, I've seen it happen before. They just write a child up a few times, and, when there's enough paperwork, they can ship the child off to a special school. Down there in Merschel County, where Davin goes to school, they'd much rather do that than try to work with the children themselves."

"Doesn't he have to be assessed before the school can do that?"

"I don't know about being assessed, but Sondra's been taking him to mental health every week now for 3 or 4 months." Violet crossed her arms, stared down the road, and sighed. "I told Sondra 'bout a year ago that Davin's temper was quicker than most—told her that maybe she should look into getting him some extra help. But it wasn't 'til this past summer that she did anything. I suppose she put it off 'til it was too late."

"Didn't she think he needed help?" asked Carrie.

"I suppose she knew it, all right, but she didn't want to admit it."

"Why?"

"Sondra's been through a lot," answered Violet. "Her daughter got mixed up with the wrong crowd early on. Drugs . . . boys . . . ran off a few times. Sondra's practically raised Davin and his brother. The brother's been called a behavior-disturbed child." Violet bent down to pick up a cigarette butt off the ground and said, "That one's in a special place now. . . ." Her voice trailed to a whisper, then she took a deep breath and turned toward the door.

"Would you mind if I made a couple of calls before we talk about Nathan?" asked Violet. "I want to see if there's anything I can do to get Davin's care covered for the days he's suspended." As they walked inside, Violet seemed to transform—she drew herself up and seemed to walk in a more determined and business-like manner than she usually did.

As Violet dialed the phone, Carrie sat in the chair across the table from Violet. Carrie sensed that she was seeing Violet the business-woman, the Violet who spoke to social workers and bankers instead of to children and parents. Carrie watched closely as Violet deftly negotiated funding for Davin's care at Smiling Faces.

Handling Davin

After hanging up the phone, Violet smiled and seemed to relax into the Violet that Carrie knew better—a warm and relaxed motherly figure the children at Smiling Faces adored. They walked outside, and, by the time they helped Jenny to put the pail of sand back into the sandbox twice more, Sondra was back with Davin in tow.

"How's my beautiful Davin child?" yelled Violet when Sondra drove up. Davin waited for Sondra to come around and unhook his seat belt before he bounded out of the car and ran over to Violet. Violet reached down and enveloped the child in the big folds of her arms. "You want to go in and play, like a good boy?"

"Yeah."

"What was that? 'Yeah?' Is that how I taught you to answer?"

"I mean, yes, ma'am. I want to go play."

"Okay. You go on in and play with that bucket and shovel over in the yard there. That one over there . . . the red one. And you can help Jenny keep the sand in the sandbox, too."

"Yes, ma'am," said Davin, hurrying toward the gate and letting himself in.

"I have good news," Violet told Sondra. "They're letting us treat the 2 suspension days as if they were teacher workdays, so Social Services will pay for his care."

"Well, that's a relief. Thank you so—" Sondra was distracted by the sight of Davin climbing the ladder of the sliding board. "Davin! What are you doing up there? I thought Violet told you to play in the sandbox."

"That's okay, Sondra," said Violet. "That's what those people over at the school don't seem to understand. With Davin, you got to let him win some every now and then. You can't win every time with him—not with everything."

"He's a lot like his grandfather sometimes. That man is as hard-headed as anyone I've ever seen!" Sondra said, shaking her head and smiling.

"It's not just that," said Violet. "Davin gets comfortable with a situation, and then someone goes and changes the rules on him. He just can't take it sometimes. He's one of the smartest kids I've had here, but you can't go changing things on him. He'll balk just like a mule."

"You try tellin' that to those folks over at the school."

"Oh, I've tried. Tried to get them to send the teachers to a behavior management class like the one I send my staff to. The principal seems to think it's a good idea, but I don't think she's sent anyone yet."

"When I got to the school, he was just sitting there on a bench in the office, quiet as a mouse," said Sondra. "I asked the secretary how long he'd been there like that, and she said an hour or so. How can they say he's out of control if he'll sit there on a bench like that, with not a toy or a book, for more than an hour?"

Getting Involved

While Sondra and Violet talked, Carrie's mind raced. She had a friend whose husband was on the Merschel County school board. Maybe she would give her friend a call when she got home tonight. There must be a way to get Davin back in school. And she had more questions on her mind. If Davin was receiving counseling or therapy through mental health, wouldn't he have been given a diagnosis? And if he'd been diagnosed as having behavior or emotional problems, how could the school suspend him for acting out? That would amount to suspending him for having a disability. What kind of programming, if any, did the school have in place for this little boy? The more Carrie thought about it, the more she believed she should do something to help.

"He's so happy here," Carrie heard Sondra say. "I'll bet he wishes he could stay suspended for good."

Discussion Questions

1. Was it appropriate for Carrie to initiate or participate in discussions with Violet about Davin and his grandmother Sondra? Has either Carrie or Violet breached confidentiality?

2. Although Carrie has never been directly involved with Davin and his grandmother, she is a consultant to Smiling Faces Day Care. Is it appropriate for her to become involved in Davin's problems? Should she feel responsible to help?

3. If Carrie decides to involve herself in the situation, what role should she play? What would be the best course of action for her to take?

4. If Carrie had been directly involved with Davin while he was enrolled in Smiling Faces Day Care prior to entering public kindergarten, would her responsibilities to this family be different?

5. Could Davin's difficulties have been prevented or lessened if a preschool consultant had provided services for him while he was enrolled in Smiling Faces Day Care? How could a preschool consultant have facilitated a more successful transition to kindergarten?

chapter 9

The Need to Know

P.J. McWilliam

The brass and marble decor of the lobby was no different from that of similarly large hotels in Atlanta, Boston, Chicago, or Denver. A gold plaque directing guests to the beach was the only indication that white sands and the mighty Pacific Ocean lay just beyond the walls. Sherra Nowell-Hill searched for directions to Sebastian's, the restaurant where Paula Goldman worked. At the far end of the lobby, beside a bank of elevators, an advertisement for the restaurant sat on an easel. Following its directions, Sherra turned right and walked down a long corridor.

A teal-jacketed maitre d' approached Sherra as she entered the restaurant. His gold name tag proclaimed him to be Toby. "Good afternoon, ma'am. Welcome to Sebastian's. Will you be dining alone today?"

"Well, actually, no." Sherra looked over Toby's shoulder in search of Paula, but she didn't see her.

"Would you like to wait here, or shall I find a table for you?"

"I'm supposed to be meeting Paula Goldman. She works here. Do you know if she's working today?"

"I'm not sure, ma'am. I suppose I could check in the back. Perhaps you might like to—"

"Hi, Sherra!" Paula removed her apron as she approached them. "Toby, this is Sherra. She works with my son, Jeffrey. She's . . . well, she's sort of his teacher, I suppose." Paula glanced over at Sherra and smiled.

"Nice to meet you," said Toby.

"Nice to meet you, too." Sherra smiled politely and then looked to Paula for directions.

"Well, would you like to sit down?" asked Paula. "The lunch special looks great today."

"I'm not really hungry, but I'd love a cup of hot tea."

"Sure thing," said Paula. "But I'm afraid we'll have to sit in the back. I didn't bring a change of clothes, and they don't approve of us sitting with the guests while we're wearing our uniforms."

Paula escorted Sherra to a small table at the rear of the restaurant and went off to punch her time card and get the tea. Paula's short, dark hair bounced with each step as she hurried toward the door to the kitchen area. It's good to see her looking so perky again, thought Sherra.

A Sensitive Topic

While she waited for Paula to return, Sherra pulled some papers out of her briefcase and sifted through them. Although she hadn't seen Paula and Jeffrey for almost 2 months, she'd gathered the information on child care options that Paula had asked for early in January. Among the papers, Sherra found a photograph of Jeffrey with Santa Claus that Paula had given her when they last met. She held it up to the light. He really was an adorable child, and he resembled his mother in many ways.

Sherra couldn't help noticing that his hemiplegia had completely eluded the camera's lens. What a shame, she thought, that Jeffrey would bear the effects of his early birth for the rest of his life. Then again, many babies who are born 2 months premature don't do nearly as well as Jeffrey had. It's all a matter of perspective, she supposed.

The aroma of strong coffee drifted from the sideboard a few yards away, making Sherra feel a bit queasy. She thought she had passed the morning-sickness stage of pregnancy, but apparently she hadn't. She put the picture of Jeffrey back into her briefcase, grabbed a breadstick from the center of the table, and began to look over her notes.

Sherra had agreed to help Paula look into child care options for Jeffrey, even though she had mixed feelings about the decision. Paula's mother, a retired school teacher, had been caring for Jeffrey since Paula started working full time in August. This arrangement seemed to be working out well, and Sherra couldn't understand why Paula would want to change it.

Paula lived at home, so Sherra had met Paula's parents on numerous occasions, and she thought that they seemed like very nice people. It was obvious that Paula's mother loved Jeffrey and took very good care of him. She also seemed sensitive to her daughter's situation in that she always acknowledged Paula's role as the decision maker in matters concerning Jeffrey. Sherra knew that this wasn't always the case when young, single mothers lived with their parents.

Paula's father taught at the local university and usually wasn't home during Sherra's visits. The few times she had talked with him, however, he had been the picture of courtesy, and he spoke fondly of his daughter and grandson. All in all, Paula's parents appeared to be quite supportive, and Sherra admired them for this. Heaven knows, it couldn't have been easy for them when their daughter went off to college and returned home a year later as an unwed mother.

Sherra had planned to talk further with Paula about her decision to place Jeffrey in child care, but Paula came down with a bad case of the flu in late January. She was sick for weeks and had even been in the hospital with pneumonia and dehydration. Sherra had visited her only once during all of February and March, and then she had only taken flowers to the hospital. She had offered to stop by the house after Paula was back at home, but Paula had said she wasn't feeling up to a visit and preferred that Sherra wait until she had fully recovered.

Sherra hoped that she would be able to talk more with Paula about putting Jeffrey in a child care center before Paula made her final decision. After all, Paula was a bright girl from a well-educated family. What future was there for her working in this hotel restaurant? Paula had never mentioned going back to college, but surely her parents would support her if she decided she wanted to return. Paula was young. Maybe she didn't realize how important an education was for her future—and for Jeffrey's. Wasn't it at least worth bringing up the topic for discussion?

Meeting Resistance

Returning from the back room with two cups of tea, Paula said, "Here you go. Sorry it took so long. There was some mix-up about next week's schedule."

"No problem. I was enjoying the rest." Sherra squeezed a lemon wedge into her cup and reached for the honey. "It's good to see you back in the land of the living. I was really beginning to worry about you. I take it you're feeling better now?"

"Yeah, I am. Thanks." Paula picked up her cup.

There was a brief silence as each sipped the tea.

"Paula, I brought along the information you wanted about child care centers and their fees."

"Oh, thanks. I'd nearly forgotten that I'd asked you. Does anything look good?" Paula paused. "Ummm . . . you know I don't make a whole lot of money here. At least, not yet."

"I know you don't. You have a few choices, though, and Jeffrey is eligible for some programs that don't charge fees for children with special needs."

"Boy, that would really help. So, what have you got?" Paula peered at the papers sitting in front of Sherra.

Sherra folded her hands on top of the papers and leaned forward. "Paula, before we talk about the particulars, I was wondering if we could talk for just a few minutes about why it is that you want to enroll Jeffrey in a child care center."

Paula's brown eyes stared across the table. She said nothing.

"I don't mean to be nosy or anything," Sherra added quickly. "I just thought that if I had a better understanding of why you needed a different child care arrangement it would help me to find a program that suits your needs."

"Uh, sure." Paula looked a bit bewildered. "Well, I suppose I just thought it wasn't very fair that Mom has to take care of Jeffrey every day while I'm at work."

"Has she said something to you about it?"

"No, not really."

"I always thought she enjoyed being home with Jeffrey. Has something changed at home?"

"I don't know . . . maybe." Paula looked down at the table and started picking at the corner of her napkin.

"It must be hard sometimes, being a mother yourself and living with your own parents," Sherra suggested.

"No, not really." Paula spoke quietly and did not look up. She slid her hand back and forth along the crease of the napkin. "They're good to me—maybe they're too good."

"I don't understand. What do you mean, 'They're too good?'"

"I know they were disappointed with me when I got pregnant, but they never said a word. They stuck by me even though I disgraced them."

"They love you, Paula."

"I know." Paula refolded her napkin. "Sometimes I wish they didn't."

"Why do you say that?"

"I'm afraid I'll disappoint them again."

"How?" No sooner had the words come out of Sherra's mouth than she thought of the answer. "You're pregnant again?"

Paula looked up at Sherra. "No, I'm not pregnant." A faint smile passed across her lips, but Sherra could see that she was on the verge of tears. "That's one lesson that doesn't need repeating."

Sherra felt relieved, but she still didn't understand what was going on. Maybe she should try another angle.

"I've been wondering, Paula. Have you given any thought to the possibility of going back to school?"

"No, not really."

"I know how important it is to be independent, but if you could tolerate living at home long enough to finish school, you could earn the salary you need to get your own place."

"I don't know if I can do that."

"Is it because of your parents?"

"No. I just can't." The tears welled up in Paula's eyes.

Sherra was as confused as ever and a little frustrated about Paula's unwillingness to communicate. How could she help if Paula wouldn't tell her what was wrong?

"Oh, Paula, I'm sorry. I didn't mean to push school on you. Of course, that's your decision to make." Sherra reached across the table and gently placed her hand over Paula's. "Life's been a little rough on you lately. I know it must seem like the end of the world to you sometimes. But you're young, and you've got a long life ahead of you. It'll get better, you'll see."

A stream of tears fell down Paula's cheeks, and she breathed deeply to control the flow.

"And Jeffrey is doing so well," continued Sherra. "Even with the cerebral palsy, he's doing almost everything that other 17-month-olds are doing. You've been a great mom and—"

Paula suddenly withdrew her hand from Sherra's and pushed herself away from the table. She grabbed her purse from the floor, rushed past the sideboard, and exited through a side door. Sherra could hear Paula's throaty sobs as the door closed behind her.

A Secret Fear

Outside, the salted breezes coming off the ocean settled Sherra's stomach. She drew in a long breath and instinctively turned left on the weathered wood planks—toward the beach. A few yards ahead, Paula was sitting on a bench that looked out over the dunes. Sherra approached cautiously.

"Paula?" she called softly.

Paula did not respond. She was looking out somewhere beyond the horizon as the wind toyed with strands of her dark hair.

Sherra braved a step closer and perched on the far corner of the bench. "Paula, I'm so sorry I've upset you. Please forgive me. I shouldn't have been so pushy."

"It's okay." Paula wiped a single tear from her cheek. "You didn't do anything. . . . It's me."

Sherra laid a hand on Paula's shoulder and edged closer. "I hope you know how much I admire you. I really do. Please, if there's anything I can do to help, let me know." She lightly squeezed Paula's shoulder.

Paula gasped, trying to hold back her tears, but they came anyway. She leaned into Sherra's shoulder and sobbed uncontrollably. Sherra enveloped her with both arms and patted her back. The source of Paula's upset remained a mystery, but the immediate solution seemed obvious. Sherra let her cry and said nothing.

A few minutes later, her tears subsided. Paula sat up and moved toward the other side of the bench while Sherra rummaged through her purse and found a tissue.

"Thank you," said Paula, dabbing at her reddened eyes and cheeks. "I'm sorry for acting like this. It's just . . . it's just that . . . I need to tell somebody. . . ." She stared at the tissue in her hand.

"What is it, Paula? What do you need to tell somebody?"

Paula took a deep breath and shuddered. Then she looked out over the dunes. "Well, when I was in the hospital last month, I got so scared."

"I can understand that."

"No, I don't think you can." Paula turned toward Sherra, and their eyes met. "I'm HIV-positive."

A sudden chill ran through Sherra's arms and legs. How could this be? She sat back against the bench and groped for her voice. "What do you mean? Are you sure?"

Paula nodded her head slowly.

"When did you find out?" asked Sherra, still trying to make sense of Paula's revelation.

"I've known for almost a year. But when I got so sick with the flu and pneumonia, I was afraid I had AIDS. I thought I was dying—that I wouldn't see Jeffrey. . . ." Again, tears came to her eyes.

"What about Jeffrey? Is he—?"

Paula looked down and nodded her head.

Sherra's hand went up to cover her open mouth. Oh, dear God! She immediately thought of death, and her nausea returned.

"When he was sick so often his first 6 months, they did a blood test, and it came up positive." Tears rolled down Paula's cheeks, but her voice was steady and low. "That meant I had it, too, and—and that I was the one—the one who gave it to him."

"But how? Didn't you know you had it before Jeffrey was born?" By now, Sherra's mind was crowded with questions and emotion. How long would Jeffrey live? How long would Paula be able to care for him? How could Paula have let this happen? Maybe there was more about Paula that she didn't know.

Then another thought crossed Sherra's mind—had she been exposed to the virus? For more than a year and a half, she had played and cuddled with Jeffrey every week without knowing. Could she have it, too? She fought the urge to vomit.

They sat on either end of the bench, both women staring out at the endless, flat line that separated the earth from the sky. Paula began her story about how she became infected with HIV.

A Chance Encounter

Paula's father had wanted her to go to college, but she had been reluctant to leave home. She had always lived beside the ocean and didn't want to leave her lifelong friends. In the end, they reached a compromise: Paula and two of her high school friends applied for and were accepted by a small, nearby university. The three of them decided to rent an off-campus apartment together.

Paula did well in her studies and enjoyed her new independence. She and her friends often traveled to a nearby town on the weekends to enjoy the night life. The town bordered a naval base, so servicemen on leave often hung out in its bars and nightclubs. Paula's first sexual experience was with a sailor.

Their love affair ended almost as quickly as it had begun. The young man was shipped out 2 months after they met, and Paula discovered she was pregnant a few weeks after that. She didn't even think of marriage—she knew it wasn't that kind of love. Even so, she couldn't bring herself to have an abortion. Telling her parents she was pregnant was the hardest thing she had ever had to do.

Paula finished her second semester of college, went home for the summer, and started working full time at Sebastian's in August. Jeffrey was born the day before Thanksgiving, weighing only 2 pounds and fighting for his life.

None Shall Know

Paula folded her hands in her lap. "I can't help thinking how different my life would be if I had had an abortion." she said softly.

"Oh, Paula, don't—"

"No, that's not what I'm saying. I'm glad I had Jeffrey. What makes me feel bad is that I'm *not* sorry I had him. I feel so selfish." Then Paula looked into Sherra's eyes and added, "But you must believe me. I had no idea that I was HIV-positive when I was pregnant."

"I believe you." Sherra wanted to hug Paula, but she held back. "Do your parents know?"

"No. I can't tell them—I just can't. It would kill them if they found out."

"But, Paula, they're going to find out eventually."

"Later, then, but not now." She picked at the shredded tissue in her hands. "Maybe after Jeffrey is in child care, when Mom isn't watching him for me."

Child care. Sherra had completely forgotten. So this was why Paula wanted Jeffrey in child care. The issue seemed so different now— now that she knew Jeffrey was HIV-positive.

"Did you say you had the information on child care centers with you?" asked Paula.

"Uh, yes." Sherra fumbled for her bag and pulled out the manila folder. "Here it is." She began to hand the file to Paula but then hesitated. She pulled the file back, laid it on her own lap, and folded her hands on top of it.

"What is it?" asked Paula.

"I was wondering. . . Are you going to tell the child care center about Jeffrey's being HIV-positive?"

"No," Paula replied flatly. Sherra had never seen this look on Paula's face before. Was it anger? Or maybe hurt? It was difficult to read.

"Don't you think they have a right to know?"

"I can't do that to Jeffrey. I saw the looks on the nurses' and doctors' faces when I was in the hospital. Their rubber gloves and their masks. . . . Oh, they said all the right things, but they stayed as far away from me as possible. I don't want Jeffrey to go through that. He's too young and innocent."

"I understand, but—"

"No, you *don't* understand. I know you want to, but you can't understand unless you've been through it. I have. And I go through it over and over again in my nightmares."

Sherra relinquished the file to Paula, acutely aware of their hands brushing each other's in the transfer.

Issues of transportation, distance, and schedules automatically eliminated some of the choices for child care that Sherra had presented to Paula. Cost or lack of openings eliminated others. They eventually whittled the list down to three options. Two of these were private child care centers. The third option was the center-based program for children with special needs that Sherra's agency sponsored. Approximately half of the children attending the program had disabilities, and the rest were typically developing children from the surrounding community. The program had an excellent reputation, and there was a long waiting list for children without disabilities.

In the end, the program for children with special needs seemed most attractive to Paula. Her preference was clearly influenced by the fact that Jeffrey would be eligible for free services as a child with an identified disability.

Paula frequently visited the program because a few of the children on her caseload attended, and a number of the children she had served in the past had made the transition into the classroom. In fact, one of her favorite colleagues, Marcia, was the teacher in the toddler classroom. Marcia was wonderful with the children, and the parents loved her.

Sherra agreed to find out if there were any openings and told Paula that she would stop by the center on her way back to the office. She would call Paula at work tomorrow to let her know if the center could accommodate Jeffrey. Sherra wasn't sure why she said this; after all, she knew perfectly well that there were at least two openings for children with disabilities. There had been an announcement about it at the general staff meeting just last Tuesday.

The Lives of Many

Sherra's long day was finally coming to an end. The garage door groaned closed behind her as she walked into the kitchen. Inside, the smell of sautéed onions and garlic filled the air, and Sherra's husband Mark greeted her with a kiss on the cheek.

"Hey! You're late," he said with a smile.

"What are you doing home?"

"Isn't that what husbands are supposed to do—come home?"

"But why so early?"

"In truth, my afternoon meeting was cancelled, but . . ." Mark took Sherra by the shoulders and led her into the dining room where the table was handsomely set with their fine china and candles. "What I really want you to believe," he continued, "is that this wonderful husband of yours dragged himself away from his work to come home and cook an exquisite dinner for his tired, pregnant wife."

"This certainly is a surprise!" said Sherra, allowing Mark to seat her in a chair. "And I suppose I can believe you're wonderful—if you really want me to."

Mark brought her a glass of sparkling water with a lime wedge and went back into the kitchen to finish preparing dinner. Sherra tried to relax and enjoy Mark's surprise, but her mind would not let go of the day's events. Images of the scene at the child care center flashed though her mind over and over again.

Sherra had stopped by on her way home to talk to Marcia about Jeffrey. Marcia let her know that there were still two openings for children with disabilities at the center, one of them in Marcia's room. Although Sherra knew that the center's teaching staff had been trained in safety precautions against HIV and other communicable diseases, what she had seen today had sent shivers through her body.

A toddler walking toward a table of toys had tripped and hit her mouth on a wooden chair. The little girl cried hysterically as blood spilled out of her split lip. A nearby adult hurried to comfort the child. She held her hand under the child's chin to catch the blood while she carried her to the bathroom for first aid. A washcloth and some ice were all she needed to stop the bleeding—a common accident among the preschool set. But what if the child had been HIV-positive? What if the child had been Jeffrey? Didn't the staff have the right to know that he was HIV-positive?

"You look awfully serious," commented Mark as he returned with two salad plates.

"Oh, sorry. Just thinking, I suppose."

"Time to stop thinking and start eating," he said in a mock tone of authority.

"You're right. Time to eat." Sherra poured salad dressing and picked up her fork. "So, how was your day?"

Mark began to tell her about an account he had been working on for the past month. The account was one of the company's top clients, and he was very excited about the presentation he would be delivering to them next week. Sherra tried to listen attentively, but her mind kept wandering.

She thought about Paula and Jeffrey—it was hard to believe that they would someday die of AIDS. It was so sad. And had she put herself and her unborn child at risk? Sherra looked at Mark, so excited about his latest campaign. She wanted to tell him all about what had happened and what was on her mind, but she was reluctant.

She remembered how Mark had insisted on driving her to an evening home visit 2 weeks ago because the family lived in a less than desirable section of town. How would he respond if he knew she was working with a baby who was HIV-positive? Did she really want to confront him with this issue?

Mark stopped talking and leaned forward in his chair. "Sherra? Where are you?"

"Oh, I'm sorry, Mark. I guess I'm just tired."

"That's all right. I guess I am going on too much about this campaign. How was your day? Anything exciting happen in the baby business?"

"No. Not really."

The conversation shifted to their plans for the weekend, and Mark started telling her about a new play that had just opened downtown. Sherra tried to push her worries aside and make eye contact with Mark as he spoke. Maybe it's best that he doesn't know, she thought. Then again, wasn't the baby his, too?

Discussion Questions

1. Did Sherra do or say anything that may have contributed to Paula's emotional outburst at the restaurant? If so, how could Sherra have handled the situation differently?

2. Once Paula was upset, did Sherra handle the situation appropriately? What specifically did she do or say that may have been helpful to or supportive of Paula? Would you have said or done anything differently?

3. Does the fact that Jeffrey and Paula are HIV-positive present a real threat to Sherra and her unborn child? To Paula's parents? To other children or staff at the child care center?

4. Should Sherra feel responsible for protecting Paula's parents or the child care staff from contracting HIV from Jeffrey? If so, what course of action should she take?

5. To whom, if anyone, should Sherra divulge information about Jeffrey's HIV status?

6. What steps can Sherra take to protect herself and her unborn child against contracting HIV from Jeffrey? Would such steps have any impact on Paula and Jeffrey or the quality of service she provides to them?

7. How might the news of Paula's and Jeffrey's HIV status influence service delivery in general to this family? Should intervention goals or service needs be revised? If so, how?

8. Who can provide Sherra with information and support as she makes decisions about the issues she now faces in working with this family?

9. Should Sherra inform Mark that she is working with a mother and son who are HIV-positive?

10. What legal issues concerning confidentiality or public health would apply to this situation in your state?

11. Would the decisions you would make regarding this situation hold true for any family whose child is HIV-positive? If not, what factors are likely to influence your decisions?

chapter 10

Daria's Silence

P.J. McWilliam

Gayle disconnected the mobile phone and surveyed the neighborhood before she got out. The rows of townhouses that lined Morrison and Grady Streets seemed bleaker than usual in the morning mist. Twenty years ago the housing project was built to replace the high-rise projects that had stood only a few blocks away. Although once lauded as innovative and attractive, the charm of the project had long since faded along with the paint.

Gayle locked the phone in the trunk and pocketed her keys. Kendra Edwards, Daria's 7-year-old sister, and another little girl were playing with Barbie dolls on the front stoop. The girls looked up from their play as Gayle approached.

"Daria's in the house," announced Kendra.

"Thanks," said Gayle, pausing to look at the dolls and clothes spread out on the stoop. "You know, I used to have Barbie dolls when I was your age. My friend and I would play with them for hours and hours."

"Yeah," replied Kendra flatly. She was obviously not interested in Gayle's childhood. "Daria's real mad," she added.

"Yeah, she be *real* mad," chimed in the other little girl.

"We come out here," said Kendra.

"What's Daria so mad about?" asked Gayle.

The two girls just shrugged and went back to dressing their Barbie dolls.

Gayle knocked on the front door, and a pair of brown eyes peeked out at her from behind a broken venetian blind in the living room window. The eyes belonged to 4-year-old Lavar, Daria's little brother. Gayle waved, and Lavar flashed her a shy grin before he disappeared from the window.

Daria's mother opened the front door with one hand while holding her housecoat closed with the other. Gayle stepped inside.

"Hi, Renee!" said Gayle, but her greeting was not returned.

Renee Edwards turned toward the living room. "Daria!" she shouted. "Daria! The lady's here to drive you to the hospital. You best come on now." Then she walked toward the kitchen at the back of the house, leaving Gayle alone at the door.

Gayle waited a moment, then walked to the living room and stood in the doorway. The room was dimmed by the half-closed venetian blinds. Daria's stepfather, Raymond, was sitting in his vinyl recliner watching television. Lavar played with two plastic action figures on the floor in front of his father. He knocked them together again and again, softly murmuring "Pow! Pow! Pow!" with every impact. Then he threw one of the figures—obviously the loser of the battle—a few feet away. Scooting across the floor on his knees, Lavar retrieved the figure, and the battle began again.

Daria was sitting on the floor at the far end of the room, propped against the end of the sofa. She was on the telephone, but the sound of the television drowned out her voice. Fourteen-month-old Andre was sleeping on the sofa.

Uncertain whether Daria knew she had arrived, Gayle walked into the living room and stood near the end of the sofa. The expression on Daria's face when she looked up made it clear that she wasn't happy to see Gayle. Daria held up an index finger to indicate that she would be finished soon then continued talking on the phone.

Gayle sat down on the sofa to wait, careful not to wake up Andre. As she watched him sleep, she noticed that his breathing was somewhat labored and his nose was stuffed up. She reached over to touch his cheeks and forehead. He seemed a little warm. She wondered whether Daria had noticed.

Gayle glanced around the room and caught Raymond watching her. "It's a little chilly out there this morning," she said.

Raymond issued a barely audible "Hmmpf."

"They say we're supposed to get some rain later today," she continued. But her effort to start a conversation was futile because Raymond had begun to watch television again.

Gayle had, however, succeeded in attracting Lavar's attention. He stared at Gayle from across the room. Gayle smiled at him, and he grinned back. She patted the sofa cushion, encouraging him to come and sit beside her. Lavar approached cautiously with the two figures still in his hands. In no time at all, Gayle had him talking about the names and special powers of each figure. She prided herself on her way with children and, at times like this, wondered whether she wouldn't be happier in a job that didn't involve home visiting.

Lavar started talking about the various battles his superheroes had fought and won, and, in his excitement, he accidently sent one of the figures flying across the sofa. It hit Andre on the head, causing him to wake up and cry. Gayle resisted the urge to comfort Andre, hoping that his crying would force Daria to hang up the phone.

"DARIA! Get off that damn phone NOW!" boomed Raymond. "And tend to that baby."

Daria stood up slowly, the telephone still to her ear, and gave Raymond a piercing scowl. "Well, I gotta go now. . . . Call you later." She hung up the receiver and glared at Raymond again before turning around to pick up Andre. Lavar quickly scooted out of her way and left the room, heading toward the rear of the house.

By now, Andre was sitting up, but he was still crying. Daria grabbed the small quilt he'd been lying on, wrapped it around him, hoisted him onto her hip, and walked past Gayle without so much as glancing at her. Gayle caught up with them as Daria was opening the storm door.

"Daria, shouldn't we take a diaper bag or something?" Gayle asked.

Daria paused a moment, looked toward the street, and then abruptly stepped back inside. The door slammed behind her as she brushed past Gayle and walked into the kitchen. Gayle waited at the front door, watching Kendra and her friend play on the stoop.

"Tell her to stop off at the store so you can get Raymond some cigarettes." Renee's gruff voice traveled easily from the kitchen to the front door.

"I ain't tellin' her nothin'," answered Daria. "He can buy his own damn cigarettes. All he doin' is sittin' in there doin' nothin'."

"Now you tell me, girl, why should he have to go walkin' all the way to the store when you be drivin' right past in that car?"

"Give me some money then," said Daria. "But I ain't makin' no promises."

A few minutes later, Daria came back with Andre and a plastic baby bottle filled with a red liquid.

"Do you want to take a few diapers?" asked Gayle.

"They'll give me 'em at the clinic if he needs 'em." Daria headed toward the car, and Gayle followed behind.

"Hey, Daria!" shouted Kendra. "Daria! Where ya goin', Daria?"

"None of your business, girlfriend." Daria didn't bother to look back at her little sister.

A Quiet Drive

Gayle buckled Andre into the car seat in the back, and Daria slid into the front passenger seat. They headed north through the housing project and merged onto the parkway that would take them to St. Mark's Hospital on the west side of the city. Daria hadn't said a word since they left the house. Gayle glanced at her a few times, but Daria just stared out of the side window, holding the plastic baby bottle on her lap.

Sometimes it was tempting not to even try with Daria. For more than 7 months now, Gayle had tried to reach out to her, but all of her attempts to get Daria to open up and talk were useless. There was just no breaking through her angry silence.

Gayle constantly reminded herself that Daria was only 17 years old and that her behavior was typical of many teenagers. She also tried to keep in mind that Daria had had a rough start in life.

According to the social worker at the group home, Renee Edwards was only 14 years old when she became pregnant with Daria. Renee's own mother had been an alcoholic, and her father had abandoned the family when Renee was just a little girl. Renee's age and unstable home environment resulted in Daria's being placed in foster care when she was only a few months old. Daria was in and out of foster homes throughout most of her early childhood. When Renee married Raymond, she regained permanent custody of Daria, who by then was nearly 7 years old.

But rough start or not, it was pretty clear that Daria was not going to win anyone over with her present attitude. And just look at her, thought Gayle. She could at least have made some effort to dress decently for their appointment at the clinic. Instead, she was wearing an old flannel shirt and stretch pants that were frayed and pilled. Her hair was dry, and the clumps that had escaped from her barrette stuck straight out from her head. Maybe she didn't have a lot of money, but she could do better than this.

Sometimes Gayle wanted to take Daria by the shoulders and shake some sense into her. But Daria had already turned half the human services agencies in the city against her. What she really needed was an ally.

"Daria, is everything all right?" asked Gayle.

"Yeah. Why wouldn't it be?" She maintained her watch through the car window.

"Oh, I don't know. You just seem kind of . . . well, kind of sad."

"Then tell me. . . . How am I *supposed* to feel?" Gayle winced at the hostility in Daria's voice.

"These clinic visits must be pretty miserable for you," Gayle suggested.

"I don't have much of a choice, now, do I?"

"No, I don't suppose you do."

Daria was silent.

"When I was coming into the house today, Kendra said something about you being angry."

"That girl needs to start mindin' her own business, if she know what's good for her."

"Were you angry about something?" Gail knew that she was taking a risk. She braced herself for Daria's reaction.

"What difference does it make?"

"For what it's worth—I care."

"Yeah, right." Daria rolled her eyes toward the roof. "Like I'm supposed to believe that."

"You don't have to," replied Gayle.

They rode in silence for a few minutes, Daria looking out the side window and Gayle looking straight ahead at the road. It was Daria who broke the silence this time. "I just wish everybody would mind their own damn business and stop tellin' me how to run my life," she mumbled.

"I'll bet you do," said Gayle softly.

Morning Tests

The mist had turned into a light rain by the time they reached the clinic at St. Mark's Hospital. Gayle drove around the block to the back of the building and dropped off Daria and Andre at the clinic's entrance. She waited until they were safely inside before leaving to park the car.

When Gayle walked into the waiting room, Daria was sitting in one of the blue plastic chairs that lined the wall. She had turned the chair so that she had her back to the room, and she was staring out a narrow window, paying no attention to Andre on the floor beside her. He was holding onto her chair with one hand and banging a set of plastic keys with the other. Looking at Daria now, Gayle was reminded of the first time they met. Daria had been sitting in the same chair, staring out the same window, and had the same angry look on her face. That was when she and Andre were still living in the group home.

Daria had an extensive record on file in juvenile court. Among her numerous offenses, she had been arrested once for stealing clothes in a department store, twice for under-age drinking, and twice for disturbing the peace during street fights. For one of the fights, she was charged with assault as well, but that charge was dropped before Daria's case reached court. Daria had also run away from home for a month and a half when she was 13 years old.

Daria's latest arrest was for distributing illegal drugs—cocaine and amphetamines—which she claimed to have been delivering for her boyfriend. Because the police could not prove any money had been exchanged, Daria was convicted only of possession. Nevertheless, she was sentenced to a 12-month stay in a group home for female juvenile offenders. Many of the young women in the home were pregnant or had young babies, and Daria herself was 3 months pregnant with Andre when she entered. As a result of prenatal counseling at the home, Daria submitted to blood tests for HIV, and her results were positive.

Andre was born a month premature, weighing a little more than 5 pounds. Although he appeared to be healthy at birth, Andre was closely monitored by the regional pediatric HIV clinic at St. Mark's. The group home had provided Daria and Andre with transportation to and from the clinic and kept track of Andre's scheduled appointments.

When Daria was released from the group home, Andre was 7 months old. The clinic staff had some concerns about his development, but overall his delays were not severe. Even so, the social worker at the home obtained a court order decreeing that Daria participate in an early intervention program and continue bringing Andre to the HIV clinic at St. Mark's. Daria's keeping Andre was contingent upon her compliance with this order. Gayle could understand the need for a court order, but, at times, it made her feel like a police officer or probation officer. Perhaps Daria saw her this way, too.

Gayle walked across the room and sat in the chair next to Daria's. "Did you sign in?" she asked.

"Yeah," answered Daria. She didn't turn away from the window to look at Gayle.

"I guess it will be a while."

"You best believe it," said Daria.

Andre was still standing next to Daria's chair playing with the plastic keys. Gayle reached over and rubbed the top of his head, and he turned to face her. His round eyes took in Gayle's face, and he gave her a quick smile of recognition. Before long, the two of them were playing a game of hide-and-seek with the ring of keys, and Andre giggled in response to the silly sounds and faces that Gayle made whenever he found the keys. Daria occasionally glanced over at them but remained detached.

The clinic psychologist eventually emerged from her office, walked across the waiting room, and stopped beside Daria.

"Daria?" she called.

Daria turned to look at her.

"Hi, Daria. I'm Donna Friedman. Remember, I saw Andre a few months ago?"

"Yeah, I remember."

Donna sat in the chair on the other side of Daria. She crossed her legs, revealing a pair of taupe high heels and matching hose. Her linen suit was a soft blue, and the pattern of the scarf around her neck matched her suit perfectly.

"I'm going to be giving Andre a test today called the Bayley Scales of Infant Development," said Donna. "What the test basically amounts to is watching how Andre plays with a variety of toys. By watching how he handles the toys, we can tell if his development is similar to other children's his age. We just want to make sure his cognitive skills are still progressing at the rate they should be. Do you have any questions?"

"No," said Daria.

"Great. Then I guess we can get started." Donna stood up and straightened her skirt. "Would you like to bring Andre back?"

Daria stood up slowly and lifted Andre from Gayle's lap.

Gayle extended her hand toward Donna. "Hi, I'm Gayle Daniels from the Emery Hill Infant Program on Battle Street."

"Hi. Nice to meet you," said Donna, reaching over to shake Gayle's hand.

"I'm working with Daria and Andre," said Gayle. "I make home visits."

Donna looked a little uncertain. "Well, uh . . . would you like to come back for the testing?"

"I suppose that's up to Daria," said Gayle, and she looked toward Daria. "Would you like me to go with you, or should I wait here?"

"Suit yourself," said Daria. "It don't make no difference to me." She grabbed the plastic baby bottle from the windowsill and adjusted Andre on her hip.

"It really is your choice, Daria."

"I said it's all right, didn't I?" Daria brushed past Gayle and crossed the waiting room, trailing behind Donna by a few steps. Gayle took this to be an invitation and followed Daria down the hallway toward one of the testing rooms.

The testing room was small but attractively decorated with a colorful border of Disney characters running along all four walls. A tot-size table with two chairs sat in the middle of the room, and a Bayley test kit was carefully arranged for action on the floor. Donna took Andre from Daria and sat him in one of the small chairs. She gave him a book from the top of the test kit, sat in the chair across the table from him, and began pointing to and talking about the pictures in the book. Daria plopped down on an adult-size chair in the far corner of the room, leaving Gayle to sit in a chair just behind and to the side of Andre.

Donna was skilled at keeping Andre engaged with the test materials and eliciting his best performance. Daria didn't say a word throughout the entire testing session. She just slumped in the chair with her head down and picked at a small hole in the right knee of her pants. At one point, Gayle tried to talk about what she and Daria were working on during her home visits, but Donna didn't seem all that interested. She was polite enough about it, but Gayle could tell that she wasn't really listening.

The Bayley took about an hour, and the rest of the morning consisted of blood tests and a physical exam. The three of them spent much of the time sitting in the waiting area.

For lunch, they walked to the hospital cafeteria. Gayle and Daria both picked up a cup of soup and a sandwich and placed them on the tray Gayle had picked up. Daria asked the woman at the counter for a small plate of macaroni and cheese, saying it was for Andre. Gayle paid for the soup and sandwiches, but Daria held onto the macaroni and cheese. She pulled a dollar bill from her back pocket and paid for it herself. Gayle couldn't help wondering whether she had used Raymond's cigarette money.

They said very little, but Daria seemed more relaxed. At least she didn't make any sarcastic comments. When they were finished eating, Daria walked back to the counter, bought an oversized chocolate chip cookie, wrapped it in a napkin, and stuffed it in the pocket of her flannel shirt. Then they all walked back to the clinic.

A Fellow Inmate

Daria followed Gayle through the clinic door and walked over to her seat by the window. Andre had been fussing since midway through lunch, so Daria spread his quilt out on the floor beside her chair and laid him down with his bottle. He settled down immediately and closed his eyes as he drank. Daria sighed and slumped in her chair. Gayle picked up an old *New Yorker* from a nearby table and started to read, but what she really wanted to do was take a nap. All this waiting around was exhausting.

"Hey, Vanessa! What are you doin' here, girl?" Daria said suddenly.

Gayle looked up from her reading and saw a tall, rather attractive young woman holding a young infant wrapped in a blanket. A broad smile spread across Daria's face as she stood up.

"Hey, Daria! Same as you, I guess," answered the young woman. "How's Andre? I bet he's grown . . . and would you look at your raggedy old self?" She picked at the shoulder of Daria's shirt with her fingers and made a face. "Why, girlfriend, I thought you'd be out livin' it up!"

"Yeah, right," said Daria rolling her eyes.

"Why, sure. I know when I get out I'm gonna—" Vanessa spied Andre on the quilt sleeping and stopped talking to look at him. "Look at this boy! He grown! I've been missin' him since you been gone."

"Yeah, maybe he missed you some, too," said Daria. "When did your baby come? Is it a boy or a girl?"

"A girl . . . named her Theresa. She be 5 months come Saturday."

Daria peeked under the receiving blanket that concealed the baby's face, then she looked up at Vanessa. "Do you know?" she asked softly.

"Well, I just got through talkin' with the doctor, and she said that—"

A middle-age woman approached the two girls, and their conversation came to a sudden halt.

"Daria? Daria Edwards?" the woman asked.

"I'm Daria."

"Hi, Daria. It's nice to meet you. My name is Monica Stevens. I'm a social worker for the clinic. Would you like to come back with me now so we can talk about a few things?"

"Yeah, all right." Daria's sullen expression returned. She turned around and stooped to pick up Andre.

"I'll stay out here and keep an eye on him if you want me to," offered Gayle. "You just got him to sleep, and he's so tired."

"Yeah, okay," said Daria. She turned to face Vanessa again. "Well, good seein' you. Take care of yourself."

"Yeah," said Vanessa. "Listen, maybe I'll get up with you once I'm out. We'll have us some fun. And you tell that boy of yours I been missin' him."

Daria followed the social worker, staying a step or two behind. Vanessa sat down in Daria's vacant chair and let out a deep sigh. She adjusted the infant on her lap and leaned over to look at Andre.

"Have you known Daria a long time?" asked Gayle.

"Not real long," said Vanessa, turning to look at Gayle. "You come here with her?"

"I visit Daria and Andre at home. I'm from the Emery Hill Infant Program . . . . Gayle Daniels."

"Yeah. Well, me and Daria were at the group home together a while."

"I see. It must be nice to see each other again."

"Yeah . . . nice." Vanessa pulled a little yellow bonnet out of her shoulder bag and tied it onto the baby's head.

"Your little girl sure is beautiful," said Gayle.

"Yeah, thanks. They said that her last test was lookin' like she might be all right." A brief smile crossed her face. "Course, they can't be certain. They got to do more tests first."

"Well, it sounds promising."

"Yeah." Vanessa turned away and looked out the window. "I worry about that Daria sometimes, you know," she said softly.

"Why's that?" asked Gayle.

"Well, she don't always take care of herself like she should."

"What do you mean?"

"Oh, never mind. It not my place to be sayin' nothin' anyway."

"You sound a little worried."

"Yeah. It's just that . . ." Vanessa turned away from the window to face Gayle. "Well, when we were at the home, Daria told me that she didn't take her AZT like she was supposed to—said she didn't care, and it probably wouldn't do no good anyway."

Vanessa paused for a moment, looking down at her baby. "Well, I don't suppose that's none of my business anyway." Then she looked toward the door and stood up. "The van's here. I gotta go."

Gayle watched Vanessa walk to the door where an older woman stood waiting. Probably the van driver from the group home or from Social Services, thought Gayle.

Behind Closed Doors

When Daria returned from her talk with Monica Stevens, it was almost 2:30 P.M. Andre was still asleep. As usual, Daria had nothing to say about her meeting with the social worker—at least she had nothing to say to Gayle about it. Gayle excused herself to make a telephone call. She needed to reschedule a home visit that another family had canceled earlier in the week.

The call took longer than Gayle expected. When she returned to the waiting room, Daria was gone, and so was Andre. They must be seeing someone else, she thought, and settled back in her chair with another magazine.

Ten minutes later a nurse entered the waiting room and approached Gayle. "Ms. Daniels?" she asked.

"Yes?"

"Ms. Daniels, the doctor would like to see you for a minute, if you don't mind."

"Sure. Is something wrong?" Gayle felt a little anxious. Had something happened while she was away?

"Follow me, please."

The nurse escorted Gayle down the hallway. She stopped at a door and opened it a crack. "Right in here, please," she said and stepped aside to let Gayle enter.

One wall of the small room was lined with bookcases, and Monica Stevens and another woman sat at a table near the window on the other wall. Donna Friedman stood beside a metal pushcart clutching a mug of coffee with both hands.

"Hello," said the unfamiliar woman. "Could you pull the door shut, please?"

Gayle instinctively obeyed and then took another step into the room.

"I'm Sheila Donahan," said the woman. She stood up and shook Gayle's hand, then she motioned toward the empty chair beside her. "Please, sit down."

Again, Gayle obeyed and sat down on the edge of the chair.

"I'm the pediatrician who saw Andre today," the woman continued. "We're a little concerned about his latest test results and thought you might be able to help us out."

"Sure. I'll try," said Gayle. "Where is Daria, anyway? She wasn't in the waiting area."

"She's with the nurse getting a prescription," said Monica.

There was something about all of this that Gayle didn't like. She felt herself becoming defensive, but she wasn't sure why.

"What are you concerned about?" asked Gayle.

"We're concerned about Daria's lack of responsiveness to Andre," said Monica. "None of us have seen any type of quality interaction between her and the baby all day. According to the records, their interaction has been a concern since their first clinic visit. As you know, a strong mother–child relationship is critical for these babies."

"Yes, I know," said Gayle. "It may be that Daria—"

"We're particularly concerned after today's testing," interrupted Donna Friedman. She stepped toward the table, still clutching her coffee mug. "Andre's performance on the Bayley indicates that he may be regressing. Although he has made developmental progress over the past 6 months, the rate of that progress has slowed considerably."

"Soft signs such as these may indicate that his brain is beginning to be compromised by the virus," said Sheila, the pediatrician. "But, let's back up here a minute." She took a deep breath and continued,

"The baby's last diagnostic test for HIV was, again, positive. So, there is absolutely no doubt about a diagnosis of HIV infection."

"Does Daria know?" asked Gayle.

"I think we've been pretty straight with her. But it's not the diagnosis that's of concern to us now."

"What is it, then?"

"It's his CD4 count and his developmental status." Sheila Donahan looked down at the papers on the table in front of her. "Up until now, the baby has been asymptomatic. His cell count, however, is now below normal. By the way," she said looking up at Gayle, "do you know if the mother is giving the baby his prescribed dose of Septra?"

"I'm sure she is," said Gayle. But was she really all that sure? Or did she just want to believe that Daria would do what was right for Andre? After all, hadn't Vanessa just said that Daria hadn't always taken her AZT?

"It's very important that he takes the Septra to prevent infection," said the doctor.

"Yes, I know," said Gayle. "I'll make certain to check on it when I visit." Why did she suddenly feel as though *her* competence was being questioned?

"It may sound harsh," said Monica, "but we have to ask ourselves whether Daria is really capable of caring for Andre. There isn't sufficient evidence of negligence to remove him from the home now—and you know we don't want it to come to that—but we have to keep our eyes open to the possibility. After all, his life is at stake."

"She seems to try," said Gayle. "You know how young she is, but she does seem to try."

"Young or not, she has a baby who needs special care," said the pediatrician. "It's our responsibility to see that he's taken care of."

"Daria might feel a little intimidated when she's here surrounded by professionals," Gayle offered in Daria's defense.

"That's why we wanted to talk with you," said Monica. "We thought you might have a better idea of what's going on at home. What we've seen here doesn't look good."

Oh, Daria, thought Gayle. *Don't you know what you're doing to yourself? Why do you have to act like this? Why must you be so angry?* Then again, Daria probably had no idea she was being judged like this. This wasn't a fair trial. Gayle felt like a traitor as she sat there among the prosecutors.

"Have you talked to Daria about any of this?" Gayle asked the group.

"There's no sense in alarming her about the results of Bayley testing now," said Donna Friedman. "We'll test him again in another 4 to 6 months. We'll be more certain about what's going on then."

"We just thought you should know since you're working with Andre," added Monica. "You see them every week. Maybe there's something you can do."

"I'll do what I can," said Gayle.

"Please," said the doctor, "let me finish up here." She placed her hands flat on the papers before her and continued, "We have a 14-month-old baby who is now symptomatic for infection. His persistent diaper rash, low cell count, plateauing growth curve, and today's fever are indicative of immunological compromise. Furthermore, psychological testing indicates regression in developmental functioning. Taken together, this means—"

"But he hasn't fallen one standard deviation yet," interrupted Donna.

Sheila glared at Donna. "Yes, I know. What I'm trying to say, if I may, is that there appears to be ample evidence to warrant initiation of antiretroviral treatment." She leaned back in her chair and looked straight at Gayle. "We're starting Andre on a combination of drugs in an attempt to reduce his viral load."

"Have you told Daria?" asked Gayle.

"Of course. She's getting the prescriptions now. I told her it was a preventive measure. There's not much more to say until we're certain. He'll need careful monitoring both by us and by the local pediatrician." She opened the front cover of Andre's chart. "I see he's being followed locally by a health clinic."

"Yes," said Gayle. "It's just a few blocks away from their house."

"And what Monica said is true," added Sheila. "His life may depend upon the mother's ability to follow through. After all, medicine left in a bottle has no therapeutic value."

Sheila Donahan stood up and walked toward the door. She placed her hand on the doorknob, then looked back at the group and said, "There's also the future to consider. . . . It's going to get rough at some point. We just don't know when. And we need to remember that we have two patients here, not just one. Thank goodness the mother is asymptomatic. She probably has a long way to go."

Going Home

It was nearly 4 P.M. when Gayle and Daria left the clinic. The parkway was already congested with people leaving the city for the weekend. Inside the car it was quiet. Daria stared out the side window at the passing cars, and Andre was asleep again in the back seat. Gayle couldn't get her mind off what had happened at the clinic. She felt the need to do something. But what?

Approaching the south side of the city, Gayle realized that she hadn't said anything to Daria since they left the hospital. Then she remembered Raymond's cigarettes.

"Daria, do you need anything at the store?" she asked. "I'd be happy to stop off. I've got plenty of time."

"Nah. I don't need nothin'."

So much for Raymond's cigarettes, thought Gayle. "Do you have any plans for the weekend?"

"Nah."

"Do you have someone to watch Andre so you can go out?"

"Nah."

"How about your mother?" asked Gayle.

"She works at the Revco on the weekend."

"Oh, I didn't know she was working."

"Just started," said Daria. "To pick up extra money now that Raymond's out of work."

"Would Raymond watch Andre?"

"Ha!" said Daria rolling her eyes.

"What? He wouldn't do it?"

"I wouldn't *let* him."

"Why's that?"

"He ain't good for much . . . just sits in front of that damn TV all day."

"Oh, I see."

There was silence again as the car, inching along in rush hour traffic, neared the housing project. The words of the doctor and the social worker echoed through Gayle's mind. What did they expect her to do? There was just no reaching Daria. She had tried every way she knew, but nothing had worked.

"You got any kids?" asked Daria, still looking out the side window.

Gayle was surprised by the question. Daria rarely spoke without being prompted, and she had never asked Gayle anything about her personal life before.

"Yeah, I do," answered Gayle. "I have a little girl who's almost 4 years old."

Daria didn't say anything else, despite a few faltering attempts on Gayle's part to continue the conversation.

Soon they were pulling up in front of the house. Daria got out, retrieved Andre from the back seat, and walked toward the front door where the Barbie dolls now lay abandoned on the stoop. Gayle didn't follow. The day had been intense enough already. She watched from the curb as Daria disappeared through the front door. "Bye, Daria," Gayle said softly. Then she got the phone out of the trunk, put it in the car, and drove off. She would see Daria next week.

Discussion Questions

1. What factors may have contributed to Daria's anger and silence?

2. What strengths, if any, does the Edwards family demonstrate? What other potential strengths might the family have?

3. How well do you think Gayle has conducted her interactions with Daria? Identify any specific things Gayle did or said that you think may have been helpful in establishing a relationship with Daria.

4. Could Gayle have done or said anything differently to establish a more productive relationship with Daria?

5. Was it important for Gayle to have accompanied Daria to the pediatric HIV clinic? What may have been the outcome of Daria's visit if Gayle had not come?

6. Suppose you were a consultant to St. Mark's Hospital's pediatric HIV clinic. What comments or suggestions would you offer to assist them in becoming more family-centered?

7. Was it appropriate for the clinic staff to have enlisted Gayle's help in addressing the concerns they had about Andre and Daria?

8. If you were in Gayle's position, would you have said or done anything differently in the conversation with the pediatrician, psychologist, and social worker?

9. Should Gayle have told the clinic staff what Vanessa said about Daria not having taken her AZT when she was pregnant with Andre? Should Gayle let Daria know that Vanessa told her this?

10. In general, what strategies could Gayle employ to work collaboratively with the clinic staff at St. Mark's Hospital?

11. Should Gayle tell Daria about her conversation with the clinic staff? If so, should she reveal everything that was said in the meeting?

12. If you were Gayle, what concerns would you have about Daria and Andre? Make a list.

13. What are some possible strategies for addressing each of the concerns you listed in your answer to Question #12?

14. What types of support might be helpful to Daria during the next year or two? What resources are available in your community for families under similar circumstances?

15. If you were working with this family, what would you want to accomplish during the next few weeks or months? How would you proceed?

16. In general, how can a professional use family-centered approaches when parents are unwilling or unable to communicate, as Daria was in this story?

chapter 11

Sunset View

Wanda B. Hedrick and P.J. McWilliam

lice Kincaid was poised at the door of the trailer and ready to knock when she heard Eduardo's angry voice. "F__k that b___h!" he boomed. "Ain't no damn woman gonna tell me what I can do with my kid!"

Alice felt her face get hot. Her own worst expletive was "darn," and she used that only occasionally.

"I'll be damned if I'm gonna let them f__k me over!" he continued ranting.

Could Eduardo be mad about something she had done? Alice contemplated returning to her car. Even if he wasn't angry at her, this didn't seem like a good time for a visit. Before Alice could decide, however, a slender figure walked past the door and spied her through the small rectangular window. It was Carolyn Lopez, Eduardo's wife.

Alice knew that she and Carolyn were about the same age, but Carolyn looked much older than her years. Her long, brown hair was peppered with gray, and she had the emaciated look that some top fashion models diet to achieve. But her slouched shoulders, unflatter-ing hairstyle, and ill-fitting clothes made her look more like a refugee than a supermodel.

Carolyn's Joy

Carolyn's one joy in life is her 18-month-old son, Miguel—a beautiful child with thick, dark hair and a face as perfect as any cherub in a Re-naissance painting. Beyond his nearly flawless appearance, however, there is reason for concern. For one thing, Miguel's pleasant expression is nearly as static as those of the painted cherubs. He often sits and stares into space with a half smile on his face for long periods of time, rhyth-mically rocking to the beat of an invisible metronome. At times, it seems as though Miguel is completely unaware of all that goes on around him.

Alice has been making weekly visits to the Lopezes' home for the past 6 months to work with Miguel. She and Carolyn had been en-couraged when Miguel started talking a few months ago. His first word was "ball"—a favorite toy. A few more words followed, and he now has a vocabulary of about 20 words. His talking, however, has been in-consistent, and Alice is concerned that Miguel only parrots what is said to him. Occasionally, he seems to be labeling or requesting, such as when he says "ball" when Carolyn holds the toy before him. Even then, Miguel often repeats the same word incessantly. It is difficult to tell whether he has any true understanding of the words he uses.

Alice is also concerned that Miguel doesn't appear to enjoy the simple social games that children much younger than him find amus-ing. He doesn't giggle or smile in response to Peekaboo, he doesn't play or even respond to Pat-a-Cake, nor will he roll a ball back and forth with another person. At first, Alice had thought his lack of social play was simply a function of his overall developmental level. But now, Miguel's progress in motor development and the emergence of speech make his delays in social skills all the more obvious. Miguel's behavior has perplexed Alice for months.

Although Alice has discussed Miguel's delays with Carolyn, Caro-lyn doesn't seem to be nearly as concerned as Alice is. She appears per-fectly content with Miguel just the way he is. And Eduardo . . . well, who knew what Eduardo thought about Miguel? Alice had tried to in-clude him when she made home visits, but he made it clear from the very beginning that taking care of Miguel was Carolyn's job.

Alice hasn't yet broached with Carolyn her growing suspicion that Miguel has autism. She had planned to bring it up on a number of vis-its over the past month; but each time she arrived at the trailer, she lost her nerve. Carolyn's life seems troubled enough as it is.

Playing Games

Carolyn opened the door of the mobile home, and Alice stepped inside. "Hi, Carolyn. How are you doing today?"

As usual, Carolyn responded, "I'm fine."

"Where's Miguel?" asked Alice. "Isn't he up from his nap yet?"

Alice scanned the dimly lit room. There was no sign of Miguel, but Eduardo was sitting in his usual spot in front of the television. He turned his head and stared at Alice, making her feel uncomfortable. Alice may have been confused about Miguel, but she believed she understood his father all too well. Every time he was in the room with her, she felt his eyes looking her up and down, no matter what she was wearing. She felt silly about it, but on days she visited Miguel, Alice purposefully wore her least flattering outfits.

Last week she had worn what her friend liked to call her schoolteacher outfit: a long denim skirt with an oversized red sweater that had apples, letters of the alphabet, and other school-related paraphernalia embroidered all over it. But the outfit hadn't seemed to daunt Eduardo. He continued to eye Alice with lust, and she hated it.

"Yes, he's still sleepin'," Carolyn answered. "I need to get him up, though, or he'll never go to sleep tonight."

"Fine," said Alice. "I brought a few toys that I thought Miguel might like."

Carolyn smiled briefly, covering her lips with her chafed fingers. "I'll go and get him now," she said and walked down the narrow corridor of the trailer toward Miguel's bedroom.

Whenever Carolyn smiled or talked, she automatically covered her mouth with her hand. Alice assumed that she did so because she was sensitive about anyone seeing her decaying teeth. It was such a shame; regular brushing and dental checkups could probably have prevented the problem. Once, Alice had mentioned a program that might help Carolyn to pay for some dental work, but Eduardo had overheard the conversation. "She's fine the way she is," he had barked from the kitchen, which of course had closed the subject as far as Carolyn was concerned. She never disagreed with Eduardo, and she did everything that Eduardo told her to do. Sometimes Alice had to bite her tongue when he degraded Carolyn in front of her.

Alice sat down on the floor beside the sofa and began rummaging through the bag she'd brought. She made certain not to look in Eduardo's direction, but she could feel his stare.

Carolyn soon returned with a sleepy-eyed toddler in her arms. As she entered the living room, Eduardo shifted his weight in the chair. "Hey, get me some iced tea," he commanded.

Carolyn rushed into the kitchen, depositing Miguel onto Alice's lap on her way.

"And pick up that cigarette pack on the dresser while you're at it," Eduardo yelled through to the kitchen.

Carolyn came back with the iced tea and put it on the table beside Eduardo. "I'll be there in a second," she mumbled to Alice as she edged past the footstool on which Eduardo's feet were propped. She walked quickly back to the bedroom. When she returned with the cigarettes, Carolyn looked at Eduardo in anticipation of another request. Eduardo just lit a cigarette and stared at the television.

"I'm sorry," apologized Carolyn. "I should have been ready when you got here."

Alice shook her head and smiled, implying that she didn't mind. She thought about a visit she'd made a few months ago when Eduardo made Carolyn wash the dishes before she could sit down with Miguel and Alice. Alice couldn't imagine a woman staying in a relationship like this one, but Carolyn seemed to accept it as normal.

The hour passed slowly. Miguel was pleasant as usual and showed some interest in the toys that Alice and Carolyn had laid on the kitchen floor. He picked up a few toys and tapped them on the floor or waved them back and forth with outstretched arms. Alice tried to follow his lead as he handled each toy and encouraged him to engage in more advanced levels of play, but Miguel was unresponsive. Carolyn tried, too, but she wasn't any more successful. Even so, Carolyn beamed with pride after each and every thing her son did.

While packing up the toys at the end of her visit, Alice rolled a yellow and red ball to Miguel. "Here you go, buddy," she said. "I wanted to leave this one with you. I know how much you like balls." She was quite surprised when Miguel picked up the ball and threw it back in her direction.

"Good throw, Miguel!" she praised. "Here you go. Your turn to catch it." Alice threw the ball gently toward him. The ball bounced off Miguel's chest and landed on the floor between his legs. He made no attempt to catch it and seemed oblivious that it had come back to him. He just stared off into a corner of the room. Alice picked up the ball and placed it in Miguel's hands, but he didn't grasp it. Alice let go of the ball, and it rolled to the floor. After several more unsuccessful attempts, Alice stood up to leave. "Well, maybe you'll want to play with it later."

She took out her big, black appointment book and removed the rubber band that held it together. She flipped through the frayed pages. "Is it okay if I see you the same time next week?" she asked.

Carolyn nodded.

"I want Kim to come here with me and do a speech-language assessment with Miguel the next time," said Alice. "It's been a while since she was here. Will that be okay?" Before Carolyn could answer, Alice was already writing in her appointment book. Carolyn always agreed to whatever she requested. She wished Carolyn would say "no" just once.

"That will be fine," Carolyn responded.

A Ring of Purple

Kim took off her high heels and tugged at her skirt as Alice drove the car out of the parking lot.

"Push the seat back if it's up too far," suggested Alice.

"Thanks, I will. My legs are so long, I always feel like I'm eating my knees when I ride in someone else's car." She pushed down the lever and slid the seat back. "Wow! That's better."

"It's been a while since you've been out to Miguel's. Remember, the father has a rough vocabulary." Alice felt compelled to prepare Kim for Eduardo. "Frankly, he gives me the creeps sometimes."

"Don't worry about me. I've heard it all," Kim laughed. "But now that you mention it, I do remember him. Don't they live in that little trailer park?"

"That's right."

"Oh, yes. . . . And the father asked the mother who the hell I was." Kim chuckled again. "It was a good question, though. You know, I ask myself that one all the time."

Alice relaxed. Being with Kim made her put things into perspective. Kim was fun-loving but not flippant. She didn't seem to let things bother her; rather, she took whatever came her way and rolled with the punches. Alice envied that quality and was trying to emulate it.

When they arrived at the Lopezes' trailer, they locked their purses in the trunk and carried the test kit Kim had brought to the front door. Carolyn answered their knock.

"What on earth happened to your eye?!" Alice exclaimed. But as soon as she said it, she wished she hadn't. Carolyn's right eye was ringed in deep purple and cut at the outside corner.

Carolyn's fingers gingerly touched her swollen eye. "Oh, it's okay. I was hangin' up the ironing board, and it fell off the hook and hit me."

Alice and Kim exchanged glances, each knowing what the other was thinking.

"Well, you sure got a shiner!" Kim quickly commented. "Where is that little guy of yours?"

"Playin' under the kitchen table with the cat," answered Carolyn. She walked toward the kitchen, and Alice and Kim followed her.

After the language assessment, the two women said their good-byes to Carolyn and Miguel and packed up to leave. As they walked back through the living room, Alice saw Eduardo sitting in his chair in front of the television. He hadn't been there when they arrived.

"I suspect that bruise wasn't from any ironing board," said Kim shortly after their car left the trailer park. "It looked like a battle scar to me."

"I know," said Alice. "I wish I hadn't reacted like I did."

"Don't worry about it. Have you ever noticed anything like that before?"

"Unfortunately, yes. She had a busted lip one day, and I've seen bruises on her arms before."

"What about Miguel?" asked Kim. "Anything suspicious there?"

"No. Just regular little-boy bumps . . . cat scratches, mostly."

"Have you ever mentioned the women's shelter to Carolyn?"

"No. Do you think I should?"

"I don't know," said Kim. "Maybe you could mention it to her and see whether she acts interested. I'm not sure.

"Me either," said Alice.

The Morning News

The secretary buzzed Alice's number. "Phone call on line two," she announced.

"Thank you," replied Alice. She swallowed a bite of her lunch and punched the button on the phone. "Hello, this is Alice Kincaid. May I help you?"

"Hello, Alice? This is Kim."

"Hi, Kim. I've been meaning to call you. I was wondering about—"

"Have you looked at this morning's paper?"

"No, I picked it up on my way out of the driveway. It's right here on my desk." Alice rummaged through her papers and pulled it out from under a Big Mac wrapper. "Here it is. What's up?"

"Read the article on the front page of section B," said Kim. "It starts out 'Man murders—.' I've got to get to a meeting now, but read that article. Give me a call later, if you want to. Bye."

Alice hung up the receiver and opened the paper. Her eyes widened as she read the article in Section B.

Sunset View was the mobile home park where the Lopez family lived. Alice suddenly felt lightheaded. Of course, that was partly because it was 2:30 P.M., and she was just beginning to eat her lunch. Two bites of hamburger hadn't raised her blood sugar level yet. She looked at the article again. It couldn't have happened too far from Car-

Man Murders Estranged Wife's Boyfriend, Shoots Self

CLARKSBURG—A Clark County woman's estranged husband and boyfriend are dead in what law officers called a murder–suicide Wednesday.

James Michael Williams, 36, was found dead inside the mobile home of his estranged wife, Peggy Williams, after going on a rampage through the home Wednesday morning, according to Chief Deputy Bobby Moore of the Clark County Sheriff's Department.

Mrs. Williams and her 2-year-old daughter escaped without injury. Maurice Johnson, 29, was shot twice as he tried to escape and was found dead outside the mobile home when officers arrived.

Neighbors at the Sunset View Mobile Home Park said that the couple had been separated for about two months.

olyn's and Miguel's mobile home. After all, there were only 15 or 20 trailers in the trailer park. Alice suddenly felt sick to her stomach. She had never knowingly been close to a crime scene of any type, much less a murder.

Alice thought about what her fiancé Andy had said about that neighborhood. Andy had been working near the trailer park installing cable television and had referred to the people living at Sunset View as "low lifes." She had sharply criticized him for making judgments about people whose values were different from his own. But maybe Andy was right. After all, what kind of people went around killing each other? Alice thought about Miguel's family and wondered how different they were from the people in the newspaper article.

She picked up her Big Mac but then dropped it back down onto the wrapper. She couldn't eat. She began her paperwork again, hoping to take her mind off the murder, but it was no use. It wasn't just the murder that bothered Alice; it was also the thought of Miguel and Carolyn living in the trailer with Eduardo. And what about her own safety? Alice couldn't stop the flood of questions as she contemplated what she should do during her next visit.

Discussion Questions

1. Do Alice and Kim have reasonable cause for suspecting that Carolyn is being physically abused by Eduardo?

2. Should Alice do anything about her suspicions that Carolyn is being abused? If so, what options does Alice have for handling the situation? Make a list.

3. Should Alice and Kim have done anything differently on the day they arrived and saw Carolyn's blackened eye?

4. Kim suggested that Alice mention the women's shelter to Carolyn on a future home visit. If you were Alice, would you do so? And, if so, how would you bring it up?

5. Should Alice be concerned that Miguel might be harmed by Eduardo? Is there anything she should do to ensure Miguel's safety?

6. Alice apparently tried to involve Eduardo when she first began visiting this family. Should she do more now to encourage his involvement? If so, what could she try?

7. Alice obviously feels uncomfortable about being around Eduardo. Does she have reason to feel this way? What, if anything, should she do about it?

8. Are Alice's concerns about her own safety at Sunset View justified? Is there anything that she could do to protect herself when she visits Carolyn and Miguel?

9. What, if anything, should Alice do about Carolyn's passive agreement to any suggestions she makes about Miguel?

10. What should Alice do about her suspicion that Miguel has autism? What options does she have? Make a list. If you were Alice, which of these options would you choose?

11. Should Alice do anything more to ensure that Carolyn fully understands the extent of Miguel's delays? If so, what?

12. What are the legal criteria for spousal abuse in your state? What are the legal obligations of professionals regarding the reporting of such offenses?

13. What resources are available in your community for women who are abused by their spouses or partners, and what agencies become involved in domestic violence situations?

14. In general, to what degree should early intervention professionals be responsible for taking action when they suspect family violence?

c h a p t e r 12

A Family Feud

Miki Kersgard

The rusty door hinges squeaked behind her as Hannah Osborne entered the screened-in porch of the Catesville Community Child Care Center. A recent delivery of food supplies lined one side of the porch, the labels on the cardboard boxes identifying their contents: industrial-size cans of pears, chili con carne, fruit cocktail, and chicken gumbo soup. There was little variety in the lunches served at the center from week to week. When Hannah had first started coming here to see Conrad Brown, the center's dark rooms, mismatched furniture, and worn-out toys had made her question whether it was an appropriate place for him. During the past year and a half, however, Hannah had grown accustomed to the shabbiness of the place and had come to appreciate what they'd accomplished with so little.

The staff consisted of the director, Maura Desmond, and three older women from the Catesville community. The women were all rather old-fashioned in their approach to child care, but they were cheerful and affectionate with the children. As Hannah once told her colleagues, "huggin' and smoochin'" appeared to be a high priority in the early childhood curriculum at the Catesville Community Child Care Center. Hannah realized that the center provided a vital service to the community by offering affordable child care for working parents with modest salaries. Catesville was a relatively stable and tightly knit community, and Maura Desmond seemed to know everything there was to know about the parents whose children attended the center.

Like the other children, Conrad received a healthy share of huggin' and smoochin' from the women who worked at the center and, for the most part, was included in activities with the other children. Conrad, now almost 3 years old, had been born 2 months premature and had sustained an intraventricular bleed while in neonatal intensive care. The bleed resulted in a hemiplegia of Conrad's right side. Six months ago, Conrad had started walking, albeit with an awkward gait, and Hannah thought that his self-help and play skills were progressing nicely. Even so, Conrad was still a year behind other 3-year-olds in most areas of development. Hannah's major concern at the moment was his speech delay. Conrad did use single words to communicate and was even attempting some two-word combinations, but his speech was extremely difficult to understand. He often had to resort to gesturing to make his wishes known, even to Hannah and the women who worked at the center.

The staff had been suspicious of Hannah's presence at first, but they'd gradually warmed up to her. Now Hannah felt quite welcome when she arrived for her weekly visits at the center. The women had implemented a good portion of Hannah's suggestions for working with Conrad, but they also had their own ideas about what Conrad needed to learn and how to go about teaching him. Conrad's feeding was a case in point. Hannah had recommended a built-up spoon and a scoop plate to help Conrad learn to feed himself at mealtimes. She had even brought a spoon and plate to the center and left them there for the staff to use with Conrad. Maura Desmond and the teachers had certainly seen to it that Conrad learned how to feed himself, but they did it without the aid of a special spoon and plate. In fact, Hannah didn't see the spoon and plate again until months after Conrad had become proficient at self-feeding. She came across them one day while playing with the children in the little kitchen area: They were at the back of the toy cupboard among the plastic food, plates, and cups.

More recently, the child care staff had decided that Conrad should be toilet trained. Hannah had questioned whether he was ready for toilet training and expressed her reservations to Maura and the woman in whose room Conrad spent most of the day. Despite Hannah's explanations about prerequisite skills for toilet training and her opinion that the staff should focus their energies on speech development first, Conrad was in training pants when she came to visit the next week. And much to her surprise, Conrad was nearly fully trained in a matter of 2 months.

Where's Conrad?

Within moments of entering the center, Hannah was surrounded by a group of toddlers and fully incorporated into their play. All of the children wore dress-up clothes and were acting out an imaginary scene for which Hannah was chosen to be the grandmother. After a few minutes, Hannah realized that Conrad was nowhere in sight. That's odd, she thought. Conrad was devoted to her and usually came scrambling over as soon as she came into the room. She told the children that the grandmother needed to go to the grocery store and stole away from the group to look for Conrad. But she didn't find him anywhere.

The clack of high-heeled shoes stopped abruptly behind Hannah, and she heard someone harshly whisper, "Mercy!" Hannah turned around toward the voice and came face-to-face with Maura Desmond. "I don't know if you're ever gonna forgive me," exclaimed Maura. "I've been meaning to call you this whole morning, and the time just flew by, what with—"

"Is Conrad sick?" interrupted Hannah. She knew she was being rather rude, but she had learned from experience that Maura would talk on and on, providing a detailed account of her entire morning. It drove Hannah crazy when Maura took forever to get to the point.

"Come on into my office, and I'll tell you all about it," said Maura.

The two women walked to the office, skirting a maze of metal storage closets and filing cabinets that formed a staggered line on both sides of the hallway. Hannah ducked to avoid the fronds of a plant outside Maura's door and followed the director into her office. Maura removed a stack of file folders and what looked like a week's worth of mail from the seat of a chair, then dropped the whole pile onto the floor. Hannah sat down next to the table that held the Mr. Coffee machine. Like the eternal flame, the machine was never off or empty. "Coffee?" asked Maura.

"No, thank you. Too much caffeine makes my hands shake." Hannah watched Maura drain what was left in her coffee cup and then pour herself some more. "So," Hannah said in a cheery voice, "what did you want to tell me about Conrad?"

Maura shook her head as she took a large gulp of coffee. "Shonda came to pick him up Friday afternoon, just like always, and she says in a voice as casual as could be, 'By the way, I've enrolled my boy in another day care program. He won't be coming here after today.' As far as I know, he's been at the new place this whole week."

"Why would she do that?" asked Hannah. "Did Shonda say there was something wrong? I mean . . . I thought she was happy with Conrad's progress here."

"Well, that's just what I asked her. She said she has no complaints with me or the center. It's Louise she's having problems with."

Hannah was surprised—Conrad's grandmother had always been a big help to Shonda, and the two women seemed to get along well even though Shonda was no longer married to Louise's son, Robert. Louise had provided child care for Conrad from the time he was a few months old until she went back to work about a year ago. In fact, before Conrad began coming to the center, Hannah had conducted a number of her home visits at Louise's house. Even after starting at the center, Conrad spent many evenings with Louise while Shonda worked a second or third shift at the clothing factory. Robert couldn't always be counted on to arrive on time and stay with his son, but Louise was more than glad to fill in for him. On more than one occasion, Hannah had listened to Louise go on about her "darling Robert" and how busy he was all of the time. Hannah had long suspected that, without Louise, Robert and Shonda's marriage may not have lasted as long as it did. Even after their separation last year, Louise had been a big help, taking care of Conrad when Shonda needed her.

"I thought Louise and Shonda were very close," said Hannah. "Doesn't Conrad still spend a lot of time with his grandmother?"

"As much time as Louise can get him," responded Maura. "But it seems that lately she might have been overstepping her bounds just a little. Either that or Shonda's exaggerating. All I know is what Shonda told me, and that was that she was putting Conrad in a different center so that—and these are her words, not mine—Louise couldn't steal her baby from her."

Hannah looked at Maura in amazement. "Do you really think that Louise would do something like that?"

"Well, I'll put it to you this way. I don't think Louise is actually trying to steal Conrad away from Shonda in the literal sense of the word. What I think is that the two of them have very different ideas about how Conrad should be brought up and that Louise is more of an emotional threat to Shonda than a physical one."

Hannah gave Maura a questioning shrug and was about to ask her a question when Maura started talking again. "I can't really go into detail without going beyond my own rules of confidentiality with my parents here. If you want to know any more about it, I think you'd better talk with Shonda herself."

"Of course, I understand," said Hannah. "Can you tell me where Conrad is, though? Maybe I could stop by and see him. I need to finish up the developmental profile that I've been working on the past few weeks. You remember, we wanted to get it done so we could write his new intervention plan?"

"Well, that's another thing," said Maura. "I know I should have checked with Shonda yesterday, but it just slipped my mind. She asked me not to tell anyone where Conrad was. Now, I know that she probably just meant Louise or someone else from the family, and I should have asked if she was going to call you, but like I said . . . things just happened so fast."

"That's okay." Hannah stood up and smoothed the pockets of her jacket. "I'll just call Shonda and make arrangements with her."

Maura walked Hannah through the door and out onto the porch, where the two women parted company. Well, thought Hannah, what a strange turn of events. Hannah would miss coming to Catesville Community. Maura certainly had her own way of doing things; but her heart was always in the right place, and Conrad seemed to like being there. Where was Conrad now? She groaned inwardly. Hannah would have to go through the arduous process of developing relationships with new people at whichever program he was attending. And how was she supposed to complete Conrad's intervention plan now? It was already 2 weeks overdue.

A Quick Call

When she left the center, it was 12:00 P.M. Hannah thought about going to a restaurant where she could sit down for a relaxed meal; but instead, she stopped off at the drive-in window of a fast-food restaurant and brought her lunch back to the office with her. After gulping down some food, she reached over and dialed Shonda Brown's work number. On the one hand, Hannah knew that Shonda's supervisors wouldn't appreciate her being interrupted at the factory—it would be better to call her at home in the evening. On the other hand, Shonda should have told her that Conrad was no longer enrolled in Maura's center. Hannah did her best to be respectful of parents, but she wished they would show her the same respect. Trips to visit children who weren't there didn't count as time on her monthly record of child contact hours.

Two different people at the clothing factory picked up the telephone and put Hannah on hold before she could find someone willing to pass the call to Shonda.

"Shonda?" asked Hannah finally, yelling over the din of sewing machines driving through miles of cloth.

"Yes . . ."

"Shonda, this is Hannah . . ."

"Yes . . . ?" It sounded as if her name hadn't rung a bell with Shonda.

"Hannah Osborne?" Hannah clarified.

"Yes . . . yes, I know who you are. Is something wrong? Is something wrong with my son? Why are you calling me here at work?"

"I'm calling because . . . well, when I went to the child care center today to see him, they said that you—"

"Oh! I'm so sorry! Didn't Maura tell you where he was?" asked Shonda.

"Maura said that you asked her not to tell anyone where you had taken him. She thought it best if I called you."

There was an incoherent moment on Shonda's end of the line as a loud whistle blew. The sound of the sewing machines whirred to a halt as the workers left for lunch. "I can't tell you how sorry I am that you made the trip there for nothing. I didn't mean to put you out like that," said Shonda. "He's at the Woodmere Children's Center, out in Donsbridge. Do you know where that is?"

"Yes," replied Hannah. "Shonda, would it be all right if I stopped by to see him there this afternoon? I need to finish up his developmental profile."

"Yes, of course. Look . . . I'm so sorry about this, but I really have to go now. We only get a half hour to eat lunch."

"Don't worry about it, Shonda. But before you go, do you think you could call the Woodmere Children's Center to say that I'll be by this afternoon?"

"Sure. I'll call now."

"Just one more thing," said Hannah, sensing Shonda's impatience to hang up the phone. "Would it be all right if I came by your house this evening so we can talk some more about this? I'm a bit confused about what's happening."

"Yes, that'd be fine. I'll be home after 6 o'clock. Could you come then?"

"Great," said Hannah. "I'll see you around 6 o'clock."

Fancy Digs

Hannah pulled into the long driveway that led to the Woodmere Children's Center. How in the world, she thought, did Shonda end up bringing Conrad all the way out here? It's miles from her home and from the factory. Besides, Conrad is probably the only child here who isn't white and, more than likely, the only one who has disabilities. She parked her car in the section of the parking lot marked "Visitors" and walked toward the big double doors. Her feet sank into the lobby's thick carpeting, and her bare upper arms prickled with the chill from the air conditioning. She wished she'd brought her sweater with her, the one she usually brought into large office buildings that were chronically overcooled in the summer.

"Can I help you?" asked a woman who was tacking up a poster in a glass case by the doors.

"My name is Hannah Osborne. I'm here to work with Conrad Brown. His mother was supposed to have called to say I was coming."

"Conrad Brown?" She walked over to the reception desk and flipped through a list of names on a clipboard. "I'm afraid we don't have anyone here by that name."

Maybe Shonda had instructed them not to let anyone see Conrad for fear that Louise might locate him here. Hannah reassured the woman at the desk, "I'm a consultant for children with disabilities. I've been working with him at the Catesville Community Child Care Center, but his mother registered him here just last week."

"Let's see," she said as she flipped through the pages again. "Brown . . . Brown. Oh yes, he's that little handicapped boy." The woman flipped to the last page on the clipboard. "Yes. Here he is . . . Kareem Brown. Go on back to the last room on the right—Leila Russell's room."

"Uh, thank you," replied Hannah. "I'll just go on back there, then." Kareem? Why was she calling him Kareem? There must be some kind of mistake, thought Hannah. She walked down the corridor, astounded by the plush quality of the rooms she passed. It must cost a fortune to send a child here, she thought. How could Shonda afford a place like this?

Gazing through the window of the door to the last room, Hannah spotted Conrad. He was sitting on the floor with a toy truck in front of him, but he wasn't doing anything with it. He was just staring off into space with his back to the rest of the room. She gently pushed the door open, stuck her head inside, and raised her hand to get the attention of a woman helping a child get her pink suspenders on her shoulders. "Can I help you?" asked the woman.

"Yes. I'm looking for Leila Russell?"

"That would be me," said the woman with a smile. Two teenage girls who were there, Hannah guessed, as part of a high school work-study program were supervising a fingerpainting project. They looked up as Leila Russell crossed the room.

"What can I do for you?" asked Leila.

"I'm here to work with Conrad Brown. My name is Hannah Osborne."

"Oh, you must mean Kareem. Yes, his mother called earlier about your coming here to work with him. It's nice to meet you," Leila stepped toward Hannah and shook her hand. "You know," she whispered, "we've never had a handicapped child here before. You just have to wonder why his mother would want to send him here. I mean, aren't there special places for children like him? You know, where he could be with other handicapped children?"

Hannah felt the hairs on the back of her neck bristle. "Actually, he's a rather bright little guy, and he does quite well around typically developing children," said Hannah. She wanted to say a lot more but thought it best to hold her tongue for now. Just who did this woman think she was talking to? Even if she thought such things, what nerve she must have to say them aloud! Then again, maybe she was just that naive.

"Now, don't get me wrong," continued Leila. "We're very happy to have Kareem here with us. You just have to wonder if it's what's best for him. You know what I mean?"

Hannah gave her a cold stare. "Yes, I'm sure we all want what's best for Con . . . Kareem." What was this confusion over his name, anyway?

"Well, I really admire people like you who work with handicapped children," said Leila. "I assumed you would need some privacy, so I've arranged for you to have the spare room in back that we use for naptime."

"Actually, I'd prefer to work with him in the classroom. If it's all right with you, we can just continue with whatever activity you had planned for the afternoon." To heck with the developmental profile, thought Hannah. I've just got to see how they include Conrad in the classroom. Besides, if she took Conrad out of class to do the profile, she would be giving this woman the wrong idea about her role and her expectations for Conrad.

"Oh. . . ." Leila seemed a little confused. "I hadn't really planned anything for Kareem. To be honest, we're not sure what he's capable of handling, and I haven't yet worked out which activities he could be involved in."

Hannah couldn't believe her ears. If they knew so little about working with children with disabilities here, why would they have admitted him? For that matter, why didn't Shonda check out the place more thoroughly before she enrolled Conrad here? Then again, if they needed the enrollment, perhaps they didn't divulge any misgivings they might have to Shonda.

Leila and the two teenage girls gathered the children together to go outside to the playground. Hannah walked over to Conrad.

She knelt down beside the little boy and whispered, "Conrad. . . ." He turned when he heard her voice, and a smile burst across his face.

"Ah-ah," he squealed.

Hannah pulled Conrad to her chest and gave him a big hug. Then she stood up and held out her hand for him to grab. "Let's go outside to play, big guy," she said. "We'll show them what you can do, won't we?"

They walked toward the door, hand-in-hand, with Conrad's right foot dragging more than usual because he was craning his neck to look up at Hannah.

A Concerned Grandmother

There was an hour and a half between Hannah's last visit of the day and the time she had to be at Shonda's house. She decided to go back to the office to catch up on some paperwork and make a few phone calls. As she sifted through the pink message slips in her box, a name jumped out at her.

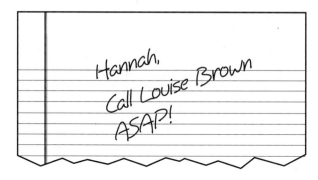

It seemed like the Brown family drama was not going to calm down for a minute today. Hannah dialed, and Louise picked up the phone on the second ring.

"Hello, Mrs. Brown. It's Hannah Osborne."

"Oh, honey, bless you for calling back so soon. I've been beside myself with worry. It's about my boy, Conrad. I hope you don't mind me calling you like this."

"Well," replied Hannah, "it's a bit of a surprise, but, no, it's fine."

"Shonda and I had a disagreement, and I didn't want to bother her right now, but I wanted to know how my grandson was doing."

"He's fine, Mrs. Brown. I saw him just a couple of hours ago. He was doing just fine."

"I thought he would be, but I wanted to make sure. He's such a good boy. He just needs a lot of love, and he'll do fine. You just make sure those people at that new place he's at give him the love he needs."

"Yes, Mrs. Brown, I'll do that."

"Well, I don't want to keep you. I know you're busy. You don't mind if I call now and then, do you? . . . Just to see how he's doing?"

"Well, I suppose that would be okay," said Hannah.

The Name Game

Shonda let Hannah into the small house on Marlette Street where she and Conrad lived. She cradled a portable phone between her shoulder and her ear and held up a finger to Hannah, signaling that she would be off the phone in a minute. Then she waved Hannah into the house and over to the couch in the living room. The house smelled of incense and spicy food. Colorfully printed African fabrics hung on the walls like tropical paintings, and carved wooden statuettes sat on the tables.

"Okay, Letticia, I'll talk to you later. Really, I've got to go—I've got company. Yes . . . I'll call you." Shonda clicked off the phone and pushed its antenna down. "Sorry, I have a time getting that girl to hang up sometimes."

"I hope I haven't interrupted anything."

"Just Letticia's latest report on where she saw Robert and who she saw him with. Like I need to know anything about his newest girlfriend or that he's spending $40 each on tickets to a show at the Memorial Amphitheater. And he has the nerve to give me some story about why he's 2 months late on his child support. In the meantime, all the money I saved up to start my own clothes shop is going right out the window."

Shonda raised the hem of the long skirt she was wearing to step over a toy army tank on the floor. "I asked that woman time and again not to give those war toys to my son, but does she listen? Not for a moment! Then, if I try to take them away from him, I become the mean mommy."

"You mean Louise?" asked Hannah.

"Who else?" asked Shonda. "And she has the nerve to defend that son of hers to me. Telling me, 'Men just do things like that,' and 'Maybe if you'd done things different, he'd still be here.'. . . Like I'd *have* him back!"

"I'm not so sure I understand what's going on," said Hannah.

"All you need to know is that Robert is a good-for-nothing drunk and that he's run off with another woman. Well, he can take his women and his booze, and they can all go—"

"Shonda, I know that already. What does all of this have to do with Louise and your moving Conrad to another child care center?"

"I've changed his name to Kareem, you know."

"You have?" So it wasn't a mistake, thought Hannah.

"It's his African name. I think he should be more in touch with his heritage. Even his father agreed with me on that when he was born; but then Louise threw such a fit about it, saying we were turning her grandson into a savage and going on about how Robert had sworn to name his first child after his uncle. So we ended up putting 'Conrad' on his birth certificate. Now I've changed it back. I feel that a child should be introduced to his real heritage, not just some slave name a relative got when he was brought to this country. And I don't see why he should accept his enslaver's religion, either."

Hannah was dumbfounded. She searched for the right words to say, but before she found them, Shonda started talking again. "I'm sorry. I don't mean to go on at you about this. It's just that Louise has crossed way over the line this time."

"What did she do?" asked Hannah.

"She took Kareem to her church last week and had him baptized behind my back. I heard about it from Letticia and only because her mother goes to the same church as Louise. It's been an ongoing battle with me and Louise . . . this having him baptized. And Robert never would back me up on it. He never would back me up on anything if it meant crossing his momma. She thinks that just because she took care of Kareem when he was a baby, he's her child now. Well, she can just think again."

Hannah thought for a moment, then put her hand on Shonda's arm. "I know you love Con—Kareem. It might take me a while to get used to the name change. Anyway, I know how much you love him and that you'd do anything for him. I also know you want him to grow up with a sense of heritage. But have you given much thought to how the change in child care programs and the change of his name might affect him?"

"How do you mean?" asked Shonda.

"I'm not exactly sure, but I think we should keep an eye out for any signals he might give us." Hannah thought about telling her what she saw and heard at the Woodmere Children's Center but decided that she should wait.

Shonda looked at Hannah. Her face looked angry at first, but the tiny lines around her mouth quickly smoothed out, and her brows relaxed. "I'll have to give that some more thought. I'm not taking him back to Maura's, though. Letticia told me that Louise said I was a heathen and didn't deserve to raise a child. I'm not taking any chances with that woman. For all I know, she could try to go out there and take away my boy. I won't risk that."

"Of course not," agreed Hannah. "But have you talked to Louise herself about all of this? Maybe there's been some exaggeration about what she's said."

"She had him baptized, didn't she? No, there's no way I'm going to talk to that woman now. And I'll not have her messing with my son again."

They talked for a while longer and decided that Hannah would make two more visits to the Woodmere Children's Center, then meet with Shonda again to let her know how the visits were going.

Hannah thought about Shonda and Louise for days afterward. What a shame they couldn't seem to work out their differences. Shonda had relied so much on Louise's support in the past. Would she have to turn down opportunities for extra work if Louise wasn't available to look after Conrad? Hannah thought about the money that Shonda must have saved on the clothes and shoes that Louise used to buy for Conrad. And where would Shonda get the money for the extra transportation costs and tuition for Conrad to attend the Woodmere Children's Center? All of these changes would amount to a substantial burden on Shonda's financial budget. Hannah felt sorry for Louise, too. She had sounded so sad on the phone. And what would Hannah do the next time Louise called? Shonda probably wouldn't approve of her talking to Louise, but it seemed that Louise at least had a right to hear how her grandson was doing.

Discussion Questions

1. Should Hannah have told Shonda her impression of the Woodmere Children's Center? For example, should she have told Shonda what Conrad's new teacher said about children with disabilities or that the center doesn't seem to know how to include Conrad in the classroom? Is Hannah justified in having such negative feelings about the Woodmere Children's Center?

2. Should Hannah discuss her concerns about changing Conrad's placement any further with Shonda at this point? If so, what issues should she raise, and how might she broach each topic with Shonda?

3. If Conrad remains at the Woodmere Children's Center, what does Hannah need to do to ensure that he is receiving appropriate services? Make a list of the steps you would take if you were in Hannah's position.

4. In general, when a therapist or consultant encounters a situation in which classroom staff are uneasy or reluctant about including a child with a disability, what is the best way to approach the situation?

5. Hannah is concerned about how Shonda's decision to place Conrad at the Woodmere Children's Center will affect the family's finances. Should Hannah discuss this issue with Shonda? If so, how should she approach the topic?

6. Shonda appears to have severed her ties with Louise. We know that Hannah is concerned about their relationship, but should she act on her concerns? If so, what might Hannah do?

7. What are Hannah's options if Louise calls her next week wanting to know how Conrad is doing?

8. Should Hannah let Shonda know how she feels about Louise being excluded from Conrad's life?

c h a p t e r *13*

Grandpa's Lap

P.J. McWilliam

Walking along the sidewalk that connected the elementary school to the preschool building, Lori Skidmore could already hear the morning chatter of children coming from the play yard. As she neared the preschool's entrance, a little girl appeared from behind the building and scampered down the sidewalk. It was Takesha Carey, full of energy and eager to start another day of preschool. The 3-year-old was carrying a brown paper bag that whisked back and forth across the ruffle of her bright yellow sundress, and the matching beads in her hair clicked with each hurried step. Takesha spotted Lori at the junction of the two walkways and headed straight toward her.

"Hi, Takesha!" greeted Lori. "Don't you look like a little sunshine girl today?"

Takesha stopped abruptly, and the paper bag struck her leg, almost toppling her over. "I gotsa bunny!" she proudly announced. Takesha set the bag on the sidewalk, opened it, and pulled out a cloth rabbit. "He name Hop-Hoppy."

Lori crouched down to admire the rabbit. "Oh, look at him! What a beautiful bunny. Is he new?"

Before Takesha could answer, Lori was distracted by the sight of a woman hurrying along the path that Takesha had just taken. Lori immediately recognized her as Takesha's grandmother, Evelyn Carey. She was wearing a floral cotton dress and blue house slippers that whistled along the sidewalk as she hurried toward Takesha and Lori.

"Whoowee, child! I told you not to go runnin' off like that without me." The woman stood beside Takesha, breathing heavily.

"Hi, Mrs. Carey," Lori said with a smile. "They sure are quick at this age, aren't they?"

"You're tellin' me! I'm gettin' too old for this. My legs can't take it no more." She pulled a white handkerchief from her pocket and mopped her cheeks and brow.

"Well, she certainly looks pretty this morning." said Lori. She stooped again to meet Takesha at eye level and patted the cloth rabbit. "And she was just showing me her beautiful bunny."

"Momma brung me bunny," said Takesha. "He name Hop-Hoppy."

"Her momma give it to her for her birthday last week," explained Mrs. Carey. "You'd a-thought it was sewed with gold thread the way this girl carries on." Mrs. Carey didn't exactly sound pleased about the rabbit.

Her attention still focused on Takesha, Lori asked, "Are you taking your bunny to school today?"

Takesha nodded and smiled.

"C'mon, Takesha," said Mrs. Carey, reaching for the child's hand. "We best be gettin' you to school 'afore it too late."

Lori stood up quickly. "Excuse me, Mrs. Carey, but is Demitrius here today? I wanted to do some therapy with him while I was here."

Mrs. Carey stared at the sidewalk. "He's home with his grandpa," she said softly.

"Oh, is he sick?"

"I think he's tryin' to catch hisself a cold." Still holding Takesha's hand, Mrs. Carey turned toward the door to the preschool. Takesha reached down with her other hand to pick up the paper bag, but she dropped her rabbit.

"I hope he's feeling better," said Lori as she picked up the rabbit and placed it in the crook of Takesha's arm. Without looking at Lori, Mrs. Carey gave a quick nod and continued toward the door with Takesha in tow.

Lori wasn't sure what had just happened. Had she offended Mrs. Carey? If she did, she didn't know what she had said that could have offended her. Maybe she shouldn't have asked her about Demitrius.

But she was responsible for providing him with physical therapy, so why shouldn't she ask about him? She was deeply concerned that he hadn't been getting the therapy he needed. A child with muscles as tight as his were couldn't afford to go for weeks on end without physical therapy. Lori decided to have a talk with Demitrius's teacher, Pam Bowman.

A Questionable Illness

The classroom was buzzing with activity. "Bombs away!" a 4-year-old voice yelled as Lori entered. A tower of multicolored blocks crashed in front of her, narrowly missing her feet. The bombardier, a husky little boy in a baseball cap, flashed a sheepish grin in Lori's direction. His companion sat cross-legged on the floor amidst the pile of blocks. Although the companion's facial features immediately identified him as having Down syndrome, his giggle and the mischievous look in his eyes were the same as any other 3- or 4-year-old's. Lori just grinned at the two boys and shook her finger at them in mock reprimand.

Lori scanned the room and located Pam at a table with a group of children playing with Play-Doh. As Lori approached the table, Pam was helping a child in a travelchair to pound the pile of green dough on his tray.

"Good morning," said Lori.

"Hi, Lori," said Pam, looking up. "I nearly forgot you were coming this morning. How are you?"

"Fine, thanks."

"You want to play with some Play-Doh?" asked Pam with a smile.

"Uh, sure," said Lori. A little girl, overhearing their conversation, held up a blob of yellow dough for Lori to take. Lori accepted the dough and absently began to knead it.

Pam again directed her attention toward the child in the travelchair, holding his hands and wrists in hers to guide his play. "Who are you here to see?" she asked.

"I was hoping to see Demitrius."

"I'm afraid you're out of luck on that one," said Pam. "He's not here."

"I know. I ran into his grandmother and his sister on the way in. I asked about Demitrius and got some vague answer about him having a cold. He's only been here twice this month when I've come to get him for therapy. Is something going on?"

"Not that I know of—except, of course, the usual."

"The usual? What do you mean?" asked Lori, stepping behind the travelchair to make eye contact with Pam. "Has he really been that sick?" Lori instinctively provided support to the child's upper arms to help him manage the green dough.

"I really couldn't tell you. They rarely call to say he'll be out."

"Well, don't you call them?"

Pam lifted her hands away from the child's wrists and glared at Lori. "No. I've been a little busy lately taking care of the other nine children in this classroom."

"I'm sorry, Pam. I know you're busy. I'm just concerned about Demitrius. He's supposed to be getting physical therapy three times a week, and I'm the one who's supposed to be providing it. How can I do that if he's never here? I don't understand what's going on."

"I don't understand myself," replied Pam. She reached down to pick up a piece of Play-Doh that had fallen on the floor. "Actually, I did go out to Demitrius's grandparents' house a few weeks ago after he had been absent for nearly 2 weeks. I used the Mother's Day present he helped make for his grandmother as an excuse for dropping by."

"And what did they say?"

"The usual. Evelyn said that he had had several colds and that they thought it was best if he stayed home for a week or two to build up his strength before they brought him back to the classroom." Pam pushed back her chair, stood up, and walked around the table to intervene in a dispute over a star-shaped cookie cutter.

While Pam helped the two children reach an agreement about the cookie cutter, Lori sat down in Pam's place and took over helping the child in the travelchair.

"Do they want him in the classroom at all?" asked Lori when Pam returned.

"You know, I asked myself that same question last month," replied Pam. "So, when I made my visit, I asked Evelyn straight out. She said she knew he needed special help and that she wanted him in my class. Besides, they bring Takesha to school almost every day. Evelyn walks her here—rain or shine."

"Do they have a way to get Demitrius here?" asked Lori.

"They have that nice travelchair you ordered for him, and they only live a few blocks from here. Evelyn walks him to school along with his sister. They also have a car, and I know his grandfather drives."

"That really confuses me. Why will they bring one child and not the other?" Lori paused a moment and then asked, "Did you actually see Demitrius while you were at the house?"

"Yes, he was there," answered Pam.

"Well, what did he look like?"

"He didn't look any different than he usually does. I spoke with Evelyn in the kitchen, but I went into the living room before I left to say hello to Demitrius. He was curled up in his grandfather's lap in front of the television and looked the same as always."

"That's what I was afraid of!" exclaimed Lori. "It wouldn't surprise me if he spent all of his time like that. Having cerebral palsy as severe as he does, he needs correct positioning and stretching. He'll get contractures that are beyond the point of remediation in no time at all."

"I suppose he might," said Pam. "I don't really know what they do with him at home. You know, Lori, he's not an easy child to engage, even here in the classroom. He does, however, seem to have more going for him cognitively than you would think at first glance."

"How about his mother? Would talking with her help?"

"I've only met her once," said Pam. "She came to his initial IEP meeting in September, but she barely said anything. His grandmother did most of the talking." Pam walked around the table to where Lori was and started picking pieces of green dough off the child's tray. "I think the mother still has legal custody of Demitrius and Takesha," she continued, "but she doesn't really seem to be in the picture. I remember his grandfather making some cutting remark about her one time when I was out there. He said something about her having these babies and then leaving them for him and Evelyn to raise."

"But we don't know for sure how the mother feels about the kids, do we?"

"Lori, I don't think it's a good idea to get ourselves into that."

"Well, we have to do something, don't we?" implored Lori.

"Maybe . . . I don't know. All I know is that I have to clean up this Play-Doh and get these kids their snacks." Pam began encouraging the children to put the Play-Doh into big plastic tubs.

Lori looked at her watch. It was nearly 10:00 A.M.—time to return to the elementary school for her regular sessions with two students there. She and Pam hadn't come to any resolutions about Demitrius, and Pam didn't seem overly concerned. Didn't she care? No, that wasn't a fair question—of course Pam cared. But was she going to do anything about it?

An Angry Grandfather

Through the window, Pam watched Lori walk back up the sidewalk that led to the elementary school. She snapped the tops onto the Play-Doh tubs and ushered the children through the door to the play yard. Pam and her assistant, Cynthia, had decided to hold morning snacktime outside because the weather was so nice. Pam offered to clean up the room if Cynthia would get the children started on their snacks. Pam usually preferred to be with the children, but she wanted a few minutes to herself to think over Demitrius's situation. What did Lori expect her to do that she hadn't already done? And why was it her responsibility to talk to Demitrius's grandparents? Wasn't Lori involved with this family as well? If Lori was so worried, maybe *she* should be the one to take action. Then again, who knows what Lori might do— call Demitrius's mother!?

Pam swept crumbs of Play-Doh off the floor and drew a pail of water from the sink. Sponging down the table, she continued to think about Demitrius. She finally decided to make another attempt with his grandparents, but on what pretense could she make a visit to their house? Pam walked over to the children's cubbies and looked through Demitrius's things. There, behind the diapers, was his blue tippy cup. It wasn't much of an excuse, but it would suffice as a ticket into their house.

It was a little past 4:30 P.M. when Pam gave a good-bye hug to the last child leaving the classroom. She quickly straightened the classroom, grabbed the blue tippy cup from Demitrius's cubby, and jumped into her car. Within a few minutes, she was pulling into the Careys' driveway. She stepped up onto the porch of the white frame house and knocked on the screen door. Pam waited a minute or two, then knocked again. Demitrius's grandfather finally came to the door and looked at her through the screen. He offered no greeting.

"Hi, Mr. Carey. I'm Pam Bowman from Takesha's and Demitrius's school. Do you remember me?"

"Yeah." Mr. Carey did not open the door. He just stood and stared at her.

Then Pam remembered the tippy cup. She pulled it out of her purse and held it before her like a trophy. "I found Demitrius's blue cup in his cubby. I thought you might be missing it. It seems to be a favorite of his."

"Yeah, that be his all right," mumbled the grandfather. He opened the door a crack and took the cup from Pam's outstretched hand.

Pam decided to take a gamble. "I was sorry to hear that Demitrius has another cold. Is he up to a visitor? I've missed him."

"The boy's not been sick. He be just fine—lyin' in here on the couch. See for yourself." Mr. Carey opened the door wider and motioned Pam in.

Pam walked through a small, dark entry hall and turned the corner into the living room. Demitrius was lying on his side on the sofa, and a kitchen chair was positioned in front of him to prevent him from falling to the floor. He was sound asleep.

"That's one tired little man," commented Pam.

The grandfather grunted in reply, then walked over to an arm-chair and sat down. He turned away from Pam and looked blankly at the television set that stood a few feet in front of him.

"I was wondering," said Pam, "if maybe I could talk to Evelyn or you about when you think Demitrius might be able to come to the classroom again. We've all missed him."

"Evelyn ain't here," he said flatly.

"Oh . . . I see. Well, are you expecting her back soon?"

"She took the girl down to the store. Don't know when she be back."

Mr. Carey continued to stare at the television. Pam didn't know what to do next. Should she wait for Evelyn and Takesha to return? Should she leave? Or should she continue to pursue the issue with Mr. Carey? Heaven knows he wasn't making this easy for her. Why must he be so unfriendly? She decided to give it one more try.

"Well, I know that Evelyn said she wanted Demitrius to be in the classroom," began Pam. "I was just wondering if there was anything that we could do to help out."

Mr. Carey turned around in the chair to face Pam. He crossed his arms over his chest and cocked his head to one side. "Now, it don't much matter what Evelyn says 'bout that," he said. "I'm the one be de-cidin' what my boy's gonna do. And I made up my mind—I ain't gonna send him to that school if all they's gonna do is make him cry. He don't need to be goin' through none of that. His life be rough enough as is."

Pam was momentarily stunned. What crying was he referring to? Sure, Demitrius cried in the classroom sometimes, but all of the 4-year-olds in her class cried occasionally.

"I can understand how you'd be concerned if you thought Demi-trius was unhappy at school," said Pam. "But I'm afraid I don't under-stand why you say he's crying. I mean, he does cry sometimes but not all that often. And even when he does, it usually doesn't last very long."

"Well, I know what I seen," replied Mr. Carey firmly.

"I . . . I didn't mean to say it wasn't true," stammered Pam. "It's just that I haven't noticed that he's all that unhappy in the classroom."

"I'm not talkin' 'bout when he be with you."

"When, then?" questioned Pam. "When did you see him cry?"

"With that other woman who sees him," said Mr. Carey.

Pam could tell that he was growing increasingly irritated with her, and she was getting a little nervous. But what was he talking about? What other woman? Where would he have seen Demitrius crying? She racked her brain for answers, but none came.

"What other woman?" she finally asked.

"That woman who has all that equipment," said Mr. Carey. His voice was getting louder. "I seen her with him through that little window when I took his medicine to school."

What window? What equipment? Then it suddenly came to her. He must be talking about the therapy room—the one with the one-way mirror. And the other woman must be Lori.

"Do you mean Lori?" asked Pam. "Lori Skidmore, the physical therapist?"

"I'd a-told you her name if I'd a-known it," Mr. Carey said with an edge to his voice. "I never seen her 'afore."

"Yes, of course," said Pam quickly. "I'm sorry."

Wasn't Mr. Carey at Demitrius's last intervention plan review meeting? Pam couldn't remember. Or maybe it was Lori who wasn't there. Lori was contracted by the school to provide physical therapy 15 hours per week, and her time was divided between the elementary school and the preschool. She often didn't attend preschool planning meetings. Furthermore, Lori spent very little time meeting with parents. It bothered Pam, but what could she do about it?

The stern look on Mr. Carey's face called for Pam to respond to his accusation, but what was she supposed to say? The fact was, she didn't know what went on with Demitrius in the therapy room. It had been a long time since she had watched Lori working with Demitrius. She did, however, know that some of the children cried while Lori was working with them. The teacher whose classroom was across the hall from the therapy room sometimes joked about being next to a torture chamber.

"I'm sorry, Mr. Carey, but I don't know what Lori has been doing with Demitrius," said Pam. "I'll talk with her first thing in the morning and find out what's been going on."

"Don't bother. I done decided he don't need none of that."

"Do you mean you don't want Demitrius to get therapy from Lori?" asked Pam, trying to clarify his position.

"I said, he don't need none of it," Mr. Carey said flatly.

Pam wondered if he meant the classroom, too. "How do you feel about what we've been doing in the classroom with Demitrius?" she asked timidly.

"That was Evelyn's idea," was all he said.

Pam wished Evelyn would walk through the door right now. She was so much easier to talk to. Pam still didn't know whether Mr. Carey wanted Demitrius to attend the classroom, and she didn't want to ask again and give him the opportunity to say no while he was angry. She decided to let it drop for now. She needed time to think and to develop a strategy.

"Mr. Carey, I really am sorry that you're unhappy with the program," said Pam. "If it's all right with you, I'd still like to talk with Lori tomorrow and find out what's been going on. Then I'll get back to you and Evelyn. Will that be okay?"

"Hmmmpf," he grunted.

"Well, I guess I better be going now," said Pam. She turned away from Mr. Carey and started walking toward the door. As she passed the sofa, she looked down at Demitrius, who was still sound asleep. Pam wanted to stop and touch his head or stroke his cheek, but she just walked by. He needs so much, she thought. What a shame it would be if he didn't get any services. Mr. Carey followed a few paces behind Pam as she walked back through the dark entry hall and stepped outside. Without a good-bye, he pulled the screen door closed behind her.

As Pam got into her car, she stole a quick glance back toward the house, but Mr. Carey had already vanished. The driveway gravel crunched under her tires as she backed out onto the street. Thoughts of Demitrius's future raced through her mind: How could she have let this happen? Why didn't she realize what was going on before it was too late to do anything about it? Then again, maybe it wasn't too late. Surely there must be something she could do to get Demitrius back into the classroom.

Individualized Education Program
Goals and Objectives

Name: *Demitrius Carey*
Age: *4 years 2 months*

Goal/Objective	Person(s) Responsible
1. Demitrius will bring his head to midline to accept food from a spoon when properly positioned in his travelchair or corner chair.	Pam Bowman (Teacher) Cynthia Lowe (Assistant)
2. Demitrius will demonstrate complete lip closure when removing food from a spoon.	Pam Bowman (Teacher) Cynthia Lowe (Assistant)
3. Demitrius will drink fluids from a regular cup (without a spout) held by an adult.	Pam Bowman (Teacher) Cynthia Lowe (Assistant)
4. Demitrius will tolerate increased texture in foods and improve rotary chewing.	Pam Bowman (Teacher) Cynthia Lowe (Assistant)
5. Demitrius will indicate food preferences by visually orienting to one of two food choices held in front of him and spaced 12–16 inches apart.	Pam Bowman (Teacher) Cynthia Lowe (Assistant)
6. Demitrius will play with water and sand toys when positioned at the sand/water table (with adult assistance).	Pam Bowman (Teacher) Cynthia Lowe (Assistant)

(continued)

(continued)

Goal/Objective	Person(s) Responsible
7. Demitrius will independently operate a switch to activate battery-operated toys (e.g., bear with cymbals, cassette player, roller coaster) in order to entertain himself for 10 minutes. —sidelying, corner chair, travelchair—	Pam Bowman (Teacher) Cynthia Lowe (Assistant)
8. Demitrius will indicate preferences in toys and classroom activities by visually fixating on one of two toys held before him, or by eye pointing at one of two photographs showing available activities (e.g., photo of water table, swing, Play-Doh, storybook reading).	Pam Bowman (Teacher) Cynthia Lowe (Assistant)
9. Demitrius will respond appropriately to social overtures made by other children in the classroom. —look at peers —smile —laugh —vocalize —accept offered toys	Pam Bowman (Teacher) Cynthia Lowe (Assistant)
10. Demitrius will gain attention of and initiate interactions with adults and peers by making eye contact with others, vocalizing, or banging on tray.	Pam Bowman (Teacher) Cynthia Lowe (Assistant)
11. Demitrius will actively participate in singing songs during circle time by attempting to perform hand movements of familiar songs (Itsy-Bitsy Spider, Wheels on the Bus, If You're Happy and You Know It). —cooperate with adult assistance —initiate movement —increasingly closer approximations	Pam Bowman (Teacher) Cynthia Lowe (Assistant)
12. Demitrius will participate in circle time by choosing a song to sing when asked by an adult (e.g., gesture to indicate preferred song—clasp hands for Itsy-Bitsy Spider).	Pam Bowman (Teacher) Cynthia Lowe (Assistant)
13. Provide weekly written or verbal communication to grandparents regarding Demitrius's progress and activities in the classroom.	Pam Bowman (Teacher)

(continued)

(continued)

Goal/Objective	Person(s) Responsible
14. *Investigate alternative car restraint system for Demitrius and provide information to grandparents—travelchair does not easily fit into car (family prefers some sort of seatbelt).*	*Lori Skidmore (PT) Pam Bowman (Teacher)*
15. *Experiment with various ways to administer seizure medication in order to increase Demitrius's tolerance, reduce spillage, and make dosage more accurate. Share successful strategies with grandparents.*	*Pam Bowman (Teacher) Cynthia Lowe (Assistant)*
16. *Investigate potential resources for obtaining a bath chair that grandparents can use with Demitrius at home.*	*Pam Bowman (Teacher) Lori Skidmore (PT)*
17. *Investigate sources of financial assistance to cover costs of dental care for Demitrius.*	*Pam Bowman (Teacher)*
18. Demitrius will tolerate range of motion exercises 3X a week.	Lori Skidmore (PT)
19. Demitrius will demonstrate protective balance reactions to front, side, and back when tilted on a therapy ball.	Lori Skidmore (PT)
20. Demitrius will tolerate being placed in a prone stander 3X a day for 20 minutes for joint compression.	Lori Skidmore (PT) Classroom staff
21. Demitrius will independently lift his head 4″ when placed over a therapy ball or on a wedge.	Lori Skidmore (PT)
22. Demitrius will reduce scissoring during diapering, when lifted, or when suspended.	Lori Skidmore (PT) Classroom staff
23. Demitrius will tolerate sitting in an adult's lap without demonstrating an opisthotonic reaction.	Lori Skidmore (PT) Classroom staff
24. Demitrius will sit in a corner chair, bolster chair, or travelchair, with hips, knees, and ankles flexed at 90 degrees (3X a day for 20 minutes).	Lori Skidmore (PT) Classroom staff

Discussion Questions

1. What factors may have contributed to the difficult situation that Pam Bowman now faces? Make a list.

2. Could anything have been done to prevent Demitrius's grandfather from making the decision to withdraw Demitrius from the program? If so, what?

3. Do you think Pam did the right thing by making a visit to Demitrius's grandparents' home? If not, how could she have better handled the situation?

4. How well do you feel Pam interacted with Demitrius's grandfather? Would you have said or done anything differently?

5. What options does Pam have after talking with Demitrius's grandfather? Make a list.

6. Of the options you identified in your answer to Question #5, which would you choose, and why?

7. If, in the end, the Careys decide against physical therapy for Demitrius but allow him to attend preschool, what, if anything, should Pam or Lori do? How important are the physical therapy goals that are included on Demitrius's IEP? What would the consequences of not receiving physical therapy be for Demitrius? Could the physical therapy goals on Demitrius's IEP be worked on in the classroom? If so, how?

8. Suppose the Careys tell Pam that they want to withdraw Demitrius from both physical therapy *and* the classroom. How should Pam approach such a situation? Why?

9. If, in the end, Demitrius's grandparents actually do withdraw him from the classroom as well as from physical therapy, should Pam feel responsible for ensuring that any of his physical or developmental needs are met? If so, which of Demitrius's IEP goals would be most important for Pam to attend to, and how might she go about doing it?

10. Let's assume that the mother still has legal custody of Demitrius and Takesha but that, except for the initial IEP meeting, the grandparents have been the preschool's sole contact in matters concerning the children. Should the preschool staff have continued

to contact the children's mother or tried other ways to involve her in making decisions about the children? Should they now?

11. What legal issues might arise in the grandparents' functioning as guardians for Demitrius and Takesha if, in fact, the mother has custody? Is the preschool taking any legal risks? If so, should they be taken? What, if any, safeguards could be enacted by the preschool?

12. To what extent do you think the method by which physical therapy was provided to Demitrius (e.g., contracted services, pull-out therapy) contributed to the difficulties that arose with the Carey family? If you were in charge of the preschool program described in this story, what policies and procedures would you establish for using contracted physical therapy or other related services?

13. In general, what family-centered strategies can be employed by professionals working in a full-day, center-based preschool program? What roles would various staff members have (e.g., lead teacher, teacher assistants, administrators, physical therapist, speech-language pathologist)?

chapter 14

Silent Partner

Miki Kersgard

Samantha Price waved her assistant out the door with a smile. "Go on, Jocelyn, I'll wait for Roz. Really, it's no problem."

"But you're always the one who gets stuck waiting for her."

"I know—she's late a lot," said Samantha. "I'm going to talk to her about it today. Really, though, it's no problem. I'd be here puttering around anyway."

Jocelyn shook her head and shrugged into her jacket. "Well, thanks. I'll see you tomorrow at the seminar, then."

"Okay, see you tomorrow," said Samantha.

On her way to the door, Jocelyn put Amy Polikanski's lunchbox on one of the small tables and bent down to pick up the sweater that the little girl had dropped four times in as many minutes. "Here, sweetie, hold onto your sweater like a good girl. Mommy should be here any minute, and you'll have to put it on then."

"Mama?" asked Amy, looking up from her toys.

"No, sweetie, but Mama should be here soon." Jocelyn gently pushed Amy's bangs away from her eyes and touched the little girl's cheek, then she waved good-bye and left.

Amy watched the door close behind Jocelyn, then resumed playing with the toys scattered around her. Her little hands moved tiny dolls in and out of the miniature beds and chairs of the doll house.

Samantha watched Amy's silent play. Although she was almost 4 years old, Amy's speech was more like that of a $1\frac{1}{2}$- or 2-year-old's. Her limited vocabulary consisted primarily of single words like "mama," "go," "drink," and "baby." Occasionally, she combined two words to form phrases like "more drink" and "mama bye-bye," but these word combinations usually required modeling and prompting by an adult. In fact, most of Amy's speech production required prompting. When left on her own, Amy was usually silent. Oddly enough, though, Amy seemed to understand a great deal of what others said to her. For example, if Samantha told her to get her sweater out of her cubby, she could usually be counted on to follow through without additional instruction.

The little girl's silence remained a mystery to Samantha. Although Amy was at least a year delayed in all aspects of her development, her speech-language delays seemed disproportionately severe. The test results in her file documented her speech delays but offered little in the way of explanation. Even more frustrating to Samantha was the fact that neither the therapy Amy received nor Samantha's own attempts to encourage Amy to talk had made an appreciable difference in her speech during the past 7 months. Samantha had also offered some suggestions for working on Amy's speech at home, but she suspected that her mother didn't take the activities very seriously.

The special preschool class, part of an elementary school in a lower–middle-class section of Boston, was Samantha's first teaching assignment, and she was very proud of it. Most of the children in her class were already showing improvement. In many ways, Samantha felt more secure about her work with the children in her class whose delays were more severe than Amy's. At least there were concrete reasons for their delays, and her expectations for their progress were not as high.

The Bum's Rush

This was the third time this week that Roz Polikanski was late picking up Amy. Samantha knew she had to speak to Roz about being late, but she could never decide which she wanted more: to get Amy and her mother out the door so she could go home herself or to persuade Roz not to make the end of the day any later than it had to be. Just as she was deciding that today was as good a day as any to have a talk with

Roz, Samantha saw Roz through the window. She was walking down the sidewalk accompanied by a tall man in mechanic's overalls. Together, they looked like Mutt and Jeff. Roz hardly came up to the man's chest. So much for talking to Roz, thought Samantha. No sense in creating tension by complaining in front of the guy she's with.

"Un—ca!" yelled Amy when they came in.

"Sorry we're late," said Roz. "Jimmy here had to come get my car started again."

"How's the little squirt?" asked Jimmy, as he picked up Amy and threw her in the air.

"Un—ca," yelled Amy again.

Amy seems to have quite a few uncles, thought Samantha. This is the third one who's come to school with Roz this year. Samantha tried not to judge Roz, but she wondered how stable Amy's home life was.

"Here you go, pumpkin, on with your sweater," said Roz. "We've got to hurry—we're running late already, and we've got lots to do tonight. We're going to Uncle Jimmy's. He's going to make us dinner. Isn't that nice? Now wave bye-bye to Miss Price."

Amy waved to Samantha as she peeked over Roz's shoulder on their way out the door. Roz had rushed in and out so quickly that Samantha's head was spinning. She felt like she'd been given the slip, but she couldn't figure out how or why.

Samantha was heading back to her desk when she realized that, even though she had been telling the children's parents all week that the classroom would be closed tomorrow, she hadn't reminded Roz about it tonight. I hope she'll remember, thought Samantha. Well, it's too late now. I can't call her at home. I don't even know "Uncle" Jimmy's last name.

Samantha bent down to pick up a red plastic ball that had rolled under her desk. It's always something, isn't it? she thought. As hard as she tried to keep everything in its place, something always turned up under something else. Thanks to her dad, a career military man, Samantha had a keen sense of organization and a need for everything to meet her standards. Her high expectations presented her with many challenges in her work with preschoolers, but she still managed to let the children be themselves.

Samantha enjoyed this time alone, tidying up after the children had been picked up by their parents and Jocelyn had gone home for the day. There was something almost meditative in the way she straightened each sign on the cubbies and arranged each toy just so, as if they were brand new and on display in a store window.

The last thing she always did before she left was straighten her desk. She put the pens and pencils point down in her pencil cup, filed her notes for the day in her drawer, and turned the page of her calendar to the next workday.

April

2 Friday	
8 AM	PM 1
9	2
10	3
11	4
12	5
Evening	

Early Intervention Training Seminar

Attending tomorrow's seminar meant 3 days in a row away from the children. Samantha didn't know whether she was relieved, excited, or disappointed. She usually missed the children by the end of a normal weekend, and children at this age could come back entirely different after a long weekend. The seminar, though, would be a wonderful break from her daily routine and a chance to get some new ideas for her classroom.

She flipped the calendar to Monday, then picked up the plastic bag containing the money for next week's lunches. Realizing that she had already locked her desk drawer, she put the bag back down on the desk, ran her finger over the seal, folded the bag in half, and stuck it in the corner of her desk blotter. No one will notice it, she thought. You can hardly even tell there's money in there. Besides, the classrooms are locked over the weekend. Samantha gathered her jacket and purse, checked the room one last time, and closed the door behind her as she left the room.

What's Missing?

It seemed like Monday morning took forever to arrive. Samantha had learned a lot at the early intervention training seminar and was eager to see how the new activities would fit into her classroom routine. Jocelyn was there, as usual, to take care of the few early arrivals whose parents had to be at work before 8 o'clock. The children were sitting in a circle singing "The Eensy Weensy Spider." As more children arrived, Samantha took off their sweaters and jackets and directed them toward the circle.

It wasn't until all the children were sitting in the circle that Samantha had time to go back to her desk to put away the notes and handouts she had brought back from the seminar. Funny, she thought, pushing in her desk drawer. Something looks different. Everything seems to be here, though. She had gotten a few steps away from her desk when she turned around and realized what was missing. The money! There was no Ziplock bag in the corner of the blotter! Had she put it in the drawer after all? Samantha pulled open the top drawer and pushed the notebooks and papers aside. *No, it was on the blotter. I know it was.* Samantha thought back to Thursday. *I tucked it in the corner of the blotter. I locked the door, didn't I?*

"Jocelyn?" Samantha said, in as even a tone as she could manage. "Did you see a plastic bag with some money in it on my desk this morning?"

"No. Is something wrong?"

"I'm not sure yet. I have to check on something. Can you handle things here by yourself for a while?"

"Sure, I'll be fine."

Samantha walked across the hall to Marilyn Paraka's first-grade classroom and stuck her head in the door. "Marilyn? Could I talk to you for a minute?" she asked.

When Marilyn stepped out into the hallway, Samantha told her about the missing money and asked her if the doors had been locked all weekend.

"Well, yes," said Marilyn. "They were locked. But the rest of us were here on Friday when you were gone. Maybe the cleaning people unlocked your door along with ours. I guess they wouldn't have known about the seminar. You know. . . ." Marilyn had an uneasy look on her face. "I did see a woman with a little girl coming out of your classroom Friday morning. I told her about the seminar, and she thanked me. Come to think of it, she didn't seem all that surprised or upset when I told her that there was no class. I'd probably recognize the little girl if I saw her."

The two women walked over to Samantha's classroom and opened the door. "That one there. The one in the red overalls," whispered Marilyn, pointing to Amy. "She was with a short woman in her late twenties with long blond hair about down to here." Marilyn pointed to a spot midway down her back.

I knew it, thought Samantha. She walked over to the circle of children and picked up Amy. "Come here for a minute, sweetheart," she said and carried the little girl over to her desk. "Remember when Mommy brought you to school, and no one was here?"

Amy's round eyes stared at Samantha, and she nodded her head.

"Remember, Mommy talked to Mrs. Paraka?" Samantha pointed to Marilyn.

Again, a nod from Amy and a smile of recognition.

"Hi, Amy," said Marilyn. "Remember me? I saw you and Mommy at school. Everybody was gone, and you and Mommy had to go back home."

Amy tilted her head to one side and said, "Mama?"

"That's right, Amy—Mama." Samantha turned Amy around to face the desk and patted the corner of the blotter. "Did Mama get something from here?" Samantha touched the corner of the blotter and pantomimed grabbing something with her hand. "Did Mama get the bag?. . . Mama get it?" Samantha paused and stared into the little girl's face.

"Mama. . . ." Amy's inflection was midway between a question and a statement.

"Did Mama get the bag . . . the bag with money? Did Mama put it in her pocket?"

Amy's face lit up, and she nodded her head vigorously. Then she plunged her hand into the bib of her overalls. "Pa-pa!" she exclaimed.

"Did Mama put the money in your pocket?" asked Samantha.

Amy nodded vigorously and smiled.

Samantha looked at Marilyn, then put Amy back down on the floor. "Thank you, Amy. You can go back to the circle now." Then Samantha turned to Marilyn, her cheeks flushed with anger, and she whispered, "Well, I'll put up with a lot, but I draw the line at stealing! I have a good mind to call the police right now!"

Discussion Questions

1. Was Samantha justified in suspecting Roz Polikanski of stealing the lunch money from her desk?

2. Was Samantha justified in questioning Amy about the missing money?

3. Should Samantha follow through on her threat to involve the police? If not, what other options does she have for handling this situation? Make a list. Of the options you have identified, which is Samantha's best choice?

4. Aside from the missing money, how might Samantha approach the other issues she faces in working with Roz Polikanski?

5. What, if anything, can Samantha do to confront the problem of Roz's persistent tardiness at the end of the day?

6. Should Samantha act on her concerns about Amy's home environment? If so, what should she do?

7. What can Samantha do to impress on Roz the importance of working on Amy's speech at home?

chapter 15

Recipe for Rachel

*P.J. McWilliam and
Kathryn Matthews*

*J*ingle bells, jingle bells, jingle all the way. Oh, what fun it is ride in a one-horse open sleigh. . . . HEY! As always, the children screamed the last word of the refrain. It was their favorite holiday song. The parents sang along, smiling and laughing at their preschoolers' antics. So far, the party was a big success. At least one parent for each child, except Reggie, had attended, and a handful of children had both parents or a parent plus a friend or a relative present.

Gwen Roland, the classroom teacher, eased herself away from the group. It was almost time for the main event—Santa's arrival. She was still amazed that Samuel Bevins, the director, had actually agreed to play the part of Santa Claus. He rarely involved himself in any of the children's activities, despite Gwen's numerous invitations. *Samuel may not give an Oscar-winning performance,* thought Gwen, *but at least he'll be in the classroom and get to know the children better.*

Gwen stationed herself next to the door so she would be able to see Samuel coming down the hall. She leaned against the toy shelves and watched the children singing. Andrea, her assistant, was doing a good job of keeping the group going. *I really should give Andrea more responsibility,* thought Gwen. *She's energetic and great with both the children and their parents.*

As Gwen watched, a child drifted away from the group and headed toward the table of goodies on the far side of the room. It was Rachel Stevens. Gwen quickly scanned the group of parents. Sandy Stevens's ever-vigilant eyes had already spied her daughter, and she was on her way to intervene. Gwen hurried toward Rachel, hoping to reach her first. There was no sense in having a scene that would spoil the party for everyone, including Sandy and Rachel.

Before Rachel had entered her classroom, Gwen hadn't even considered how routine it was to serve cookies, cake, candy, and other sweets to the preschoolers. Snacks, parties, field trips, and even some art and educational activities involved foods that Sandy either did not want her daughter to eat or allowed her to have only in very small quantities. Today's party was just such an occasion. By the time Gwen had caught up to Rachel, she was already standing in front of the table. The sun coming through a nearby window glinted off the 3-year-old's tawny red curls. She stared up at Gwen, awaiting a verdict. Gwen knelt beside the little redhead and smoothed the ruffles of her party dress. "You look so pretty today, Rachel."

Rachel looked at a plate of cupcakes with green and red sprinkles on top. Then she looked back up at Gwen. "Pretty cakes," she said with a smile.

"My, they are pretty, aren't they?" replied Gwen.

"We gonna eat cake?"

"Later, sweetheart. Right now, everyone is singing."

"I wanna red one. . . . I like red cakes." Rachel couldn't take her eyes off the cupcakes.

"Hey, Rachel!" said Gwen, hoping to distract her. "Do you know who's going to be here soon?"

Rachel gave her a blank look.

"Who wears a red coat, has a big white beard, and says 'Ho, ho, ho?' "

"Santa Claus!" squealed Rachel. She clasped her pudgy hands together under her chin and whispered excitedly to Gwen, "Santa Claus comin'."

"Well, he'll be here soon. Let's go over, now, and sing with your friends and your mommy." Gwen gently turned Rachel by the shoulders and nudged her back toward the singers. Sandy Stevens stood at the edge of the group waiting for her daughter. Gwen smiled nervously at her. *Oh, Sandy, please let it drop this time,* thought Gwen. *Don't make an issue out of it . . . please.* Then she went back to the door to wait for Samuel.

Growing Difficulties

From the beginning, Rachel had been a delight to have in the classroom. She was social and affectionate with adults and more verbally competent than most of the other children with disabilities in the class. Some delays, however, were evident when she was compared with the typically developing children in the class. Gwen had also been impressed by Rachel's mother. Sandy was active in the classroom, and Gwen could always count on her to lend a hand in planning special events for the children. Gwen often thought how fortunate she had been to get a classroom parent like Sandy, who was so involved, rather than getting another parent like Reggie's, who constantly had to be coaxed.

Most important, Sandy was very knowledgeable about Prader-Willi syndrome and readily participated in joint intervention planning with Rachel's team. Gwen had never heard of Prader-Willi syndrome before Rachel joined her class in late August, so Sandy's vast knowledge helped the team to understand which kinds of accommodations Rachel needed and to develop her intervention plan. Not surprisingly, Sandy's major concern had been Rachel's diet. She wanted to maintain strict control over the types of food that Rachel was given as well as the size of the portions she received. Sandy also wanted to ensure that Rachel got sufficient exercise each day, as she did not readily engage in active indoor or outdoor play. Rachel's initial intervention plan outlined a variety of language, cognitive, and self-help goals, and she began to receive both speech-language and occupational therapies.

Things went smoothly for the first month or two, with the only significant problem being Rachel's lunch. The school district's nutritionist had worked with Sandy in planning Rachel's lunches, and she, in turn, had explained to the school cafeteria staff what kinds of foods they should prepare for Rachel. The cafeteria staff, however, never quite got it right—or at least not right enough to satisfy Sandy. Despite Gwen's spending hours intervening in Sandy's arguments with the women in the cafeteria, the problem never was resolved. Sandy finally gave up in exasperation and started packing lunches for Rachel to bring to school each morning. Gwen felt somewhat guilty that she hadn't been able to work out the problem. Taking advantage of free school lunches would have been one way Sandy and her husband Dennis could have saved some money. In addition to Rachel, they had three other children: Jessica, who was 8 years old, and 13-year-old twins, Matthew and Kimberly. It wouldn't be easy for anybody to feed and clothe a family of six, but it must have been particularly difficult for the Stevenses. The only income the Stevens family had was Dennis's disability pay.

Even though Rachel now brought her lunch from home, controlling her diet still proved to be far more difficult than Gwen had ever imagined. Afternoon snacktime posed a particular problem because the children's parents took turns providing the snack. Although Gwen had always encouraged parents to send healthy snacks, this year it was essential. She worked with Sandy to develop a list of acceptable snack foods, and each parent had received a copy along with a brief explanation about Rachel's special diet. At first, most of the parents stuck to the list, but lately they had been arriving with calorie- and sugar-laden snacks that Rachel wasn't supposed to eat.

Gwen sent the list out a second time along with a gentle reminder, but it didn't seem to make much difference. In fact, in response to the reminder, one mother had complained that, although she was sympathetic to Rachel's needs, it didn't seem fair to deprive the other children of typical preschool snacks. After all, why make all the other children suffer? Another mother had recently requested to have a birthday party for her son in the classroom. Although she was willing to provide acceptable foods for Rachel, she wanted to serve ice cream and cake to the other children.

Gwen had spoken to Sandy about these problems in the hope that they'd work together toward a solution, but their conversation ended up being very short. "The fact that Rachel has Prader-Willi syndrome is not going to go away," Sandy had told Gwen. "She's going to have it for the rest of her life. She'll also be surrounded by food the rest of her life. I can't control that. She needs to learn that she's different and that she can't always have what others eat. She may as well start learning it now."

Gwen had resorted to buying appropriate snacks for Rachel herself so that she had a substitute on hand when it was needed. But even when she could offer Rachel an appropriate snack, quantity was not always easy to monitor. Rachel always wanted more. Gwen felt even more thwarted in trying to honor Sandy's requests when one day she spied Andrea giving Rachel an extra bit of fruit and a cracker. Gwen had just told Rachel that she couldn't have any more. It made Gwen wonder just how often Rachel was given contraband food.

Gwen hadn't said anything to Andrea at the time because she herself had committed similar offenses. It was difficult not to give in to Rachel when she batted her eyelashes and pleaded, "Please, one itty-

bitty?" She was just too cute! Gwen usually recounted to Sandy everything that Rachel had eaten during the day and explained any violations of her diet, but there were times when she neglected to keep
Sandy fully informed. Maybe she kept quiet because she didn't want
to upset Sandy, or maybe she didn't want to admit even to herself
what she had done. Then again, when Gwen did give in to Rachel, she
gave her only fruit or other low-calorie foods. A little extra now and
then couldn't make that much difference.

Rachel was 36 inches tall and weighed about 45 pounds. She was
definitely on the heavy side, but Gwen wondered whether Sandy was
being a bit too strict about her diet. After all, Rachel was still a growing child, and she wasn't obese; she was just chubby. Rachel had displayed several mild temper tantrums at school recently, all of them related to food. This type of behavior was new for Rachel and further
alarmed Gwen to the possibility that Sandy was being too strict.

Gwen told Sandy about the tantrums, but Sandy had just said, "It
doesn't surprise me. I've had to deal with her having fits for some time
now." Sandy explained that she usually made Rachel sit in a time-out
chair whenever she had a tantrum. "It doesn't help having the twins
spoiling her," Sandy added. "They feel sorry for her and give in to her
all the time." Sandy said, too, that she was upset by Rachel's begging
for food. From what Gwen gathered, Sandy was referring to Rachel's
saying "please" repeatedly when asking for food. Actually, the behavior she described was very similar to what Rachel did at school, and
Gwen hardly considered that "begging." In fact, it seemed quite age
appropriate and polite—not to mention cute.

Gwen was feeling more and more confused about Rachel. She
wanted to do the right thing, but she wasn't sure what the right thing
was. A week ago, Gwen had suggested to Sandy that they get together
soon to review Rachel's intervention plan to make sure that the goals
and strategies they had agreed on in August were still appropriate. Going over the intervention plan would be one way that Gwen could
broach a few topics that she wanted to discuss with Sandy. She would
have done a 3-month review and updated the plan in November, but
Rachel's sudden onset of asthma in October had thrown the schedule
off a month. Rachel's asthma attacks had required several trips to the
emergency room and were quite frightening for Sandy. It took her
doctors weeks to find the right combination of medicines for Rachel.

Santa's Visit

"Ho, ho, ho! Merry Christmas!" Samuel's attempt at a belly laugh was
pathetic, but the children didn't seem to notice. They squealed with

delight as he entered the classroom, and they all rushed over to greet him. All of them, that is, except Alicia, whose face immediately crumpled like a paper bag as she began to cry and cling to her mother's leg. *There's always one,* thought Gwen. She could have predicted it would be Alicia this year. She cried at anything new.

Samuel tried to talk to the excited children, but every time he bent over, the pillow that plumped out his costume slipped and needed readjusting. Gwen let him struggle for a few minutes, enjoying the spectacle. Then she came to his rescue and escorted him to the Santa chair she had prepared in the corner of the room. Gwen and Andrea directed the children to sit in a semicircle on the floor in front of Santa and began letting them go up one at a time to sit on his lap and receive a small gift. Reggie went first.

Gwen stood back and watched the little boy saunter up to Samuel. This was her favorite part; she loved hearing what the children said to Santa. As Reggie began to describe the action figure he wanted for Christmas, Gwen was distracted by the sound of crying behind her. She had forgotten all about Alicia.

In the far corner of the room, Alicia's mother was trying to console her daughter, who was now near hysterics. "Look, honey," her mother was saying, "Reggie is sitting with Santa Claus. Don't you want to talk with Santa and tell him what you want him to bring you for Christmas?" Alicia only screamed louder. "Let's go see if he has a present for you, okay?" Her mother tried to pry the sobbing child from her shoulder; but Alicia's grip tightened, and her legs scrambled to gain a secure hold around her mother's waist. *This is getting ridiculous,* thought Gwen, and she walked over to help.

"Hey there, Alicia! You're missing out on all the fun," said Gwen cheerily. She released Alicia's fingers from her mother's sweater and took the child into her arms. Gwen rubbed her back briskly, gave her a quick kiss on the cheek, and said, "Now then, let's stop all of this crying. You don't have to talk to Santa if you don't want to, but no more crying . . . okay?" She pulled a tissue from her pocket and wiped Alicia's cheeks and nose. "We'll just go over and see what's going on." Alicia's screaming wound down to a whimper, and she laid her head on Gwen's shoulder. Then Gwen carried Alicia back to the group and stood behind the circle of children. Alicia's mother trailed behind and stood a few feet away from her daughter and Gwen.

Reggie had stepped down, and Rachel was just approaching Samuel. She smiled coyly and stretched her arms toward Santa. "Oh my," groaned Samuel as he lifted her onto his lap. "You're a big girl, now, aren't you?" Gwen winced and glanced over at Sandy, but Sandy hadn't reacted. She just looked on somberly. "Well, well, well . . . ," continued Samuel, "who do we have here?" *Darn,* thought Gwen, *he doesn't even know the children's names!* Samuel asked Rachel a few questions about whether she had been a good girl, then he popped the big one: "So, what do you want for Christmas this year?"

A bright smile lit Rachel's face, and she answered confidently, "Cookies and juice!"

A collective "Awwww . . ." sounded from the adults around the edge of the circle, and murmurs of "Isn't that sweet!" and "How cute!" passed from one parent to another. Gwen smiled, too, until her eyes met Sandy's. Sandy was not smiling. *I hope she's not upset with me,* thought Gwen. *I wonder if she's mad about my intervening with Rachel over the cupcakes. Maybe I should have let her handle it after all.*

When each child had had a turn on Santa's lap, Gwen corralled everyone toward the table of goodies. The parents helped their children choose cupcakes and cookies as Andrea poured the punch. Gwen spent a few minutes with Reggie helping him pick out what he wanted to make certain he didn't feel left out. Then she made her way around the table, talking a few minutes with each parent about his or her child. She was talking to Tamara's mother when there was a commotion at the other end of the table.

"Now go stand against the wall," Sandy was calmly telling Rachel. She had a stern look and was pointing to a corner of the room. Rachel was in tears. She slid off her chair clumsily and walked to the corner. All eyes at the table were on Sandy. The room was uncomfortably silent. *Oh no,* thought Gwen, *this is just what I was afraid would happen.* Then Sandy glanced at Gwen. Not knowing how to respond, Gwen looked away and continued her conversation with Tamara's mother. Everyone else quickly resumed what they had been doing—everyone, that is, except Rachel. Gwen's heart ached when she looked over again and saw the little girl standing all alone, face toward the wall, scratching her upper arm.

Cleanup

Andrea picked up the stray pieces of wrapping paper and ribbons that littered the floor, then carried a plastic bag over to the snack table and began shoveling in cupcake wrappers, paper plates, waxed paper cups, and napkins. "I didn't know these kids could be so messy!" she said.

"Yeah, they're real slobs sometimes," giggled Gwen. She stooped down beside the table to wipe up the sticky remains of spilled punch. "I know what I want for Christmas . . . a maid!"

"Now wait a minute," laughed Andrea. "Last week you said you wanted a personal secretary."

"Yeah, that too."

"Hey," said Andrea, "What did you think of ol' Bevins as Santa? Wasn't he a scream?"

"Pathetic," replied Gwen. "Just pathetic." She glanced toward the door to see if anyone was within earshot, then looked back at Andrea. "It cracked me up when he couldn't get that pillow to stay under his jacket."

"Yeah," laughed Andrea, "and did you see the look on his face when he tried to hoist Rachel up onto his lap?"

"Oh, that was awful, wasn't it?" said Gwen. "I could have just died when he said, 'You're a big girl, aren't you?' "

"I know what you mean," said Andrea. She threw a few more cups and plates into the bag. "Speaking of Rachel," she continued, "I couldn't believe Sandy today. She's gone too far, if you ask me."

"What happened, anyway? I was at the other end of the table and didn't see how it started."

"I didn't see it all, either," said Andrea. "I saw Sandy dole out Rachel's snack as usual. She gave her half of a cupcake and some carrots and celery sticks that she had in her purse. The next thing I knew, Sandy was telling Rachel to go stand in the corner. I don't know for sure, but I'll bet Rachel just asked for more cupcake or candy or something."

"That's what I thought," said Gwen.

"Well, you know how I feel about it. She's gonna give that girl a complex if she keeps going on that way."

"Andrea, if Sandy thinks—"

"Now, I know you're always siding with the parents," interrupted Andrea, "and I can understand that. But aren't there limits? I mean, don't you think you should talk with her about this? Somebody sure has to do something . . . for Rachel's sake."

Gwen didn't respond. The fact was, she had already done something about it—something she wasn't very proud of. She had always asked Sandy to help out on field trips and during special events, but lately she found herself asking Sandy less and less. Gwen told herself she wanted to give other parents an opportunity to be more involved; but the truth was, she didn't like to see Sandy being strict with Rachel. Granted, Sandy was strict only when it came to food, but that was enough to make Gwen feel uncomfortable.

"Well, I'm tempted to agree with Andrea," someone said.

Gwen and Andrea immediately turned around to see who it was, but no one was there. Then they heard a toilet flush in the children's bathroom, and Laura, the speech-language pathologist, walked out of the bathroom and into the classroom. "Any port in a storm," said Laura, smiling. "You know we pregnant women are always lurking around one bathroom or another. You'd be surprised how much gossip you can pick up in bathrooms."

"You surprised me!" said Gwen, clasping her hands to her chest. "I thought you'd left."

Laura waddled over to the table. "So tell me, what's going on with Rachel's mother?" She stood before Gwen, one hand bracing the small of her back and the other rubbing her protruding abdomen. She waited for an answer.

"You know," said Gwen. "Sandy is trying to control Rachel's weight."

"And she's decided to do that by belittling Rachel in front of the other children?" Laura asked sarcastically.

"I don't think that Rachel sees it that way. Three-year-olds don't think like that."

"Okay, okay. But really, Gwen, is she going about it the right way?"

"Sandy knows more about Prader-Willi syndrome than I do," said Gwen. "She reads everything she can get her hands on. Did you know she even goes out to the group home in Quail Crossroads to talk with the staff who work with adults who have Prader-Willi syndrome?"

"Maybe that's part of the problem," said Laura. "Rachel isn't an adult. She's a little girl, and she—"

"Maybe she is just a little girl," interrupted Gwen, "but she still has Prader-Willi."

"I know that," said Laura. "What I mean is, the adults with Prader-Willi at the group home are probably already obese. Strict behavior modification may be needed to get them to lose weight. Rachel isn't obese; we just need to keep her from gaining too much weight. If you ask me, that—and the fact that she's just 3 years old—calls for a different approach."

Maybe Laura had a point. Gwen thought for a moment and looked over at Andrea, whose head was nodding in agreement. *If Laura is right—and I'm still not sure she is—what should I do about it?*

"Sandy isn't being cruel," Gwen said to Laura. "She's only strict about food with Rachel because she loves her. People with Prader-Willi need external control over their eating."

"Sandy's a great mom," said Laura. "I never said she wasn't. I'm just saying I think she's going overboard on the control." She sighed and rubbed her back. "Look, maybe I'm wrong. . . . I don't know. But it seems to me that Sandy thinks she can keep Rachel from being fat if she just works at it hard enough. Well, I don't think she can. Nobody can. That's what Prader-Willi syndrome is all about. Sure, she needs to control Rachel's eating, but maybe she doesn't understand or doesn't accept the fact that she can't perform a miracle."

"So, what do you suggest we do?" asked Gwen.

"Maybe Sandy is just scared of the future," proposed Laura.

"Well, wouldn't you be?"

"Sure, I would be," said Laura, absently rubbing her stomach. "Maybe she needs someone to talk to. Has she ever seen a counselor?"

Laura's standard answer to every issue involving parents, thought Gwen. She could just picture the response she would get from Sandy if she suggested that she see a therapist.

Laura looked up at the clock on the wall. "Oh, gosh!" she exclaimed. "I've got to run. Sorry, but I've got to pick up Melissa at day care in 15 minutes." She walked toward the door, then turned around and said, "You know, Sandy is lucky that Rachel is as far along in her speech as she is. Most kids with Prader-Willi have significant language delays. She should count her blessings that Rachel is among the few who don't."

Again, Laura walked toward the door. As she reached for the doorknob, she turned around one last time to say, "And Gwen . . . I heard what you guys said about Samuel, too. I'm not above blackmail, you know." With a wink and a smile, she was gone.

Closing Thoughts

Gwen looked at the clock on the wall of her small office. It was already 3:00 P.M. She had told herself that she would leave early and run by the mall to do some Christmas shopping before picking up her son Daniel at the babysitter's. This was the first year she had to work around a baby while preparing for the holidays, and she didn't want to drag him through the crowded stores with her today.

She started gathering her things but then decided she would jot a quick note to Samuel to thank him for playing Santa Claus. As she began to write, a picture of Rachel with her twinkling blue eyes and raised arms ready to be lifted onto Samuel's lap flashed through Gwen's mind. She had looked so sweet and innocent. It was hard to comprehend the huge difficulties that lay ahead for her and her family.

Gwen finished her note to Samuel and set it aside. Then she pulled Rachel's file from the cabinet beside her desk and grabbed a sheet of clean paper from her top drawer. She wrote "RACHEL" in large letters across the top of the page and underlined it. Then she began to list the things she wanted to discuss with Sandy ". . . tantrums, begging, snacks."

Yes, thought Gwen, *if only Sandy would allow Rachel to have low-calorie foods when she wanted more.* It would be so much easier on Rachel if she were offered a substitute rather than just being told no when she wants more to eat. Celery sticks, raw carrots, apple slices. . . . They

```
Rachel

1. Tantrums—How to deal with? Ignore?
2. Begging—Should we consequate?
   Typical for age?
3. Snacks—Birthdays/special events
   Low-cal substitutes (fruits, vegetables)?
```

would be easy to keep on hand, and they shouldn't cause her any weight gain. . . . But there was still the issue of forbidden foods at birthday parties and other special events. A carrot stick is no substitute for a cupcake piled high with frosting and sprinkles, especially not for a 3-year-old.

Gwen drummed her fingers on the desk. What else did she need to talk to Sandy about? She thought for a moment, then added to her list.

```
4. Asthma—Medicines
              Emergency procedures?
              Outdoor play
```

Some time around Thanksgiving, the Stevens family had moved from their house on the outskirts of town to a place far out in the country. Gwen had been meaning to ask Sandy if the move had in any way changed how the school should respond if Rachel had an asthma attack. She doubted that Sandy had changed Rachel's doctor, and the closest hospital would still be the one in town. Heaven knows, there wasn't much medical care available where they lived now. Gwen knew just how far away it was because she had taken Rachel home one day after the school van had broken down.

Gwen enjoyed visiting the children and parents at home, and she used to schedule visits for the late afternoons and early evenings. Since Daniel was born, however, she had cut back on the number of home visits she made. Most of the families lived nearby, so she could still make an occasional afternoon visit, but Rachel's house was too far away to get there and back before it was time to pick up Daniel at the sitter's. Daniel was also still nursing, and Gwen didn't like to be away from him in the evenings.

Sandy hadn't said much about why the family had moved. Gwen assumed they'd moved for financial reasons, but she wondered whether the savings in rent or mortgage outweighed the other costs that moving incurred. For one thing, the family lived much farther from Sandy's mother and father now, and Sandy must have to consider seriously the cost of driving anywhere. Thank goodness the program provided transportation to and from school for Rachel. Even so, it had to be a long ride in the school van for her twice a day. Living out in the country also couldn't be helping Rachel's asthma. Field upon field of allergen-rich farmland surrounded their property.

Rachel's asthma had caused some difficulties at school. During the fall allergy season, Sandy had often asked that Rachel be kept indoors. This wasn't easy because the children usually spent a lot of time outdoors in the well-equipped play yard just outside the classroom, and both Gwen and Andrea were needed to supervise them. They had tried splitting the group in two, keeping half the children indoors and half outdoors, and then switching. They had also tried substituting more physically strenuous indoor activities, such as obstacle courses, for outdoor play. Both options disrupted the normal classroom routine, and neither seemed entirely satisfactory to Gwen, Andrea, the other children, or their parents. The only one who seemed satisfied was Rachel, who preferred more sedentary indoor activities to outdoor play anyway. With the onset of winter, the problem had receded, but Gwen knew it would return in the spring when the pollen count started to rise. This, too, was an issue Gwen should probably bring up when she spoke to Sandy about Rachel's asthma.

Gwen looked at what she had just written and thought some more. If the family did move to the country because of financial difficulties, maybe she should bring up finances at the meeting, too. She added two more items to her list.

> 5. Lunch—Try school lunches again?
> 6. Finances (?)

Finances were a delicate subject to address with Sandy. Although she readily admitted that she and Dennis had to struggle to make ends meet, Sandy was very proud. She would not accept anything that remotely resembled charity and often went without things she wanted and needed. Gwen remembered when Sandy had shown her a free sample of the National Prader-Willi Association newsletter that the organization had sent to her. Sandy had read it from cover to cover. Gwen could tell how much she would have liked to receive the newsletter regularly, but Sandy said that they couldn't afford it. She said she hoped to be able to subscribe next year.

Gwen leaned back in her chair and looked at the clock. *So much for Christmas shopping, she thought.* She sat straight up again and stared at the paper before her. *What else is there?* Then she remembered what Laura had said about Rachel's speech and added three more items.

7. Speech—Emphasize the positive. Revise objectives? Ask Laura.

8. Cognitive —Update objectives.

9. Motor—Talk to Patsy on Thursday. Should we force her to exercise?

Emphasizing the positive may be a good way to begin the meeting with Sandy, thought Gwen. *Rachel certainly has a lot going for her.* On standardized assessments, she came out less than a year delayed in almost all areas of development, and she showed no delays at all in her social development. *I've also learned a lot about Rachel and Prader-Willi syndrome since she first arrived in August. It would be good to update her objectives in all areas.*

She looked at the last item on the list. Gwen wasn't certain about appropriate motor goals for Rachel. For the most part, Rachel could get around as well as any of the typically developing children in the class. She was just slower. She was also clumsier at times. *In fact,* thought Gwen, *Rachel probably took a number of more spills than the other kids did. Was it just because of her weight? Was it something to be concerned about?* She would ask Patsy, the occupational therapist who consulted in the classroom once a week.

So far, Gwen thought, *I've been thinking mostly about Rachel, but what about Sandy?* Laura had suggested counseling, but that was Laura's answer whenever she encountered a problem involving a parent's emotions. Even so, Sandy probably needed emotional support as much as any other parent did. She hesitated a moment but then wrote it down.

10. Support for Sandy (?)

Was Sandy getting the support she needed? Gwen knew that she spoke frequently with the staff at the group home, but was the support they offered appropriate for a parent of a 3-year-old? How about Sandy's husband? Gwen knew very little about Dennis or their relationship. And what about the Prader-Willi Association? . . . Was there a local chapter? How much were the national membership dues, anyway? What kind of support did Sandy want? What perplexed Gwen most was how she should broach the issue of support with Sandy. Sandy was stoic—strong and independent. How did one go about asking a woman like that if she needed emotional support?

Gwen reached across her desk for Rachel's working folder, opened it, and clipped the completed list to the inside front cover. A photocopy of a brochure from the Prader-Willi Association was in the folder along with an article that Sandy had brought for her to read. She took them out and dropped them in her brown leather bag. Maybe she should read them again. Gwen remembered that Sandy didn't have a telephone, so she wrote a quick reminder to herself on a yellow sticky note. It said, "Put note in Rachel's bag re: meeting." Gwen stuck her reminder on the face of the clock, grabbed her coat and bag, and left.

Discussion Questions

1. Gwen intervened when Rachel wandered over to the snack table in order to avoid the possibility that Sandy would scold Rachel. Was this an appropriate thing for Gwen to do?

2. Gwen chose not to do or say anything after Sandy made Rachel stand in the corner during the party. If you were in Gwen's position, would you have said anything to Sandy either then or later?

3. Andrea and Laura seem to think that Sandy has "gone overboard" in being strict with Rachel over food. Do you agree with them? If so, what would you do about it if you were Rachel's teacher?

4. Andrea and Gwen have both violated Rachel's diet on several occasions. Should they be concerned about these violations? If so, what could be done to prevent them from occurring in the future? Also, how important is it that Sandy be informed of minor violations of Rachel's diet?

5. What more, if anything, should Gwen do to enlist the support of the other parents in helping Rachel adhere to the diet Sandy has outlined? Is it, in fact, unfair that Rachel's dietary needs affect what the other children can have or do in the classroom? If so, what can Gwen do about it?

6. What options does Gwen have for meeting Rachel's need to stay indoors during allergy seasons?

7. Do you think Sandy is overreacting to Rachel's begging for food? How should Gwen respond to Sandy's concerns about this?

8. Is Gwen's strategy of reviewing Rachel's intervention plan as a way to discuss her concerns with Sandy a good idea? If not, how else might Gwen broach these issues with Sandy?

9. Re-read the list of topics that Gwen made for her upcoming meeting with Sandy. Which topics do you think are most important? Are there any items on the list you would *not* talk with Sandy about at this time? Has Gwen overlooked any topics that you think should be added to the list?

10. Is there anything Gwen could do between now and the time she meets with Sandy that might help make their meeting more successful?

11. If you were Gwen and were meeting with Sandy next week, how would you begin the meeting? How would you conduct the meeting? What would you want to accomplish? What would be your highest priority?

chapter 16

Happy Birthday!

P.J. McWilliam

Sachi slapped the kitchen table. "No, sir, this just too much!" she yelled. "I not gonna put up with it! It breaking my heart they do that to my grandson. He just a little boy. I not understand why they wanna do this. You tell me. Why they wanna do this to my grandson?"

"Sachi, maybe if we—." Allison should have known that any attempt to respond to Sachi would be fruitless.

"I do everything I can, but this. . . . This just too much!" Sachi raised her hands in exasperation, then clasped them together in front of her chest. "I not understand it. They know . . . they know this not good for my grandson. You agree, this no good for him?"

"Sachi, I know James has made a lot of progress in Mary's class. Maybe we can—." Again, a wasted attempt on Allison's part. Sachi wasn't finished.

"Aha! I tell them you think so, too. Why they so stubborn? No good reason, I tell you." Sachi turned toward the stove and raised the lid of a simmering pot. Her tiny hand waved the steam toward her face as she sniffed the soup she was making. "This rule about he 3 year old, it make no sense. It crazy. I never hear such crazy talk like this!" She gave the contents of the pot a quick stir, replaced the lid, and turned to face Allison.

Allison settled back in her chair as Sachi rattled on at high speed, her arms and hands punctuating each word. The exotic aroma of Asian spices drifted across the small, tidy kitchen.

Allison listened, nodding her head and occasionally interjecting a word or two of support. She was waiting for Sachi to run out of steam—then maybe they could discuss her options and devise a strategy. The problem was, Allison had even more bad news to deliver.

Poor Sachi, thought Allison as she watched the tiny woman rant about the injustices committed against her beloved grandson. If only she didn't take everything so personally. She wore her heart on her sleeve.

No Risk or Compromise

Sachi Daugherty had called the office on Tuesday while Allison was out making a home visit. When Allison returned to the building, Seth, one of the team members, told her about the call and noted that Sachi had seemed incredibly upset. Although his words reflected sincerity, Allison couldn't miss his mocking tone and wry smile. She chose not to comment and walked over to her desk, only to find pillows on her chair and a variety of snacks beside the telephone. *Obviously a hint that I'll be talking to Sachi all night,* she thought. The team was always teasing her about Sachi's incessant chatter and exaggerations. She turned back around and saw a knowing grin pass between two of her teammates.

Allison returned the call, and Sachi was indeed fit to be tied. Serena Culbreth, the director of Loving Arms Child Care Center, had told her that James would have to be moved from their toddler room to the room for 3- and 4-year-olds. It had been difficult for Allison to get a word in edgewise over the telephone. Sachi was far too excited, outraged, and hurt. Eventually, Allison managed to offer to stop by Sachi's home on Thursday so they could talk more about James's placement. She also offered to go to the child care center and talk with Serena Culbreth.

True to her word, Allison had arranged a meeting with Serena; in fact, she had come directly from that meeting to the Daugherty's house. Sachi was ranting in response to Allison's news that Serena wouldn't reconsider her decision to move James to the 3- and 4-year-old classroom.

Serena had acknowledged that James had made a lot of progress in the 6 months he'd attended the center. She also understood how important the relationship between James and Mary, the teacher in the toddler classroom, was to James's development. She had concluded, however, that she couldn't risk the possibility of James hurting one of the younger children in the toddler room during one of his aggressive outbursts.

Serena had emphasized that Loving Arms was a private child care center for children of working parents. Although they were willing to have James in their center, they did not have the staff or resources to make exceptions for him. The rules that applied to the other children would have to hold true for him as well—and that meant moving out of the toddler room at age 3. Even though she wished she could make an exception, Serena told Allison, she couldn't because, above all else, the other children could not be put at risk. The parents paid Loving Arms to look after their children properly, and this included providing them with a safe environment. Even placing James in the classroom for 3- and 4-year-olds was a little risky, but they were willing to take that risk—for now.

Allison wasn't in the habit of withholding information from families, but telling Sachi that James's aggression—not his age—was the real reason behind Serena's decision seemed unnecessarily cruel. Sachi would be absolutely crushed. Besides, telling her wouldn't change the fact that James had to move out of Mary's room. Serena had dug her heels in on that issue. Anyway, Allison still had that other bad piece of news to deliver: James might not be able to stay in Loving Arms at all.

Living Proof

While Allison reflected upon her meeting with Serena, Sachi continued to voice her outrage: "Why that lady she so stubborn? Maybe I need talk to Mary. She understand what my James need. What you think? You think I need go talk to Mary?" Sachi dampened a paper towel and began to wipe the counter beside the stove.

"I don't know, Sachi. Mary certainly seems to care a lot about James, but I'm not sure that she has any say-so in this matter."

"Maybe Mary need talk to that lady—tell her James do good in her class. Not good make him move now." Spying a drop of juice on the linoleum floor, Sachi bent down to wipe it up with the paper towel.

"Serena sounded awfully firm about her decision to move James to the 3- and 4-year-old class. I don't know if Mary could change her mind."

"Maybe you right." Sachi stood up and began straightening the chairs around the table. "Maybe I need go talk to this Serena. I tell her not good to move James. He need stay with Mary for little while more.

Only with her 6 month now. Maybe need stay 1 year. What you think? You think 1 year, maybe . . . ?"

A child's shrill scream interrupted their conversation, and a little girl clutching a red plastic truck ran into the kitchen. The child's long, dark ponytail swung from side to side as she ran past Allison toward Sachi. She wrapped herself around Sachi's leg and looked back in the direction of the living room. She screamed again at the sight of James bounding through the doorway in hot pursuit.

"My truck! My truck!" yelled James, his dark eyes flashing. He quickly scanned the room, then made a beeline toward the little girl. He slapped her head twice, then tugged at the truck with both hands. "No! My truck! My truck!"

"What you do? . . . No hit! No hit!" Sachi yelled. She peeled James's hands off the red truck and held him at arm's length. The little girl quickly moved away and leaned against the kitchen cabinet behind Sachi. "Why you hit Missy? You be shamed of yourself. Not good you hit!"

James yelled and struggled for a few moments as Sachi held his hands tightly in hers and continued to chastise him for his transgression. When he began to calm down, Sachi released his hands. "You know not nice you hit. You need tell Missy you sorry. You give her hug. Say you sorry."

Sachi nudged James toward Missy, whereupon he gave the little girl a quick hug and a peck on her cheek. "That good boy," said Sachi. "Maybe you need go work with Poppy a little while. Let's go see we find him."

Sachi led James by the hand to the patio door a few yards away and opened it. "Poppy!" she yelled. "What you do all this time? You need come here. I need talk Allison. No can talk with children. They just fight, fight, fight!"

Maybe Serena was right about James's posing a risk to other children, thought Allison. Although he was unlikely to seriously hurt children of his own age and size, he might injure younger children. He didn't hit often or hard, but he was just so unpredictable. You never knew what might set him off, and once his anger was sparked, he seemed unaware of the consequences of his actions.

During the 10 months she had been visiting the Daughertys, Allison had tried to help Sachi control James's aggressive outbursts. Together, they had agreed on a time-out procedure: James had to sit on the sofa for 5 minutes every time he hit someone or threw something in anger. Allison had also worked with Mary so the same procedure would be used at school. Both Sachi and Mary seemed pleased with how the time-out strategy was working whenever Allison asked about it.

The scene that Allison had just witnessed, however, led her to wonder whether Sachi had stopped using time-outs at home—and whether she had ever used them consistently. This would be a good time to bring up the topic; but if she did, they would never get around to talking about James's transition. It was already past 3:00 P.M., and she had to be back at the office by 4:00 P.M. for a meeting with her supervisor.

Curt Daugherty stuck his head through the open patio door. "Hi, Allison! Sorry, I didn't know you were here." He wiped his chin and forehead with the back of his dirty hands, leaving streaks of brown on his face. "Sure is a hot one out there today! Got a bumper crop of tomatoes and cucumbers, though. They make up some good sandwiches."

"Nothing better than home-grown tomatoes," said Allison. "How's James's pumpkin patch coming along?"

"Taking over the garden. We'll have plenty by Halloween."

"Allison not want talk about garden," interrupted Sachi. "You take James. We need talk now."

"Okay," said Curt. "Come on, fella. How about helping Poppy do some digging? Then maybe we'll pick something for dinner." He smiled and waved to Allison as he led his grandson outside. Allison returned his smile.

Curt Daugherty, a retired career serviceman in the navy, was almost always at home when Allison visited. Even so, she rarely spoke to him for more than a minute or two, as he was usually out in the garden or working in his little greenhouse. Allison sometimes wondered if Curt used his gardening as a way of escaping Sachi's constant chatter and fanatical cleaning. As sweet as she was, being married to her was bound to be challenging at times.

"You watch now. Not let him get hurt," Sachi cautioned as she closed the sliding-glass door behind them. Sachi took a deep breath and sighed as she watched Curt and James head out to the garden. Then she walked back over to Allison.

"Now we talk," said Sachi. "Come sit down, and I make you cup of tea." She handed Missy a few crackers and ushered her off to the living room to play. Then she poured two cups of tea from a ceramic pot and sat down in the chair opposite Allison.

Breaking the News

"Is Missy your grandchild, too?" asked Allison, stirring her tea.

"She my daughter's child. Daughter's husband go on trip for work—to New York City. I say, 'Why you not go with husband?' She say she need be with Missy, but I tell her bring Missy here. I take care of my granddaughter for a little while—such a beautiful child. I tell daughter she need to be with husband sometime, too."

"It must be nice for her to have you to count on."

"I keep James at home today. Think maybe grandchildren play together. Ah! Big mistake! What you think? Maybe tomorrow James go to school."

"It would be nice to spend some time with Missy alone." Allison glanced at the clock on the wall. She needed to get things back on track. "Sachi, you know how we've been talking about James being served by the school system instead of by us in September?"

"I know you say now he 3 year old and too old for you to see. I still not understand what all this '3 year' mean. It not make sense why 3 year so different—everything need to change." Sachi looked down and began rubbing a spot on the table with a cloth."

"I know. Sometimes I wonder about that, too. But the fact of the matter is, our program only gets money to serve children up until their third birthdays. The public schools are given money to provide services for children after they are 3 years old." Allison took a sip of her tea and waited for a reaction, but Sachi was silent.

"Well," continued Allison, "Last week I talked with the staff at the public school, and there appears to be some problems that we hadn't anticipated."

"What problem? Not enough problem already?" With the spot on the table successfully removed, Sachi placed both hands around the cup in front of her. "I don't know I can take more problem today," she said in a soft voice. "All this problem and just one little boy. . . ." She shook her head slowly and stared into her teacup.

"It is incredibly confusing, Sachi. I'm sorry that it has to be this way." Again, Allison waited for a response, but, again, there was only silence.

"Let me tell you what I found out," suggested Allison. "Maybe we can put our heads together and figure something out. Remember that the school system agreed to provide special education services to James at Loving Arms so that he wouldn't have to change centers?"

Sachi nodded her head.

"Well, I found out that the school system can't provide speech-language therapy in the child care center."

"What!" Sachi's dark eyes suddenly regained their spark. "Why they not have speech-language therapy at child care? He have it now. Make big difference, what you think?"

"I agree. It has made a big difference. The problem has come up because your house is in the Summit Hill school district, and Loving Arms is in the Oak Ridge school district. According to the Summit Hill school system, they can't provide related services—like speech-language therapy—outside the school district. It has something to do with their contracts."

"Then Oak Ridge need to give speech-language therapy."

"I don't think it works like that, Sachi. You see, James lives in the Summit Hill school district. Oak Ridge isn't responsible for paying for anything."

"That not against law?" By this time, Sachi was out of her chair and pacing back and forth in front of the kitchen counter. "He need speech-language therapy. They not, by law, need give to my James?"

"Yes, they do. They told me that they would provide speech-language therapy if he went to the special education preschool classroom at Peeler Elementary School. That's over on Sun River Road, behind the mall. Peeler is in the Summit Hill school district. Or, James could get speech-language therapy here in your home." Allison paused a moment. "I suppose that you also have the option of hiring a private speech-language therapist."

Sachi slapped her hands on her cheeks and shook her head. "Too much! Too much crazy stuff! I go tell these school people I not gonna put up with this. No sir, Sachi not put up with this. Too much!"

"Sachi, I'm really sorry. I didn't know this would be a problem. I just assumed that he could get speech-language therapy at Loving Arms, too."

"No. You not be sorry. Not you fault. Is crazy people at that school place."

Allison glanced at the clock. She'd never make it back to the office if she didn't leave soon. She had been late for her last meeting with her supervisor, and she couldn't have that happen this time.

"Sachi, I have a meeting with my supervisor this afternoon. Let me talk with her about all of this and see if she has any ideas about what we can do. We still have almost 2 months before school starts to work things out. I could come out again on Tuesday afternoon. Would that be all right with you?"

"You talk to supervisor. You think she know what to do?"

"Maybe. She's pretty smart about how the school system operates. It can't hurt to ask."

Allison actually had little hope that the school system would budge and little faith that her supervisor would know any more than she did. But Allison was buying time and placating Sachi. She really needed to get back to the office, and she didn't think it would help James's case if Sachi went on a tirade in the school superintendent's office. Allison needed time to think and develop a plan to keep James at Loving Arms.

"I really better be running along now," said Allison. "My meeting is at 4 o'clock. Sorry to have to rush out on you at a time like this. I hope you'll forgive me."

"We just fine," replied Sachi. "Now, you go. You not be late for meeting. No good you be late."

"Thanks, Sachi." Allison picked up her bag and headed toward the door.

"Oh, wait! Sachi almost forget. Something for you—you take home." Sachi opened the refrigerator and took out a package wrapped in aluminum foil. "I make sushi yesterday. You try? Not pretend sushi. This real Japanese sushi. Rice, seaweed, shrimp . . . lots of ginger."

Allison accepted the package. "Thank you very much. This ought to be a real treat. I can't wait to try it." She picked up her briefcase and walked toward the door. "Well, I'll see you on Tuesday, then. Bye!"

On her way out, Allison nearly tripped over a dog in the carport. The dog made no attempt to move but just stared at Allison with big, sad eyes. The poor thing was skinny and rather bedraggled. Probably another stray that Sachi took pity on, thought Allison. She checked her watch and rushed to her car.

Now and Later

Turning onto the ramp that led to I-74, Allison switched on the car radio. Listening to music on her way to and from home visits was one job perk that she took full advantage of. She leaned back in her seat and turned on the cruise control. About 5 miles along the interstate, however, the sight of the aluminum foil package on the passenger seat started her thinking about Sachi again.

What a sweet woman she was, thought Allison. Then she felt a twinge of guilt for some of the unkind thoughts about Sachi she had once voiced.

When Allison had first started working with Sachi, the woman's incessant chattering and apparent inability to listen to anything that anyone else said grated on Allison's nerves. She was forever complaining to her teammates about Sachi. During the past few months, however, Allison had grown fond of Sachi and had actually come to admire her. Here was a woman who, without speaking a word of English, left Japan to come to America as a new bride. She not only had raised her own family but had also taken on the responsibility of raising her son's child after he was killed in a car accident. James was only an infant when his father died. Allison assumed that James's mother had also died in the accident, but Sachi hadn't ever talked about her. It couldn't have been easy for Sachi and Curt to deal with the loss of their son and simultaneously take on the responsibility of caring for an infant. Curt must be well into his 50s, maybe even closer to 60. It was hard to tell how old Sachi was.

Allison regretted that she hadn't been involved with James earlier than she had been, but James hadn't been referred to the infant program until he was 2 years old. And she would miss visiting the Daughertys after the infant program wrapped up its involvement with them in September. Sure, she could follow them for a little while after James entered the public school system, but eventually she would have to break ties. What would happen to James in the years to come? It was hard to predict. James had made a lot of progress since Allison started visiting 10 months ago. Most notably, he had finally started talking. In fact, he was even using some two-word combinations. Overall, James was probably about 9 months to a year behind other 3-year-olds, but who knew how much catching up he could do if he had the right kind of help?

His unpredictable aggression was perhaps his biggest obstacle to overcome. It was already clear just how much his aggression could influence his future. Who would help Sachi with his behavior and development at home? The school system rarely provided this type of support. Looking even further down the road, how long would Sachi and Curt be able to care for James? After all, they weren't getting any younger.

The more Allison thought about these issues, the more hopeless it all seemed. This type of thinking wasn't going to solve anything. What she really needed to be thinking about was what she could do between now and September that might make a difference in the services James would receive during the next school year. Of course, she would lose some time in August when she and her husband were on their 2-week vacation in Maine. Still, there was time.

Sachi could move James to a child care center within the Summit Hill school district, but all of the programs that Allison knew about weren't nearly as nice as Loving Arms. In fact, Loving Arms was probably the highest-quality center in the county. Besides, it had been difficult enough to convince Sachi to enroll him in Loving Arms. Chances were, she wouldn't approve of the others. Still, maybe she should suggest it and let Sachi decide.

The segregated class at Peeler Elementary School wasn't all that great, either. James would certainly receive all of the specialized services he needed; but the classroom was drab compared to Loving Arms, and many of the children there had more significant delays than the ones James had.

Allison sighed and drummed her fingers on the steering wheel. Then she reached over and turned up the volume on the radio. She would think about the Daughertys later. What she wanted to do right now was relax before meeting with her supervisor.

Discussion Questions

1. List those principles of family-centered practice that Allison adhered to during her home visit and give a specific example of each.

2. Were there any instances in which you think Allison may have violated family-centered principles? If so, what could Allison have done differently to improve those aspects of the home visit?

3. Other team members don't appear to share Allison's positive feelings toward Sachi Daugherty. Should Allison feel responsible for their impressions of Sachi? Is there anything that Allison could do to change the other team members' opinions of Sachi?

4. Serena appears to feel strongly that James needs to be moved into the classroom for 3- and 4-year-olds. Sachi appears to have equally strong feelings that James needs to stay in the toddler classroom. What, if anything, might Allison do about this conflict?

5. Was there anything Allison could have done to prevent Serena from deciding that James needed to move into the classroom for 3- and 4-year-olds?

6. Allison didn't tell Sachi that James's aggression was the real reason that Serena decided to move James out of Mary's class and into the classroom for older children. Under the circumstances, was her decision appropriate?

7. Should Allison discuss James's hitting other children on a future visit to the Daugherty's home? If so, how might she initiate the conversation, and what specifically would Allison want to accomplish in discussing this topic with Sachi?

8. What intervention strategies are effective in handling aggression toward peers when it is exhibited by preschoolers?

9. Allison is concerned that Sachi will not have the support she needs at home to control James's behavior and meet his other special needs after the transition. Is there anything Allison can do to address this concern? What resources for Sachi would be available in your community?

10. What, if anything, could Allison have done to prevent the problems in James's service transition—specifically the problems related to his speech-language therapy?

11. Allison discouraged Sachi from complaining to the public school officials about not providing speech-language therapy for James at Loving Arms next year. Was this a good idea?

12. What options do Allison and Sachi have for ensuring that an appropriate placement and services are provided to James upon his entry into the public school system in the fall? Make a list.

13. Which of the options you identified in your answer to Question #12 would you choose, and why?

14. Based upon the decisions you made in your answer to Question #13, make a plan of action for Allison to follow for the next 2 months.

15. Assuming that Allison's supervisor is a program administrator, what role should he or she play in ensuring that James's transition is successful?

16. Assuming that Allison is James's primary service provider and his service coordinator, what responsibility, if any, do other team members have in James's transition to the public school system when he turns 3 years old?

17. In your community, are there any differences in policies or procedures between birth-to-3 services and 3-to-5 services that might adversely affect children or families? What differences exist between services for 3- to 5-year-olds and services for school-age children?

18. What are the federal requirements for service transitions at age 3? What, if any, additional requirements for transitions are included in regulations governing Part C services (birth to 3) in your state? If you could add two more regulatory statements to the existing policies on transition, what would they be?

c h a p t e r 17

An Uncertain Future

P.J. McWilliam

Shannon Eason was going to be a challenge. There was no doubt about it. The child had been born at 23 weeks' gestation, weighing only 1 pound 7 ounces, and had spent 5 months in the neonatal intensive care nursery before going home. Now, at 13 months of age, she still needed supplemental oxygen and an apnea monitor. What worried Beth most about working with this baby was the fact that she also had a significant visual impairment. Although Beth had worked as an early interventionist for more than 3 years, she had never felt completely comfortable working with children who had sensory impairments. After all, she hadn't specialized in that area when she was in college.

Comfortable or not, Shannon Eason would be Beth's responsibility; she didn't have much choice in the matter. The referral had come by way of Virginia Cousins, a vision specialist who was responsible for serving all children with vision impairments who lived in the district. The Eason family was apparently new to the area and had requested a vision assessment for their daughter. Virginia Cousins conducted the child's assessment and subsequently referred her to the early intervention program. According to her referral letter, Virginia Cousins believed that the child's delays might not be related to her prematurity alone and that Shannon and her family might benefit from additional assessments and services. Given her current caseload, however, Virginia could offer the family only a once-a-month consultation, and even that was questionable.

"She's not the only one with a caseload," Beth muttered. Every time they requested vision services for an infant, the vision specialists' caseloads were always too full to provide them. Beth wondered just how full their caseloads really were. Maybe they just didn't see working with children younger than school age as their responsibility. But then, who was Beth to question what they could or couldn't do? The vision specialists didn't even operate under the direction of the same state agency as her program did.

She sighed and looked at the pile of papers in front of her. Enclosed with Virginia Cousins's letter were various medical reports on Shannon Eason and a summary of her vision assessment. Beth flipped through the reports, making notes as she went along:

SHANNON EASON
Born 23 weeks' gestation—1 pound 7 ounces
3rd child, complicated pregnancy, bleeding, cesarean section.
Air transport to Level III nursery (300 miles from home)
Heart surgery (12 days old)—PDA
Bronchopulmonary dysplasia
Low blood pressure—dopamine, hydrocortisone
Hyperbilirubin—phototherapy
Ultrasound revealed no intraventricular hemorrhage
Broviac catheter inserted (6 weeks old)
Necrotizing enterocolitis—temporarily discontinued oral feedings
Gavage feeding
Retinopathy of prematurity (ROP)
Panretinal photocoagulation (8 weeks old)
Cryotherapy (10 weeks old)
Off respirator (4 months old)
Transfer to general hospital near home (for 2 weeks)
Discharge to home—5 months old (6 pounds 2 ounces)
Stage 3+ retinopathy
Apnea monitor and continuous oxygen

After she finished writing, Beth put down her pen and read through the list she had made. This baby had obviously been through a lot! Beth wondered what Shannon Eason would look like. From the reports, she could tell that Shannon still experienced medical problems and feeding difficulties. She probably also had some motor delays. But what about her cognitive development? Even without intraventricular hemorrhaging, could her cognitive abilities have remained untouched by the ordeals that follow such premature births? Beth had never worked with a child born so prematurely. Then again, how many babies weighing just a little more than 1 pound survived at all?

Beth scanned Virginia Cousins's report of the baby's vision assessment for more clues about her development.

Student: Shannon Eason   **Chronological Age:** 12 months
Grade: Infant   **Adjusted Age:** 8 months
Parents: Bruce and Kaye Eason   **Type of Assessment:** _X_ Initial
Address: 4501 Parkview Circle   _____ Reassessment

Background Information

Shannon Eason was referred by her pediatrician, Dr. Neil Kramer, for a vision assessment. Background information was provided by Dr. Kramer, Mrs. Eason, and reports from Dr. Jonathan Sharpe, pediatric opthalmologist, and Dr. Terry Pendleton, retina and vitreous specialist. Shannon was also seen by the Pulmonary Clinic at St. Agnes Hospital; however, reports from the clinic were not available at the time of this assessment.

Shannon is the product of a 23-week gestation. She was hospitalized for 5 months after her birth and underwent heart surgery (PDA ligation) during that time. She was diagnosed with bronchopulmonary dysplasia and continues to receive continuous oxygen. She is presently taking vitamins, potassium, two diuretics, and Zantac. Three weeks ago, continued feeding difficulties led to the insertion of a gastrostomy tube, and she is presently fed throughout the night. Shannon is on an apnea monitor at night; however, the mother reports no apnea episodes recently.

Shannon was diagnosed with Stage 3+ ROP and was treated with laser surgery and cryotherapy. A right esotropia, nystagmus, and myopia of both eyes was also diagnosed. Patching of the left eye 1–2 hours per day was recommended by Dr. Sharpe. A hearing test conducted at age 9 months by the NICU follow-up program indicates "abbreviated behavioral audiometry failed to show any deficiencies. She brightens and localizes to sounds and voices."

(continued)

(continued)

Assessment Results

Shannon's vision was assessed at home, using natural lighting for the majority of testing. Both eyes were clear, with no matting or redness. There was evidence of nystagmus when Shannon attempted to fixate and focus on an object at a near distance. She oriented her gaze to peripheral activity on her far left side, with this response more clearly noted when a penlight or movement was used as a stimulus. Shannon did not respond to moving stimuli in her far right periphery. Placing stimuli within 12–14 inches from Shannon's face, she visually followed objects/light across midline using her left eye, with the right eye moving as the head moved. She awkwardly tracked left to right, breaking her gaze at about 20 degrees past midline on the right. Shannon also attempted to follow a light from her visual horizon upward. Shannon was also observed to shift her gaze from one object to another by moving her head and left eye to fixate first on one object (10 inches in front of her face) and then to another object about 6 inches to the side of the first object.

With patching of the left eye, Shannon attempted to fixate on an object at a distance of 10 inches and presented centrally to her right eye. Her right eye rested close to her nose then, as the stimulus entered her field of vision, she moved her right eye from this inward position to a more central position and was able to maintain this position for a few seconds. With patching, she was also observed to follow a reflective object from right to left and vertically.

When Shannon was held by her mother, she fixated on her mother's face for at least 4 minutes. When laying on the floor, Shannon followed her mother moving away from her and up past her head. Overall, Shannon seems attracted by movement (usually a person entering the room) and will visually follow as the object/person moves closer. When left alone, Shannon was consistently observed to orient her head toward the picture window.

It should be noted that all of the above observations were conducted with Shannon positioned on her back and with maximum head support. Supported sitting and lying on her stomach do not offer enough support for Shannon to concentrate on anything but her postural security. It should also be noted that Shannon was not observed to reach for any objects presented within her field of vision. Mrs. Eason reports, however, that Shannon has recently begun to regard her own hand.

Virginia M. Cousins

Virginia M. Cousins
Vision Specialist

Virgina Cousins's report didn't help to make Beth feel more comfortable about working with this child. It only made her feel more anxious. Beth stacked the reports together in a neat pile and put them in a crisp, new manila folder. Then she wrote a note to put on Lloyd Farmington's desk that afternoon. Lloyd was the team's occupational therapist who worked 3 days a week for the early intervention program. Beth wanted him to accompany her on her initial visit with the Easons. From what Virginia Cousins had written, it sounded as though Shannon Eason could benefit from his services. At the very least, Beth would benefit from his advice about positioning and motor development.

On the way to the Easons' home the following Wednesday, Lloyd read the reports about Shannon for the first time while Beth drove the car. There was plenty of time for reading and discussion as the Easons lived out in the country—a good 45-minute drive from the program. Shannon's father, Bruce, was a manager for a company that manufactured and distributed large farm equipment. The company operated several plants across the country, and Bruce's reassignment to the plant in Paxton—the heart of the state's largest wheat-producing region—had been the reason for the family's recent move.

Beth and Lloyd pulled up to the Easons' two-story frame house, which sat about an eighth of a mile off the main road. They could see a few scattered houses beyond the Easons' where the road stretched north toward even more remote rural areas. Kaye Eason met them at the door when they arrived. She was an attractive woman in her early thirties with shoulder-length, auburn hair. A small boy accompanied her to the door, his hazel eyes staring intently at the two strangers as he clung to his mother's long denim skirt. Brett Eason was 3 years old.

Beth and Lloyd followed Kaye to the kitchen, where she had been busy preparing soup stock for that night's supper. The large windows, southern exposure, and flowered wallpaper created a cheerful atmosphere in the kitchen. Kaye immediately introduced them to Shannon, who was lying quietly on a palette in the corner of the room, facing a window. "Perhaps you could spend a few minutes getting acquainted with Shannon," suggested Kaye. "I just need to finish putting a few things into this pot, and then I'll be right with you." Beth's eyes followed Kaye as she walked over to the stove and lifted the lid on the simmering kettle. Beth couldn't help noticing the boxes of medical supplies stacked on the far corner of the counter beside the microwave oven.

Lloyd began talking to Brett about the papers and felt-tip markers lying on the kitchen table. He must have been drawing when they arrived. Within a matter of minutes, Lloyd had persuaded the shy toddler to join him at the table, and they were soon busy chattering about the rainbows, trees, and trucks that Brett had drawn. Meanwhile, Beth had knelt down on the edge of the palette to talk to Shannon.

The little girl had the unmistakable head shape of a preterm infant, and her sparse blonde hair was neatly pulled together on top with a small, lavender hair clip. The stream of light coming through the window revealed a glint of red in her hair that must have come from her mother. Shannon's nasal cannula was held in place by clear plastic tubing that looped over her tiny ears. The remainder of the tubing ran along the baseboard and disappeared around the corner and down the hallway that led to the living room.

"I really like your hairdo," Beth said to Shannon, leaning close to the little girl's face. "I'll bet your mom fixed it up for you, huh?"

Shannon turned her head away from the window and toward Beth. Her right eye lagged behind her left, never coming quite to center. Her left eye danced, searching for and quickly locating Beth's face.

"My name's Beth. Your mom invited me to come and play with you today. How about that? You think we could have some fun together?"

Shannon gave Beth a brisk smile and kicked her legs against the palette.

"Oh, good!" said Beth. "I was hoping we could have some fun."

Shannon gave Beth another quick smile and kicked her legs. Beth noted the quivering nystagmus of both eyes as she continued to talk to Shannon, and Shannon attempted to maintain her focus on Beth's face. Beth was also somewhat surprised that, although Shannon smiled and kicked in response to her prattle, she never made a sound in return. Furthermore, Shannon's arms moved only slightly in contrast to her rapidly thrusting legs. For the most part, her arms remained in a flexed and retracted position.

Beth spied a wicker basket of toys at the foot of the palette and poked around in it. There was an assortment of rattles, balls, and squeaky toys, some of them partially encased in crumpled aluminum foil. She picked out a rattle with a red-and-white candy-striped handle attached to a clear globe full of brightly colored balls. She held the rattle in front of Shannon's left eye and shook it gently. Shannon appeared to focus on the toy but made no attempt to reach for it. Beth took Shannon's hand and gently guided it to the rattle, whereupon Shannon's tiny fingers wrapped tightly around the handle. Holding Shannon's forearm, Beth helped Shannon to shake the rattle. Shannon maintained her grasp and smiled at the sound of the rattle, but she dropped her arm as soon as Beth stopped helping. Beth noticed that Shannon didn't release the rattle after her arm dropped.

"I'm afraid she's not very good at that yet."

Beth looked up at the sound of Kaye's voice, unaware that Kaye had been watching her play with Shannon.

"She likes her mobile, though," continued Kaye. "Wait just a second, and I'll set it up so you can see." Kaye quickly rinsed her hands then wiped them on a dish towel. On her way around the table, she took a few carrot sticks from the pile she had been slicing for the soup and handed them to Brett, who was still chattering away to Lloyd. "Why don't you go upstairs and find Holly," she told him. "If you give her one of your carrots, maybe she'll read you a book." Brett took the carrots from his mother's hand and scampered out the door, leaving Lloyd at the table by himself.

Kaye reached behind the walnut-stained sideboard and pulled out a baby gym made of PVC piping. A variety of toys, some wrapped in aluminum foil, dangled from the plastic link chains that were attached to the crossbar. Kaye set up the baby gym so Shannon would be able to see the dangling toys. "Virginia Cousins, the vision specialist who came out, suggested that we use the aluminum foil so Shannon could see the toys better," Kaye explained to Beth. "It helps reflect the light."

Shannon turned toward the sound of her mother's voice, smiled, and made a raspy but happy inward gasp. "Hi, sweetheart," cooed Kaye. "Have you been having a good time with Beth? Do you want to play with your mobile for a while now?" Kaye brushed a few stray wisps of blond hair off her daughter's forehead then gently unfurled Shannon's fingers from the handle of the rattle and set it aside. Kaye then shifted her weight onto her other hip to position herself behind the baby gym. "Look, sweetie! Look here!" she called, gently shaking the aluminum-covered toys on the crossbar. Shannon searched with her left eye and located her mother. "Come on. . . . Kick, kick, kick!" encouraged Kaye. "Where are those happy feet?" Shannon smiled and kicked her legs. Both heels struck the palette at the same time, and the toys on the crossbar swayed in response. "That's the way! You did it!" exclaimed Kaye. Shannon responded with another raspy, inward squeal. A little surprised that Shannon's tiny feet could produce such a large reaction, Beth glanced at the base of the baby gym. Someone had installed a circle of small springs under the base of each upright bar to make the gym more sensitive to movement. What a clever idea, thought Beth.

"That's great!" said Beth. "Does she enjoy playing with the gym a lot?"

"Yes," said Kaye. "She really does. She also likes the mobile over her crib, now that we've put things on it that she can see."

"Does she seem to know she's the one who's actually making the toys move?" asked Beth. "Or do you think she just enjoys the spectacle?"

"I think she knows she's doing it," said Kaye. "Sometimes she even seems to be analyzing how she does it. You know, she'll change how hard or how fast she kicks her feet and then stop and stare at the toys—like she's figuring out what made them move differently."

"Wow, that's wonderful!" said Beth. There was a brief, awkward silence, then Beth continued, "I noticed that she sort of squealed in delight while you were playing with her. She didn't make any sounds when I was playing with her earlier. Do you think that's just because I'm someone new?"

"I wish I could say that was all it was," replied Kaye. "It's one of the things I'm a little worried about." Kaye turned her face away from Beth and looked out the window. "I remember all the sweet baby sounds my other two made when they were infants. . . . It's only been within the last month or so that Shannon has started to coo when we talk to her, and even then she doesn't do it very often."

"It sounds as though that's something that's pretty important to you," suggested Beth.

"Oh, I don't know," said Kaye, turning around to face Beth. "Nothing's been the same with Shannon as it was with the other two. I don't suppose I should expect this to be either. I remember in the hospital when they finally took her off the respirator, and I heard her cry for the first time . . ." A bittersweet smile stretched across her face. "It was such a pitiful cry, but it was music to my ears."

"I'll bet it was," said Beth. "How long was she on the respirator?"

"Four months."

"Wow! That's a long time to wait to hear your baby's first cry."

"Could being on the respirator for so long be the reason she doesn't coo and babble as much as other babies?" Kaye's anxious eyes waited for an answer.

"Well . . . I'm not really sure." Beth looked down at Shannon and absently lifted the baby's hand with her forefinger. She hated questions like that. How was she supposed to know why Shannon wasn't making sounds like other babies? Shannon grasped Beth's finger and held on tightly.

"I guess it doesn't really matter why," said Kaye. "The important thing is that she's starting now."

Beth played with Shannon for a while longer, trying to assess her cognitive skills. It was hard to sort out the extent to which her delays were caused by her vision impairment and medical problems, and what, if any, additional problems might be responsible. On top of everything else, she had to keep in mind that Shannon had been born 4 months prematurely and had been hospitalized for nearly half of her life. That alone would be enough to cause significant delays.

Shortly after Brett had run upstairs with his carrot sticks, Lloyd joined Kaye and Beth on the floor but had remained silent throughout their conversation. He, too, now played with Shannon and asked Kaye questions about her motor skills and feeding. Kaye told them that Shannon had gotten a gastrostomy a month ago. Before that, she and Bruce had been using a combination of bottle and gavage feedings, but Shannon had begun to fight the gavage feedings. Agreeing to the gastrostomy had been a difficult decision for Kaye and Bruce to make. They had hoped that Shannon would get better at bottle feeding so they could eliminate tube feeding all together, but that hadn't happened. Kaye said they were glad now that they had decided to go ahead with the gastrostomy. Shannon was gaining weight, and they could finally get some sleep at night.

Kaye talked a bit more about Shannon's medications, her apnea monitor, and the difficulties associated with her continued need for oxygen. Overall, Kaye didn't seem all that concerned about Shannon's present health status. She said that they used the apnea monitor only at night now and that Shannon hadn't had any episodes of apnea at all over the past 2 or 3 weeks. Kaye was hopeful that this was a sign that Shannon had passed a major hurdle toward recovery. Kaye also mentioned that she felt more comfortable transporting Shannon because they no longer needed to take the apnea monitor along with them in the car. Still, she said, transporting Shannon and her oxygen wasn't exactly a picnic. Kaye also wasn't very comfortable with the stares and questions of strangers when she was out with Shannon in public.

OCCUPATIONAL THERAPY ASSESSMENT

Child's name: Shannon Eason   **Type of assessment:** Initial
Age at testing: 13 months   **Test administrator:** Lloyd Farmington
Parent(s) or guardian(s): Bruce and Kaye Eason
Age adjusted for prematurity: 9 months

Background

Shannon was born at 23 weeks' gestation and weighed 1 pound, 7 ounces at birth. She spent 5 months in the neonatal intensive care unit (NICU) before being discharged to home. Complications following birth included hyaline membrane disease, chronic lung disease,

---

(continued)

(continued)

retinopathy of prematurity, and prolonged feeding intolerance. Shannon has recently undergone surgery for the placement of a gastrostomy. More detailed medical information is available in Shannon's records. The referral to the early intervention program was made by Virginia Cousins, a vision specialist for the school district who is providing services related to Shannon's visual impairment.

Testing Situation

All observations and testing were conducted in the family's home and in an environment that is familiar to the child (a palette on the kitchen floor with natural sunlight from a nearby window). Kaye Eason, Shannon's mother, was present during the assessment and served as informant for background information and present levels of performance.

Observations and Assessment

Shannon has excess tone in her upper and lower extremities, with reduced tone in her trunk. When supported in a sitting position, her neck and back are rounded and head bobbing occurs after 20–30 seconds. Shannon displays full passive range of motion throughout; however, she has a tendency to "fix" in her shoulders initially during ranging, and there is occasional resistance to rotational movements. Some degree of tightness was noted in ankle dorsiflexion, bilaterally.

Shannon is somewhat resistant to being placed in a prone position, but she was observed to clear her head and move it to each side when placed on her stomach on a firm surface. She does not as yet use her arms to elevate her upper body when placed in prone position; however, when her arms are positioned well under her shoulders, she can clear the supporting surface and sustain this position briefly. Ms. Eason reports that Shannon spends the majority of her time lying flat on her back and that she appears most content in this position. Some hyperextension of the neck and shoulder retraction were noted in supine; but, for the most part, Shannon appears relaxed when lying on her back.

Very active symmetrical movement in her legs was observed while Shannon interacted with her mother and also while she was engaged in "playing" with a mobile suspended within her range of vision. Shannon, however, is not yet able to round her hips off the floor. Shannon can roll from her back to her left side and from either side to her back. Rolling is accomplished through hyperextension of the back with little or no abdominal support or flexion. Very few volitional arm movements were observed during the assessment session. Arm movements that were observed consisted of Shannon's bringing her hands together at midline and bringing a hand to her mouth. All arm movements are

(continued)

primarily from the elbow, with shoulder stiffness limiting her range of motion. Ms. Eason reported that Shannon does not reach out to touch toys; however, she has been bringing her hands together and to her mouth more often over the past few weeks. Shannon's hands are primarily opened, and although she will grasp an object that is placed in either hand, volitional release is not yet present. It is difficult at this point to determine the degree to which Shannon's delays in reaching and grasping are attributable to her visual impairment. It should be noted, however, that delays in reaching and grasping are not unusual for children with significant visual impairments.

Shannon was observed while being bottle-fed by her mother. Shannon does not have sufficient strength and speed to receive total nutrition by mouth and has a tendency to gag. She is bottle-fed throughout the day and drip-fed through her gastrostomy at night. Gavage feeding was eliminated after placement of the gastrostomy. Shannon was also observed while her mother attempted to feed her semi-solid foods (strained bananas). Ms. Eason has only recently begun offering semi-solid foods, and she reports that Shannon frequently gags and spits out food that is placed in her mouth. Observations verified Ms. Eason's description of Shannon's response to spoon feeding. At most, Shannon consumes 1–2 teaspoons of strained fruits or cereal at a feeding.

Test Results

Bayley Scales of Infant Development (Motor Scale)
Psychomotor Developmental Index (PDI): less than 50 (Greater than 2.3 standard deviations)

(*Note:* PDI below 70 and standard deviations greater than 1.5 standard deviations below the mean are considered to be significant)

Lloyd S. Farmington, OTR/L
Lloyd S. Farmington, OTR/L

Discussion Questions

1. Was it a good idea for Beth to have taken Lloyd with her on her first visit with the Easons? How might the visit have been different if Lloyd had not accompanied Beth?

2. How important was it for Beth to have read Virginia Cousins's report and the medical information about Shannon before making the home visit? What additional information, if any, would have been important for her to have before the visit?

3. Did Beth and Lloyd conduct themselves appropriately on this home visit? What did you like about their interactions with the Easons? What, if anything, would you have done differently?

4. Beth seemed to have difficulty determining the level of Shannon's cognitive abilities. What can you conclude about Shannon's developmental status based on her medical history, Virginia Cousins's assessment, Beth's own observations of Shannon, and Lloyd's occupational therapy assessment? Venture a prediction as to what Shannon will be like in 6 months, 1 year, 3 years, and at school age.

5. Would additional testing or other forms of assessment be helpful in determining Shannon's current level of cognitive functioning? If so, which instruments or strategies might be employed, and should these be mentioned to Kaye now?

6. How much of what Beth and Lloyd observed or thought about Shannon's development should they share with Kaye at the end of this first home visit? Make a list of the information that they should share with the family and rank the items from most to least important. Choose one of the top three items on your list and write down the exact words you would use to give this information to Kaye.

7. In your opinion, what are the most important skills for Shannon to develop during the next few months?

8. What types of services might be useful to Shannon and her family? Make a list. If all of these services were available, which would you tell the Easons about right now?

9. In your community, which of the services you listed in your answer to Question #8 are available to families like the Easons? Are

there fees for each of these services? If so, how are fees assessed (e.g., sliding scales, flat rate, insurance/Medicaid reimbursements)?

10. What are the Easons' concerns about and priorities for Shannon and the rest of the family? What do we know about the Eason family's resources?

11. What concerns would you have about Shannon and her family? What additional information, if any, would you need if you were responsible for providing home-based intervention to Shannon Eason and her family? How would you obtain this additional information?

12. Beth appears to be somewhat uncomfortable working with Shannon because she has a visual impairment. To what extent should all early intervention practitioners be knowledgeable and skilled in working with children who have sensory impairments?

13. How can Beth coordinate the services her program provides to the Easons with the services provided by Virginia Cousins?

c h a p t e r 18

cc: Parker Ellis

P.J. McWilliam

The Wednesday afternoon preschool services meeting droned on as usual. Dana Tolliver doodled on the paper in front of her, glancing every few minutes at the clock on the far wall. It was already 3:20 P.M., and her mother was coming in from Phoenix on a 5:15 P.M. flight. Dana would have to leave for the airport by 4:00 P.M. if she wanted to park the car and meet her at the gate. Glen Atwater, the preschool services coordinator for Lochridge Children's Center, was in charge of the Wednesday meetings, and he always let them run long by at least 20 or 30 minutes. Nothing they discussed was all that earth-shattering—just the usual updates on the children and families they served and perhaps a few administrative items. Dana didn't understand why the group needed weekly meetings at all. Meetings every other week would work just as well and free a lot of valuable staff time in the process.

The meeting finally adjourned at 3:35 P.M. Dana quickly gathered her things and hurried down the hall to the small office she shared

with Karen, the team's occupational therapist. A small pile of pink messages sat beside the phone on her desk. The past 2 months had consisted of one phone call or meeting after another as she tried to secure
placements and complete IEPs for the children at Lochridge who would
enter kindergarten in the fall. Six children were leaving Lochridge this
year, and Dana was responsible for all their transitions into the public
school system. Because Lochridge had a wide catchment area, Dana
had been dealing with three different school districts in planning the
children's transitions.

Dana flipped through the pink slips. Most could wait until tomorrow, but she wondered why Yolanda Powell had called. There was no
message, just a phone number. Maybe there was time for one quick
call before leaving for the airport.

"Hi, Yolanda. This is Dana Tolliver at Lochridge Children's Center.
I have a message that you called."

"Oh, yes. Thanks for calling me back. I wanted to talk to you
about Lucas Coleman."

"Is the meeting still on for this Friday?"

"Yes, the meeting's still on," said Yolanda, "but there's something
you should probably know ahead of time."

"What's that?"

"Well, the placement committee met earlier this week," said Yolanda. "Sorry, but it looks as though they're going to recommend that
Lucas attend the self-contained class at Sandalwood Elementary School
next year."

"What?" exclaimed Dana. "What do you mean? What happened?"

Yolanda was the preschool coordinator for Clarksburg City Schools
and facilitated transitions into the public school system for all children
with special needs. Over the past 3 months, Dana and Yolanda had spent
hours planning Lucas's transition to kindergarten. They had had two
meetings with Lucas's parents, Natalie and Brian, to discuss Lucas's
needs for kindergarten. Dana had even managed to arrange for Yolanda
to spend a morning observing Lucas at the child care center he currently attended. Yolanda knew the Colemans wanted Lucas to attend a
general kindergarten classroom in the fall. What had gone wrong?

"I'm sorry," said Yolanda, "but it doesn't look as though the committee is going to recommend an inclusive placement. . . . I tried."

"I don't think the parents are going to be satisfied with just 'I'm
sorry,'" replied Dana.

"It wasn't my decision to make," said Yolanda. "I told both you
and the parents that my job was to collect information and present my
recommendations to the committee."

"Well, when did they make their decision?"

"The committee met on Monday."

"Monday! Why didn't you call and tell me sooner?"

"I didn't have to call you at all," Yolanda said a little curtly. "I knew you were counting on inclusion, so I thought I'd prepare you."

"Have you told Natalie and Brian?" asked Dana. "This will come as a huge shock to them. They feel very strongly that Lucas should be in a regular kindergarten class at Mason Elementary."

"No, I haven't told them," said Yolanda. "Technically, the decision won't be made until Lucas's IEP and placement meeting this Friday."

Dana looked at her watch. It was already 3:50 P.M., but Natalie and Brian needed to know about this now. She ended her conversation with Yolanda as quickly as possible then flipped through her Rolodex, found the Colemans' number, picked up the receiver, and started to dial. As the phone rang she looked at her watch again—3:54 P.M. Maybe it would be better to wait until she had more time to talk. Dana replaced the receiver, deciding she could call Lucas's parents from home after dinner.

A Promising Start

Visits with the Colemans were always pleasant. Brian owned and managed his own tropical fish store in town. For years, he had been a firefighter, but he'd left the fire department 3 years ago to try his hand at turning his hobby into a business. Natalie was a dental hygienist. Although Natalie used to work full time, Brian's growing business had made it possible for her to drop back to three-quarter time last year so she could spend more time at home with Lucas and their 7-year-old daughter, Christine. Natalie and Brian put a lot of effort into working with Lucas, and, although they wanted very strongly for him to reach his full potential, they seemed to understand Lucas's limitations and set realistic goals for him. In thinking about their son's future, Natalie's and Brian's primary concern was that Lucas be socially accepted by his peers and included in the community as much as possible.

Lucas was diagnosed at birth as having Down syndrome and began receiving services from Lochridge Children's Center when he was just 6 weeks old. He started in the infant home-visiting program and moved into Lochridge's toddler classroom when he was 18 months old. When he was 3 years old, Natalie and Brian decided to place him in a regular child care center in the community, and Lochridge provided ongoing consultation and therapy to support his inclusion. Dana was one of the consultants who made visits to the child care center, and she had also served as Lucas's service coordinator for the full 2 years he had been there.

Lucas loved going to child care every morning and often talked excitedly about what he and his "buddies" did at "school." Although he required extra assistance from his teachers, he followed classroom routines reasonably well and could usually keep up with his peers. Nevertheless, the differences between Lucas and his buddies had become more apparent during the past year.

Overall, Lucas's abilities were at a 36- to 42-month level. He was a little less coordinated than other children his age in running, climbing, and jumping. His fine motor skills were even further behind and affected both his ability to play with more sophisticated toys and his mastery of self-help skills such as buttoning, zipping, and snapping clothes. His most noticeable delays, however, were in his speech. Signing had been faded out over the past year and a half as he had become more proficient at talking; but his vocabulary was still limited, and his speech was sometimes difficult for the teachers and the other children to understand, especially when Lucas became upset or excited.

Nevertheless, Lucas was a charmer. Always ready for fun and adventure, he was extremely sociable, and his winning smile and funny antics had endeared him to many an adult's heart. Dana felt certain that his charm had played a big role in his successful inclusion in the child care center he now attended. Shelly Leonard had been his teacher at the center for a year and a half, and he had won her over easily. Shelly was young and energetic and had worked well with the consultants from Lochridge. She was firmly invested in Lucas's inclusion and did whatever she could to facilitate his learning and development.

During the past few months, however, Lucas had developed some behavior problems in the classroom—nothing all that dramatic, but serious enough to warrant some type of intervention. Hitting was the major problem. Occasionally, Lucas slapped other children when he wanted something they had or if he was otherwise upset with them. He didn't hit very hard or very often, but Shelly was certainly concerned. At first, she had tried to teach Lucas alternatives to slapping, but his hitting continued. During the past few weeks, Shelly had implemented a time-out procedure in the classroom: Whenever Lucas hit another child, he had to sit in a chair in the corner of the room for 5 minutes. Natalie and Brian were also using time-outs at home because Lucas had started slapping his sister. Although it was too early to tell whether the time-out procedure was working, Lucas seemed to understand the new rules, and everyone hoped this phase would soon pass.

In addition to hitting, Lucas had started running away from the classroom. Every once in a while, he would spy the classroom door open and take off down the hallway. If caught in the act, he was easily retrieved. But when his escape wasn't noticed, he usually wandered into a nearby classroom and had to be brought back to Shelly's room by another teacher or aide. Lucas didn't resist being brought back and, in fact, seemed to enjoy being chased and caught. Shelly was concerned, however, that he might wander off and get hurt. So far, the only intervention had been one of prevention—making sure the classroom door was kept shut.

Preparing for Conflict

Because of bad weather, Dana's mother's flight arrived more than an hour late. Dana took her out to dinner, stopped by her sister's house for a brief visit, and didn't get back to her apartment until after 10:00 P.M. It wasn't until after her mother went to bed that Dana remembered she was supposed to call the Colemans, but, by then, it was too late.

The next morning Dana had an early meeting about another child's transition and didn't get back to her office until 11:00 A.M. She called Brian at the fish store because she was more likely to reach him than Natalie during the day. She thought she might be able to meet Brian for lunch to tell him about Yolanda's call and they could plan their strategy for Friday's meeting. Brian, however, had already arranged a lunch meeting with an important distributor. If he could work out a deal with this distributor, he might be able to expand his business. Dana didn't want to arrange an evening visit and leave her mother alone, so she decided to tell Brian over the phone that the school district wanted to place Lucas in the self-contained class at Sandalwood Elementary.

"What do you mean, they won't do it?" exclaimed Brian. "I thought that's what we all agreed on."

"Well, I thought we did, too, but the final decision is really up to the school placement committee," explained Dana.

"It seems to me that we wasted a lot of time doing all that planning with that Yolanda what's-her-name from the school."

"I wouldn't say it was wasted time, Brian. I think the time we spent talking about Lucas's—"

"Well, I think it was wasted," interrupted Brian. "What good did all that talking do if my son ends up in some trailer out behind the school?"

"That's not going to happen, Brian."

"Can you promise me that it won't?" he asked.

Could she? There was a brief silence as Dana considered her reply. This avenue of conversation was not very productive. They needed to talk about what to do next—about how they should respond to the committee.

"We might be able to convince them to change their minds at the meeting," suggested Dana. "Even if we can't, you don't have to agree with their decision, you know. You can always appeal it."

"You mean, take them to court?" asked Brian.

"That's always an option, but I think there are things you can try before that becomes necessary."

"And what happens to Lucas while we're doing all of this fighting? Is he stuck in the trailer?" Brian said with a hint of laughter. He was forever teasing Dana about one thing or another.

"Brian! Would you stop it?" Dana laughed. It was fortunate she knew Brian long enough and well enough to understand when he was kidding her and to be able to kid him back. "He is *not* going to be stuck in some trailer. That sounds just awful!"

"How do you know?" teased Brian. "I just picture this great big, yellow trailer in the back of the school. You know, like the Goodwill trailers they have in the Wal-Mart parking lot. All the kids who don't pass the 'normal test' get dumped back there."

"That is not what a self-contained class is like, and you know it," she said with mock authority.

"Do I?" There was a sudden change in Brian's voice. "That's sort of what they were like when I was in school," he said softly. He was no longer teasing.

"Listen, Brian, I know you need to go soon," Dana said more seriously. "Your lunch meeting sounds important. Let's see where we are . . . . It's probably best not to go into the meeting on Friday fighting. Let them talk first. Then, if you don't agree, let them know that you don't. Remember, you don't have to sign anything that you don't agree with. If you have a few minutes, you might want to look over the booklet on parents' rights that I gave you. The most important thing to remember is that, even if they insist on a self-contained class at this meeting, you still have options." Dana paused for a moment then asked, "By the way, do you and Natalie still want me to go with you to the meeting?"

"Yes, of course," answered Brian.

"Then, I'll be there. I'll meet you in the lobby a few minutes before 9 o'clock."

"Thanks Dana, but before you go, tell me this—why are they fighting us? Why wouldn't they want Lucas to be in a regular kindergarten class? I just don't understand."

"I'm not so sure I understand, either," answered Dana. "It may be a matter of the money they'd need to pay the extra classroom aide we're asking for."

"Do you think Lucas really needs an individual aide?" asked Brian. "Maybe if we didn't ask for the aide, they'd let him in the class."

"I don't know how much learning he'd do without an aide. A classroom of 22 or 23 kindergartners takes a lot of teacher attention. You and Natalie can think it over a little more, but I don't think I'd back down on that quite yet."

"Okay," said Brian. "I guess we'll see you tomorrow, then."

"Yes, I'll see you then. Meanwhile, tell Natalie I said hello. Oh, and good luck on your meeting with the distributor."

Meeting the Opposition

Everyone assembled around the conference table by 9:15 A.M. on Friday and exchanged niceties before beginning to talk about Lucas's placement. Representatives from both Lochridge Children's Center and the Clarksburg City Schools were there. Dana and the Colemans had also invited Shelly Leonard, but she couldn't leave the classroom to be at the meeting. Dana was glad that Yolanda had at least had an opportunity to talk with Shelly when she had gone to the child care center to observe Lucas.

Yolanda began the meeting by introducing everyone, then asking all the professionals who had tested Lucas to present their findings. Following the assessment reports, Yolanda summarized her observations of Lucas at the child care center and related the Colemans' request that Lucas be placed in a regular kindergarten classroom. She then offered Brian and Natalie an opportunity to talk. Brian reiterated their desire for Lucas to attend George Mason Elementary, where Christine was currently in second grade. Brian also told the committee that they hoped to get a full-time assistant in the classroom to help Lucas in addition to the speech-language services and occupational therapy that Lucas would receive. Natalie then added that they were concerned about Lucas's social acceptance and thought the assistant would play an important role in facilitating friendships between Lucas and the other children.

Lynette Williams, who hadn't said anything up to this point, now spoke up. "Are you asking for a full-time individual assistant?" she asked. Lynette was the Assistant Principal of George Mason Elementary School and chairperson of the school placement committee.

Casting a quick glance at Dana, Brian said, "Yes, we thought it would be important for the assistant to be around whenever Lucas needed help." The silence and grim look from Lynette Williams led Brian to add, "But, maybe we could consider a part-time assistant if she were available during the times she was needed most."

Lynette Williams just gave him a stony look, then jotted a quick note on her pad of paper. Brian looked to Dana for guidance, but Dana didn't say anything. She thought it was best to wait for the committee's verdict before fighting. Even so, Lynette Williams's intimidation tactics infuriated her. There was no excuse for acting so cool and aloof with parents and for purposefully making Natalie and Brian feel uncomfortable. Dana fiddled with her pen, absent-mindedly loosening the top then snapping it back on. She repeated the motions over and over as she focused her gaze on the wall behind Lynette Williams's left shoulder.

The verdict was soon handed down. Lucas would be placed in the self-contained class at Sandalwood Elementary School. Lynette Williams pronounced the committee's reasons for the decision in a syrupy-sweet voice. She said Lucas's cognitive skills were far below those of entering kindergartners and that he could receive more related services at Sandalwood than he could at Mason because the special class allowed for more therapist time to be designated to the school. She also noted that Yolanda's report mentioned some behavior problems and that these could best be handled in a smaller classroom by a teacher who was experienced in coping with such matters—like the self-contained class at Sandalwood. "Besides," she added, "the safety of the other kindergartners must be considered. It wouldn't be fair to subject them to being hit by Lucas."

Tears welled up in Natalie's eyes as Lynette Williams discussed Lucas's behavior problems and the need to protect other children from him. Dana could only watch as Brian subtly reached an arm behind Natalie's chair and patted her back. How heartless, thought Dana, as she watched Lynette Williams continue with a half-smile, seemingly oblivious to the emotional damage she was inflicting. According to Lynette Williams, the committee only had Lucas's best interests in mind.

When Lynette Williams finished speaking, Dana waited for a moment to give Brian and Natalie the chance to respond first. Brian, however, looked stunned and said nothing, and all of Natalie's efforts seemed concentrated on holding back her tears.

"I can understand some of your concerns about including Lucas in a regular classroom," said Dana, looking first at Lynette Williams and then glancing around the table at the other members of the group. "But Brian and Natalie want Lucas to be given an opportunity to attend the elementary school in their neighborhood and be included with his peers. After all, he's been attending a regular child care center for the past 2 years, and his inclusion there has been reasonably successful."

Brian and Natalie nodded their heads in agreement, so Dana continued, "I believe that some of the concerns you mentioned could be addressed by having an assistant for Lucas . . . at least while he was adjusting to the school and learning new routines. Perhaps the need for an assistant could be re-evaluated periodically."

"Doesn't my son at least deserve a chance to *try* being in a regular classroom?" asked Brian. "How can you say he won't make it if he isn't even given an opportunity to try?"

"Isn't that a little like throwing someone into the middle of a lake to find out if he can swim?" said Lynette Williams. "Would that be fair to Lucas?"

"Well . . . uh," stammered Brian.

Dana wanted to scream; but Brian was handling things now, and she didn't want to interfere. After all, he might have to deal with Lynette Williams and the rest of this group for a number of years to come, and she wouldn't always be around to help out. To prevent herself from speaking out, Dana busied herself by pretending to look through the folder she had brought with her that contained Lucas's test reports and progress notes. Her frustration, however, kept her from concentrating on any one thing as she flipped through the pages in the folder.

In spite of Lynette Williams's snide remark, Brian continued to advocate for Lucas's right to have a chance to be in a regular kindergarten. He and Lynette went back and forth for a while, then Yolanda Powell interrupted to suggest a compromise. "Perhaps Lucas could be placed in the self-contained classroom at Sandalwood but be included in a regular kindergarten classroom there for part of the day. If it works out, we could gradually increase the time he spends in the general classroom. Who knows," Yolanda said with a broad smile, "maybe by next year he could be transferred to Mason Elementary and be in a regular first-grade classroom."

Yeah, right, thought Dana. *And it might snow in July, too.* She flipped more rapidly through the pages in the folder to avoid speaking her mind. From what she had seen, once children were placed in a self-contained classroom, they were there for good. No exit.

Lynette Williams and the other members of the committee agreed to the self-contained placement with partial inclusion at Sandalwood. Then they began discussing activities in which Lucas might be included with general kindergartners. Committee members suggested lunchtime, physical education, and morning circle, and Yolanda wrote these down on the IEP and placement forms.

With a smile of contentment, Yolanda pushed the forms across the table for Brian and Natalie to sign. Brian hesitated as he held the pen above the page. Dana could tell by the expressions on their faces that they were still uncertain about the decision. After all, this was not what they had wanted. They had been railroaded, and Lynette Williams had been the chief engineer. Dana could keep her silence no longer.

"You don't have to sign it if you don't agree," she told Brian matter-of-factly.

Brian put the pen down and gently pushed the forms an arm's length away from himself and Natalie. "No," he said softly, eyes cast downward. "This isn't what we want for Lucas. We don't agree." He stood up, touched Natalie on the shoulder, and held her chair for her while she got up. Natalie picked up her purse, and they turned to leave. Dana could see a slight tremor in Brian's hand as he held the door for Natalie. The door clicked closed behind them, and they were gone.

Out in the parking lot, Natalie was sobbing in Brian's arms. Dana decided that this was probably not a good time to talk about what had just happened. She walked over and told them that she was sorry and that she would call them next week to arrange a time when they could talk about what to do next. She said good-bye and walked across the lot to her car.

Making Sacrifices

Dana didn't return to the office until Wednesday, having taken off Monday and Tuesday to spend some time with her mother. She had driven her mother to the airport early Wednesday morning to catch an 8:30 A.M. flight back to Phoenix; but the traffic from the airport to Lochridge was hectic, so it was nearly 10:00 A.M. by the time Dana got in to work. Beside her phone sat the usual pile of pink messages along with a note written on legal-size yellow paper. The note said, "See me ASAP!—Glen."

Dana's officemate, Karen, turned around in her chair to look at Dana. "Did you see the note from Glen?" she asked.

"Yeah. Did he say what he wanted?" asked Dana.

"No," said Karen, "but he's been by here every 15 minutes since a little after 8 o'clock. What's up?"

"Beats me," said Dana.

"Well, I think I'd go see him right away. He looked pretty serious about whatever's on his mind."

Dana set her briefcase beside the file cabinet and walked down the hall to Glen's office. His door was open, so she knocked gently on the frame. "Morning, Glen. You wanted to see me about something?"

"Yes," he said somberly. "Come in and pull the door closed."

A closed door, thought Dana. *He must be serious.* She approached his desk.

"Have a seat," Glen said. Dana perched on the edge of the chair beside his desk.

"I got a letter yesterday," continued Glen. He picked up a sheet of paper from the top of a pile on his desk and handed it to Dana. "Can you tell me what this is all about?" It was a letter from Lynette Williams on George Mason Elementary School letterhead addressed to Glen. Dana glanced quickly down the page.

George Mason Elementary School
124 Turner Drive

Glen Atwater
Coordinator of Preschool Services
Lochridge Children's Center
1032 Northwestern Boulevard

Dear Glen,

I was dismayed by the conduct of one of your staff members, Dana Tolliver, at a school placement committee meeting held at George Mason Elementary School this past Friday. Ms. Tolliver attended the meeting for the purpose of facilitating the transition of Lucas Coleman from your program into the public school system. I was shocked by the unprofessional conduct displayed by Ms. Tolliver. She outwardly encourged the parents to be hostile and uncooperative, aggressively flipped through the child's records, and further disrupted the proceedings by continuously clicking a pen while others discussed important issues.

I feel this matter needs to be brought to your attention because Ms. Tolliver's behavior reflects poorly on the Lochridge Children's Center. I am also concerned that Ms. Tolliver has caused unnecessary stress for the parents and may have jeopardized the future educational progress of the child. I regret to inform you that I consider this matter to be serious enough to take action on my own in order to prevent future incidents of this sort. Ms. Tolliver will no longer be allowed to attend meetings at our school regarding the transition or placement of a child without my express permission and unless she is accompanied by yourself or another supervisor from the Lochridge Children's Center.

Sincerely yours,

Lynette A. Williams

Lynette A. Williams
Assistant Principal

cc: Laura Sims, Principal, George Mason Elementary School
     Kent Norwood, Director, Lochridge Children's Center
     Parker Ellis, Superintendent, Clarksburg City Schools

How dare Lynette Williams accuse her of engaging in unprofessional conduct! Lynette was the one who tried to railroad Lucas's parents into accepting a placement in the self-contained classroom. *All I did was inform them of their rights,* thought Dana. *Isn't that my job? And where did Lynette Williams come up with all that stuff about disruptive pen clicking and aggressive paper flipping? That's just plain ridiculous! Surely Glen can see through that.* But when Dana looked up at Glen, his stern eyes told a different story.

"This is going to cause some big waves," he said, reaching for the letter. Dana knew immediately what he was talking about—copies had been sent to Kent Norwood, the Director of the Lochridge Children's Center and Glen's immediate supervisor, and Parker Ellis, the superintendent of Clarksburg City Schools. Lynette Williams had really pulled out the big guns. What a malicious and vindictive woman she was!

Dana started telling Glen her side of the story, beginning with the contact she and Lucas's parents had had with Yolanda Powell prior to the placement committee meeting. Dana was only halfway through her recounting of Friday's events when Glen's phone rang. It was Kent Norwood. He had received his copy of Lynette's letter and wanted to speak to Glen right away. *Glen was right about the big waves,* thought Dana. She could feel them crashing over her already. Glen went off to talk with Kent, and Dana went back to her own office to wait for the next surge.

Within an hour, Glen called for her again. Dana tried to continue telling her side of the story, but Glen seemed much less interested in hearing it now. He said he was already late for a meeting, but he would be back around 1:00 P.M., and they would discuss ways to "repair the damage" then.

"You know me," Dana pleaded as Glen packed a few folders into his briefcase. "You know I wouldn't ever do the things that Lynette Williams is accusing me of."

"Well, you can be a little brusque sometimes," he said. "Maybe all that's needed is an apology." Glen snapped his briefcase closed. "We'll talk more about it at 1 o'clock," he said, grabbing his suit jacket and heading toward the door.

An apology! Did Glen really expect her to apologize to Lynette Williams? For what? She hadn't done anything wrong. As the initial wave of indignation washed over her, a picture started coming into focus, and Dana didn't like what she saw. She was being offered up as a sacrificial lamb. Glen had to answer to Kent Norwood, and Kent had to answer to Parker Ellis. If they supported Dana, they might risk their standings in Clarksburg's "ol' boy" network. It was far easier for them to ask Dana to humiliate herself by apologizing to Lynette Williams in order to smooth things over. It just wasn't fair.

And what about Lucas and his parents? Were they also being offered up as a sacrifice? Dana hadn't talked to Brian and Natalie since Friday. What would she say to them now? Should she tell them about Lynette Williams's letter? Didn't they have a right to know what was going on? After all, the situation most certainly would affect them. *If I apologize to Lynette,* thought Dana, *and encourage Brian and Natalie to accept the placement at Sandalwood, I'll be the one who's sacrificing Lucas.*

Dana went back to her office and sat down heavily in her chair. Karen immediately read the concern on Dana's face and asked her what was wrong. Dana pushed the door closed and started telling Karen what had happened, but she didn't get very far before the tears began to flow. Here, in the safety of someone she trusted, her defenses were down. Karen handed Dana the box of tissues and listened intently until the entire story was told.

Discussion Questions

1. Could Dana have done anything differently prior to or during the placement meeting to improve the chances of securing an inclusive placement for Lucas?

2. In this story, Lynette Williams's motives are unclear. What are some possible reasons that a school system would deny an inclusive placement for a child like Lucas?

3. Make a list of the pros and cons of placing Lucas in a regular kindergarten class. Based on your list, what placement decision would you recommend?

4. Did Dana adequately prepare Brian and Natalie Coleman for Lucas's placement committee meeting? What do you think Dana did that was helpful? What, if anything, would you have done differently if you had been responsible for preparing the Colemans for the meeting?

5. What do you think about the way Dana handled herself at Lucas's placement committee meeting? Did she provide adequate support to Brian and Natalie? Did she do anything to create animosity between herself and Lynette Williams? What, if anything, should she have done differently?

6. On several occasions, Dana tells Brian that he and Natalie can appeal the committee's decision—that it's not final. If the Colemans lived in your state or community, what legal rights would they have to appeal the decision? Who would they contact and what would the appeal process involve?

7. What approach should Dana take in working with Brian and Natalie when she next talks with them?

8. Dana felt that Lynette's letter to Glen Atwater was vindictive and malicious. Were any of the concerns that Lynette Williams expressed in the letter valid? If so, was writing and sending the letter an appropriate way of handling her concerns? Would other strategies have been more appropriate or effective?

9. Given the pressures that Glen may be under to smooth the situation over, how could he have been more supportive of Dana in handling this situation?

10. What option does Dana have for handling this situation with Lynette Williams? Should she apologize as Glen has advised her to?

11. What, if anything, should Dana say to Brian and Natalie about Lynette Williams's letter and Glen's response to it?

12. Make a list of "do's and don'ts" for transitions from preschool to kindergarten that would provide helpful advice to other early interventionists.

13. Suppose a public school system has hired you to advise them on appropriate criteria for including children with disabilities in regular kindergarten classrooms. Develop a brief document (e.g., guidelines, criteria, factors to consider) that placement committees could consult in making their decisions.

chapter 19

La Maestra

P.J. McWilliam and Nancy Frame

nne Lowrey hadn't planned to visit the Martinez family until after lunch, but now she felt that she should rearrange her schedule and make a visit this morning. The mounting paperwork on her desk would just have to wait. Maybe she could catch up on some of it this evening after the children were in bed. Of course, Steve wouldn't like it. He didn't think she should have to work at home without being paid for her time. But Steve hadn't spent the past 2 days at home with a sick baby, either. She was the one who had taken Paul to the doctor and stayed home with him through his fever while her in-box filled at the office. Steve had gone to work. Juggling time and responsibilities seemed so much more complicated now that they had two children. Maybe it would get easier when Colette started kindergarten in the fall. They'd thought about sending her to kindergarten this year, but her birthday was so close to the cutoff date that they had decided to wait. Anne re-read the phone message on her desk.

```
┌─────────────────────────────────────┐
│  WHILE YOU WERE OUT                  │
│  DAY: Monday TIME: 10:27 am          │
│                                      │
│  TO: Anne L                          │
│  FROM: Michael Santos                │
│                                      │
│  Julio Martinez has been arrested    │
│  and is in jail. Call ASAP.          │
│                                      │
│                                      │
└─────────────────────────────────────┘
```

What does he expect me to do about it? she thought. But she knew she had to do something.

Michael Santos was the Child Protective Services worker who handled the Martinez family, and he wouldn't think twice about taking the Martinez children out of their home a third time—maybe even permanently. If it hadn't been for Anne, he probably would have done that 3 months ago when Carina Martinez's preschool teacher had called protective services to report Julio for suspected abuse. Julio wasn't exactly a model father, but he certainly didn't abuse his children. Anne knew that he and his wife, Elena, loved their children dearly—all five of them.

Anne suddenly noticed the date and time at the top of the message. Michael Santos had called on Monday morning, and it was already Wednesday! If only she hadn't been out with a sick child. . . . There was no telling what might have happened to the Martinez family over the past 2 days. Instead of calling Michael Santos, she decided to go straight to the source to find out for herself.

Anne signed out a car at the front desk and left the building. Out in the parking lot, she walked over to her own car and retrieved the things she had brought for Carina. Anne lifted the lid of a small shoe box before putting it on the back seat of the county car. She couldn't help but smile. Carina's face would light up when she opened the box and saw glossy black patent leather shoes with silver linings! Then Anne carefully laid a yellow taffeta dress across the back seat. Colette had worn the shoes and dress only for Easter and a few times afterward before she'd outgrown them. Finally, Anne tossed a grocery bag full of Colette's old play clothes on the floor behind the driver's seat.

While Anne and Colette sorted through Colette's drawers and closet over the weekend and packed up the things that no longer fit her, Colette had asked Anne if she was going to give her old clothes to Carina and Isabella. Anne often talked to Colette about the two little girls. She told her how poor the Martinez family was and how much the girls would appreciate the old toys and clothes. Anne wanted Colette and Paul to grow up to be generous and sensitive to the needs of those who were less fortunate than they were. Colette had obviously been impressed by Anne's stories about Carina and Isabella, as she often asked about the girls by name, wanting to know what they were wearing and whether they were playing with her old toys when Anne had last seen them. Colette had even named her new doll Isabella.

Anne settled behind the wheel and headed east toward the small town on the other side of the county where many immigrant farm workers lived. The little town had been mentioned frequently in the newspapers during the past several months. It was an election year, and the crop losses caused by the unusually harsh winter had given rise to the popular political stance of cracking down on illegal immigrants, who supposedly were stealing the jobs of hard-working, tax-paying citizens. Funny, how little attention the news paid to illegal immigrants during years when the harvest was good, Anne thought as she headed toward the Martinezes'.

A Life in America

Julio and Elena had immigrated from a small town in Mexico about 4 years ago to take advantage of the agricultural work opportunities they had heard were available in California. There had been work in Mexico, they told Anne, "*pero no pagaba bien* [but the work did not pay well]." Julio and Elena already had three young children when they arrived in California: Guerrero, who was now 10 years old; Rosita, who was 8 years old; and Carlos, who was almost 6 years old. Since they had moved to the United States, they had had two more daughters: Carina, who was 4 years old, and Isabella, who was 19 months old. All three of the Martinez girls were profoundly deaf.

Julio and Elena had immigrated to the United States illegally, but they purchased false identification cards so they could work in the fields and the fruit warehouses when work was available. Three of Julio's brothers and one of his sisters had immigrated to the United States during the past 4 years. Elena told Anne that Julio had another brother and two more sisters who still lived in Mexico in the town where they had all grown up together. Elena spoke proudly of being a part of Julio's large family. Elena herself had only one sister who was still living in Mexico. Her parents died when she and her sister were still very young, and the girls were raised by their grandparents.

During the past year, Anne had met most of Julio's siblings, their spouses, and their children. It seemed as though nearly all of them had, at one time or another, lived with Julio and Elena. Julio's oldest brother, Umberto, and his wife, Luisa, seemed to be more or less permanent fixtures in the Martinez house. Anne had been careful not to ask about the legal status of any of Julio's extended family members. If she didn't know about their immigration status, she couldn't be held legally responsible for not reporting them.

For the first 3 years after Julio and Elena moved to California, there was ample work. Julio's mother even came to stay with them during the first two harvest seasons to help care for the little ones so that Julio and Elena could both work in the fields and make extra money. With the recent crackdown on illegal immigrants, however, they had found very little work this past year. Most weekday mornings, Julio joined the group of Mexican men who stood on the corner of the town's courthouse square, drinking coffee and hoping that some construction company or farmer would need a few pairs of extra hands for the day. The men began arriving at daybreak and stood around talking to one another, waiting for a truck to pull up to the curb. Whenever one did, the driver would jump out, point to a few of the men, and the men would quickly jump into the back of the truck. These were the lucky ones. They would have a job for the day.

Julio had no specific job skills except those of a manual laborer; but he appeared to be very strong, and his dark eyes sparked with seemingly boundless energy. Julio told Anne that he did not like school as a child and that he had stopped attending when he was 7 years old. Elena said that she also did not like school, but her grandparents made her attend until she was almost 12 years old. When her grandfather became very ill, Elena and her sister were sent to live with an aunt and uncle in another town. After Elena moved out of her grandparents' home, she never returned to school. Neither Julio nor Elena was able to speak English, and even in their own language, they were functionally illiterate. Elena could, however, read some elementary Spanish printing.

Without any other hope for work, Julio and Elena somehow managed to support their children and pay their rent with the Supplemental Security Income (SSI) payments they received on behalf of Carina and Isabella each month. They could not collect SSI payments for Rosita, because, although she was also profoundly deaf, she had not been born in the United States.

Questioned by Authorities

Child Protective Services was already involved with the Martinez family when Anne was asked to provide services for Isabella. In fact, it was

Michael Santos who had called and asked her to get involved. That was about a year ago, when Isabella was just 7 months old and had first been diagnosed as being profoundly deaf. Rosita had already been attending a public school program for children with hearing impairments, and Carina was enrolled in a state-sponsored classroom program for preschoolers with hearing impairments.

When Anne received the first call from Michael Santos, all of the Martinez children had been taken out of their home and placed in temporary foster care. According to Michael, the children had been found in their home under the supervision of a 13-year-old girl. The girl claimed to be the children's cousin and said that she was babysitting for her aunt and uncle. It was unclear how long Julio and Elena had been gone and when—or if—they were expected to return home. All of the children had lice, and Isabella had a fever and a severe diaper rash. Michael had placed the children in foster care that day. Later, Child Protective Services discovered that Isabella had not been seen by a doctor or nurse since she was 2 months old, and she had not been immunized.

By the time Anne actually visited Isabella for the first time, she and the other children had been returned to Julio and Elena—but now they were under the protective watch of Michael Santos. In the weeks that followed, Julio and Elena eventually explained the incident to Anne. They said they had heard that there were jobs for field workers in a neighboring town, so Julio, Elena, and a number of other family members had gone to work the harvest to make money. They had left Theresa, Umberto's and Luisa's daughter, to watch the children. They were gone for only 3 days, and Theresa knew that she should ask the lady who lived up the street for help if any of the children were hurt or became very sick. Theresa hadn't known that Isabella had bronchitis; she had only thought the baby was a little fussy from teething, so she hadn't gone for help.

Julio and Elena also told Anne that Carina's preschool teacher was the one who had gotten them into trouble. Theresa had told them that the teacher came out to the house looking for Julio and Elena the same afternoon that the children had been taken away. They also suspected that Carina's teacher was responsible once before for a woman from Protective Services coming out to their home. That time the children had also had lice, and the woman sent a nurse over to help Julio and Elena shampoo the children's hair and spray the bed clothes.

Because they thought it was the preschool teacher who had the children taken away, Julio and Elena had stopped sending Carina to her preschool class. They were also suspicious of Anne at first, but the fact that Anne spoke some Spanish helped her to gain Julio's and

Elena's trust. Within a few months, Julio and Elena counted on Anne for many things. She made phone calls for them when no one on the other end of the line spoke Spanish, and they saved their mail and the papers the children brought home from school for Anne to read and explain when she arrived for home visits. Letters and forms that were written in Spanish were actually the most problematic because they often included words that were beyond Elena's reading level and above Anne's mastery of Spanish vocabulary.

Within a few months, Julio and Elena trusted Anne fully and referred to her as *la maestra*—the teacher. Anne often talked with them about Carina's need to learn to use sign language and eventually convinced them to send Carina back to her preschool program. Perhaps Anne wouldn't have pushed them so much if Julio and Elena were better about signing with Carina and the other girls. Despite Anne's constant reminders about the need to sign, much of the communication around the Martinez house still consisted of pointing, pulling, yelling, and pushing. And Anne wasn't even sure that they truly acknowledged Isabella's profound hearing loss. Why else would Elena keep trying to convince Anne that Isabella made more sounds than her other daughters had made when they were babies?

Carina's returning to preschool had been a relief to Anne. For 6 months, Carina went to the classroom at least 3 or 4 days a week, and the only complaint from the teacher had been that Julio and Elena didn't consistently put Carina's hearing aids on her or that her hearing aids had dead batteries. To reduce the risk of continued confrontation with Carina's teacher, Anne had bought some batteries with her own money and given them to Elena and Julio, telling them that they had been donated by the program. She had also given them a calendar that she found in the supply closet at the office. Anne reminded Elena how to check the batteries in the girls' hearing aids and showed Elena how to use the calendar to remind herself to do it regularly.

After several months of working with the Martinezes, Anne had believed that she and the family had made real progress. But 3 months ago it all blew up again. Once again, the children had been taken away by Protective Services, and, once again, it was Carina's preschool teacher who had reported the suspected abuse. According to Michael Santos, Carina had arrived at preschool with a cut and bruising under her eye. When the teacher asked Carina what had happened, the 4-year-old had repeatedly signed: "Papa—Shoe." Given her limited sign language—Carina's vocabulary consisted of about 50–60 signs, and she was just starting to combine 2 signs—that was all anyone could get out of her. But that was evidently enough reason for Michael to remove all of the children from their home.

As soon as possible after the incident, Anne had gone out to talk to Julio and Elena to find out what had happened. She just knew that Julio would never strike one of his children hard enough to cause injury. She also felt badly that she had perhaps set them up for another conflict with Protective Services by encouraging them to send Carina back to school. With much fear and outrage, Julio and Elena told their story to Anne. Their sons Guerrero and Carlos had been fighting over the television, and, when they continued to yell after being told several times to stop, Julio had taken off his soft moccasin and thrown it at the boys. Unfortunately, little Carina had been passing through the room just as he threw the shoe. Startled by the flying moccasin, she'd lost her balance and hit her face on the corner of the coffee table when she fell. "*¡Era un accidente!* [It was an accident!]" Julio exclaimed at the end of the story.

Anne told Michael how Carina had been injured. She also explained how limited Carina's language skills were. By and large, Michael seemed to accept the story, but he told Anne that she would have to provide the same explanation to the judge at Julio and Elena's hearing. In the end, the judge allowed the children to be returned to Julio and Elena, but she made it clear that she still did not approve of throwing shoes at children—not even soft ones. And because they had a record of past neglect, Julio and Elena were made to attend parenting classes in order to maintain custody of the children. Julio and Elena actually seemed to enjoy the classes. On one home visit, they even told Anne all about time-out and said they might try it to see if it really worked.

Overwhelming Responsibilities

For 3 months now, ever since the children were taken away for the second time, Carina had not attended preschool. The preschool teacher was concerned that Julio and Elena were being unlawfully negligent by not sending her and had called Michael Santos again 2 weeks ago. Uncertain whether this constituted neglect, Michael had called Anne to find out why Carina hadn't been to preschool. Anne explained to him that, after the last incident, Julio and Elena did not trust Carina's preschool teacher. She also told him that she had a good relationship with the Martinez family, so she eventually might be able to encourage Julio and Elena to put Carina back in school. Meanwhile, Anne said that she would take responsibility for teaching Carina sign language when she went out to see Isabella.

As Anne now approached Julio's and Elena's neighborhood, she became increasingly worried about what she would find. Had Julio been accused of abuse again? Had Michael Santos removed the children from their home for a third time? Was it possible that Julio had really hurt one of the children this time? Was it possible that Julio and Elena had lied to her before and that she had been duped into believing a false story about the moccasin? . . . No, it just couldn't be true. They would never lie to her, and Julio would never hurt his children. He just wasn't that kind of a man. But then, why had Julio been arrested and put in jail?

Anne parked the car by the curb in front of the Martinez house. She heard loud voices coming from within as she climbed the front steps and knocked on the door. Elena opened the door. "*Pensé que iba a venir esta tarde* [I thought you were coming this afternoon]," she said.

"*Sí. Pero Michael Santos me llamó por teléfono* [Yes. But Michael Santos called me on the phone]," began Anne. Upon hearing Michael's name, a worried look passed across Elena's face. "*Dijo que la policía a llevado a Julio* [He said the police took Julio away]," Anne continued in broken Spanish.

"*Sí. La policía lo llevó pero está aquí ahora. . . . ¡Venga!* [Yes. The police took him away but he's here now. . . . Come in!]" Elena's eyes brightened, and she led Anne to the living room.

How could Julio have gotten out of jail so quickly? Maybe his arrest had been a mistake, thought Anne. As they walked into the living room, Anne was relieved to see Carina and Isabella playing on the floor. Isabella looked up from where she sat and smiled, and Carina's dark curls bounced as she rushed over to greet Anne then pulled her by the hands over to where she and Isabella had been playing with their dolls and a little tea set. The tea set had been Colette's. Anne had given it to the girls when Steve's parents gave Colette a new and much bigger set last Christmas.

Julio and Umberto were sitting on the couch talking loudly, but Anne couldn't follow their conversation. Umberto's wife Luisa was putting her 5-month-old in the baby swing beside the television set. She gave the swing a loud crank to start it in motion, then she greeted Anne and excused herself from the room.

Carina shoved a tiny cup and saucer into Anne's hand and signed "DRINK—WANT?"

"YES," Anne signed in return. "THANK YOU." Anne pretended to drink from the little cup. "HOT!" she signed and fanned her mouth furiously. "DRINK HOT!"

Carina's face instantly lit up with a smile, then she laughed—a hoarse, guttural sound that came from somewhere deep inside her small body. Anne had always thought that the laughter of a child who is deaf was the sincerest of all human sounds. She smiled back at Carina.

Anne played with the two girls for a while longer, signing with them as they conducted their tea party. Elena, Julio, and Umberto sat on the couch and watched. As always, Anne spoke Spanish as she signed with the girls. She knew that Carina's preschool teacher spoke English in the classroom, but Anne thought it was more important for Elena and Julio to understand the meaning of the signs she was using than for her to be consistent with the school. After all, both of the girls heard very little, so it probably didn't matter which spoken language she used. Maybe it would matter later as they learned to read lips, but, for now, teaching the children English didn't seem to be a high priority.

Anne tried to involve Julio and Elena in her play with the children by having Carina offer them some pretend tea and cookies. They accepted the toy dishes from Carina and pretended to drink and eat, but they never once signed to either of the girls. That was the way it always was. Anne was *la maestra*. She was the one who knew how to teach the children. Julio and Elena trusted her and did not consider themselves to be equals where the children's learning was concerned.

Anne noticed that the girls weren't wearing their hearing aids, but she chose not to deal with that issue today. She wanted to know more about Julio's being arrested. So, when the children had tired of playing with her, she asked Julio and Elena what had happened.

From what she gathered, Julio had been pulled over by the police while he was driving. When the officers discovered that he had a false identification card, no driver's license, and no car insurance, he was arrested and put in jail. When Anne asked how he had gotten out of jail, they told her that they had paid $1,000 to get him out. They showed Anne the paperwork from his release. The $1,000 was bond money; he would still be tried in court in a few months. Did they understand that? "*¿Quién pagó para que Julio podría salir?* [Who paid bail so that Julio could get out of jail?]" Anne asked. Elena said that she paid $400, and Umberto gave her the other $600. Anne wondered how Elena and Umberto had come up with that much money in such a short time, but she thought it was better not to ask. Anne only hoped that there would be enough money in the house to feed the children for the rest of the month.

When they had finished telling their tale, Anne looked at Julio and told him that he *had* to stop driving. Julio smiled sheepishly and said, "*Sí, maestra, yo tengo que manejar despacio* [Yes, teacher, I need to drive slowly]." Anne just looked into his dark, innocent eyes and thought to herself. . . . *What will happen to you, Julio? The system is going to eat you alive.*

Anne tried to explain that Julio was not free yet, that he would still have to appear in court. She wanted to talk with them about finding a lawyer, but she knew that they wouldn't have the money to hire one. She would have to see what help was available first.

It was getting late, and Anne had to get back to the office. She had already been gone longer than she had planned. As she stood and said good-bye, she looked around the room. The furniture was old and tattered, and the paint was peeling off the walls. Over the couch hung a large painting of *The Last Supper,* and a crucifix hung on the wall above the television set. Anne knew that the family, like herself, was Catholic because she had talked to them about their religion several times during the past year. Julio and Elena had gone to church regularly when they lived in Mexico and when they had first come to California. But now, they said, there were just too many babies for them to go to church. Maybe it's their faith that keeps them going, thought Anne as she walked to the front door.

As Anne opened the door to leave, she remembered the clothes she had brought for the girls. She went back into the living room and signed to Carina that she had a surprise for her in her car. Hand-in-hand, Anne and Carina walked outside, and Elena followed carrying little Isabella in her arms.

Carina was thrilled when she saw the yellow dress and the shoes with the silver linings. Carina took the shoe box in her arms and hugged it tightly. Anne handed Elena the dress and the bag of clothes and patted Isabella on the top of her head. Then she waved good-bye to the girls and Elena and watched as they headed back to the house.

Anne thought about her work with the Martinez family as she drove back to the office. She was already going to Julio and Elena's home twice a week. The girls needed so much. Most important, they needed a signing environment, and Elena and Julio were not yet providing it for them. And now she felt more responsible than ever for Carina's development because, despite her assurance to Michael Santos that she would try to get Carina back into preschool, Anne doubted that Elena and Julio would ever voluntarily send her back to the classroom. As long as she could demonstrate that Carina was learning at home, perhaps Michael and Protective Services could be kept at bay. On top of everything else, though, Anne now felt responsible for helping with Julio's legal problems. *Surely I'm not the only one responsible for helping this family stay afloat,* she thought. *But who else will do it if I don't?*

Discussion Questions

1. Do you approve of the way Anne Lowrey has worked with the Martinez family so far? What specifically has she said or done that you admire? What, if anything, would you have done differently before or during the home visit described in the story if you had been in Anne's position?

2. What are the major challenges and issues that Anne faces in providing services to the Martinez family? Make a list.

3. For each of the issues or challenges you identified in your answer to Question #2, what, if anything, could Anne have done to prevent the problem from occurring in the first place?

4. What are the strengths of the Martinez family? Make a list. Would Julio and Elena identify these same strengths?

5. To what extent could the Martinez family's cultural/ethnic heritage contribute to the difficulties described in the story? Provide specific examples to support your position.

6. Select three of the issues or challenges you identified in your answer to Question #2. For each issue, make a list of strategies that Anne could employ to help the Martinezes. Then identify which strategy you would select and explain why.

7. Anne apparently feels overwhelmed by the many needs of the Martinez family, and she's concerned about her ability to meet them all. Is Anne taking on more responsibility for this family than she should? If so, what can she do to relieve herself from some of the responsibilities she now feels are hers to handle?

8. Is Anne justified in her attempts to keep the Martinez children from being removed from their home and Julio from being jailed or deported? Is it in the children's best interest to safeguard Elena and Julio from further conflict with Child Protective Services?

9. Which potentially useful services or resources would be available to the Martinez family in your community? Would the services be available to illegal immigrants or children of illegal immigrants who were born in the United States?

10. In your state, which legal issues would be involved in serving families like the Martinez family? Would Anne be operating outside the law by not reporting the illegal status of Julio, Elena, and members of their extended family?

11. What is likely to happen to this family if Julio is jailed or deported as a result of his upcoming trial? Should Anne help the family to avoid such possibilities? And, should Julio be jailed or deported, how might the focus and scope of Anne's work with the family change?

c h a p t e r 20

Heaven's Glory

P.J. McWilliam

After a full morning of home visits and an afternoon meeting of the interagency council, Sharon Keyes returned to the office. She was glad to have gotten back in enough time to catch up on a little paperwork before she went home. Tomorrow morning would be much more pleasant if she could get some reports, forms, and filing out of the way this afternoon. Besides, it would be a relief to sit by herself and not have to talk to anyone. She had done enough talking for one day. She stopped by the front desk to return the keys to the car she had signed out and to pick up her mail. Then she walked down the hall toward her office, stopping by the soda machine to buy a Coke.

Rounding the corner at the end of the hallway, Sharon saw Wayne, the team's occupational therapist, through his open door and waved politely. Fortunately, he was on the phone, so there was no pressure to stop and chat. Sharon entered her own office across the hall from Wayne's and closed the door to prevent unwanted interruptions. Settling down in her chair, Sharon popped the top of her Coke, took a sip, and began sorting through her mail. There didn't seem to be much she would need to respond to—a memo about new referrals, another memo announcing a blood drive next week, and a third one from the state office notifying employees about rate changes in the group insurance policy. There was also a catalog from an adaptive equipment company and a letter from the secretary requiring Sharon's signature.

Just as Sharon had finished sorting the mail and started to update some progress notes, the secretary let her know that Dr. Ann Harrington was on the telephone and wanted to speak with her. Ann Harrington was a private pediatrician who provided medical care for several children on Sharon's caseload. Sharon would have liked to have put off talking with Ann Harrington this afternoon but decided that she should in case there was some sort of emergency involving one of the children. She reluctantly asked the secretary to transfer the call.

"Hello, Ann. How are you?"

"Hi, Sharon. I'm just fine, thanks. I've got a family I'd like you to see. They have a male infant, about 9 months old, who I've been seeing since birth. Anencephalic. This little guy's head lights up like a jack o' lantern—brainstem and just a shell of a cortex. You know what I mean? Anyway, I don't know if much more can be done for him, but the parents have had it pretty rough. I thought maybe you could get involved—talk with the family, see the baby, and work with them for a while."

"I'd be happy to," said Sharon, "but we really should—"

"Good," interrupted the doctor. "They're coming in tomorrow afternoon, I think around 3 o'clock. Could you stop by then?"

"Tomorrow afternoon is open for me," said Sharon, "but I'd like to know—"

"I know, you need more information. I'll make sure you get all that tomorrow. Maybe you could come in 5 or 10 minutes before the family gets here, and we can talk a little. Let me put my nurse on now to confirm that appointment time. I'm sorry to sound so rushed, but I've got a patient waiting." With that, Ann transferred Sharon to the nurse, who confirmed that the family had an appointment at 3:00 P.M.

Sharon replaced the receiver and stared at it for a few moments, feeling her back tense with anger. Once again, she felt pushed around by Ann Harrington, and it made her furious. That woman never went through the proper channels in referring families to the program! Sharon had explained the referral procedures to Ann numerous times and had mailed several brochures to her office with the correct phone numbers clearly circled, but she continued to call Sharon directly whenever she wanted to refer a child for services. Maybe Ann did so because she knew Sharon from their shared work with other children, but most likely she did it because she assumed Sharon would handle the details that she couldn't be bothered to deal with herself. This time Sharon wasn't even sure if the family knew she was coming to meet them. *It would be just like her,* thought Sharon, *to presume to act in the best interest of the family without involving this child's parents in decisions about their own lives.* As usual, Ann seemed to be calling all the shots, and Sharon felt she had little choice but to follow along. She thought about going across the hall to complain to Wayne but decided to stick to her original plan and get her paperwork done. She wouldn't let Ann affect her entire afternoon.

Doctor's Orders

The next day, Sharon arrived at Ann's office at 2:45 P.M. and was immediately escorted to a small office where Ann was writing notes in a file. The pediatrician looked over the top of her reading glasses, silently motioned with her free hand for Sharon to have a seat, and resumed her writing. Ann was in her late 40s or early 50s, but she struck Sharon as quite grandmotherly—a small, somewhat stocky woman with a soft, round face and rosy cheeks. Her graying hair was pulled tightly into a knot at the back of her head, and the reading glasses perched on the end of her nose looked as if they could fall at any moment.

"Hi, Sharon," Ann said, putting the cap on her pen and closing the file. "I'm glad you could make it."

"It's good to see you again," replied Sharon.

"Let's see now . . . ," Ann said as she fumbled through the papers and files on her desk. She found the folder she was searching for and pushed it across the desk to Sharon. "Here are the latest CT scan and MRI results on our little fellow. They're not very different from the ones done in the NICU, so we don't seem to be dealing with any continuing deterioration. I suppose we should consider that a blessing." Ann slipped her reading glasses into her coat pocket as she stood up. "Why don't you look through the folder a little before the family arrives. I need to finish up with a baby in the other room." She brushed by Sharon on her way out the door and padded down the hall.

Sharon opened the folder and looked at the CT scan. A series of frames, each containing a white, slightly elongated disc, filled several pages. Each frame represented a different slice of the brain, and the black spaces within the ever-present discs indicated where fluid had replaced brain matter. Each disc was slightly different, but most were riddled with large black spots. Sharon wondered what could have caused such massive destruction to a baby's brain within the protective walls of a mother's womb. She also became increasingly anxious about what she would say to the baby's parents. What could she possibly offer this family that would be of any help?

About 10 minutes later, a nurse came to the door to tell Sharon that Ann was talking with the parents and would like to introduce them to her now. Sharon followed the nurse to another office around the corner. Ann introduced Sharon and explained that she was from the Lakewood Early Intervention Program. Sharon spotted an empty chair against the wall and pulled it up to Ann's desk so she could face the parents.

The baby's mother, Emily Turner, was a tall, somewhat heavy woman with cropped brown hair. Her pleasant smile, however, belied her plainness and made her seem friendly and approachable. In contrast, Steve Turner, the baby's father, looked stiff and sullen. Although not a tall man, he had a muscular build, and his sharp features and weathered skin made him seem hard and distant. He only half stood and awkwardly shook hands with Sharon when they were introduced.

Following formal exchanges among the adults, Emily introduced her son Robert, who lied quietly in an infant carrier between the two parents. Sharon realized that this was the first time she had heard the baby's name mentioned. Robert seemed to be about average size for a 9-month-old. He sat perfectly still in a reclined position in the baby seat, which wouldn't have looked unusual if he'd been sleeping; but his hazel eyes were wide open, staring blankly at the wall. His hair was sparse, and the translucent skin of his head and face revealed delicate ribbons of blue veins just below the surface. Sharon approached the baby, addressed him by name, and stroked his cheek and brow. He didn't even blink in response to her touch. As Sharon rose to return to her chair, she brushed her hand across the downy hair on his head and said it was nice to meet such a handsome young man. All the while, she could only think about the gaping blackness within his skull.

Sharon told the family about the services offered by the Lakewood Early Intervention Program and gave them a brochure and an application form. She also told them that, since they lived in Garrett County, she would probably be the staff member who would provide home visits. Emily asked a few questions about payment for services and the frequency of home visits, then turned to Steve. "I suppose that would be all right, wouldn't it?" she asked him.

"You don't have to make a decision right now," explained Sharon. "Why don't you go home and talk about it? I'll call you sometime next week to see what you've decided."

"We don't need to," said Steve matter-of-factly. "If Emily thinks it'll help, you can come on out to the house."

Sharon again asked Emily if she was sure that she wanted services, and Emily said that she did. "Well, then, it'll be a pleasure to work with you and Robert," concluded Sharon. "How about if I give you a call sometime tomorrow so we can set up a time that's convenient to you for me to come out and visit?" Emily nodded. "And remember," added Sharon, "if for some reason after you go home you change your mind, that'll be fine. I don't want you to feel as though you have to do this."

"Well," said Ann, "I suppose that's settled." She pulled out her reading glasses, perched them on the tip of her nose, and flipped through Robert's folder to the skull series that Sharon had looked at when she first arrived. "I received the brain scans that were done last week. They don't look all that different from the first ones." She looked up at the Turners. "I suppose that's good. There's no further damage showing up. But you understand that it still shows a massive loss of brain tissue? That's not going to change . . . , and I'm afraid it doesn't paint a very bright future for this little one."

Emily's eyes glazed over with tears. Steve was expressionless as he stared at the diplomas and certificates on the wall behind Ann's right shoulder.

Sharon desperately wanted to say something that would lift the gloom that hung so heavily over everyone's heads—to provide some measure of hope. But what was there to say? What hope was there to find in this situation?

"Well," continued Ann, pulling a sheet of paper with handwritten notes on it from the back of the folder. "I did get some of the information you wanted about residential placement."

Residential placement? Sharon was stunned. *What was Ann doing talking about residential placement for a 9-month-old? Surely this couldn't be happening—not in this day and age.*

"I had my nurse make some calls," continued the pediatrician, "but nothing was available, and I'm afraid your chances don't look too promising right now. It's not going to be easy to find a placement for a child as young as your son. We'll keep looking, though."

The parents nodded slightly but were otherwise silent. A single tear slid down Emily's cheek, and she quickly wiped it away with the back of her hand.

Is residential placement something the parents want, wondered Sharon, *or was it Ann's idea? And if the parents had been talking about institutionalization all along, why had Ann waited 9 months to get Lakewood involved? Just who did she think she was? Who gave her the right to determine when and if parents were informed about early intervention services?* Then another thought came to mind: *Why had Ann felt the need to involve early intervention at this late point?* Suddenly, Sharon felt used.

"Well, I'm glad you got to meet Sharon," Ann said, summing up the meeting and closing Robert's folder. She took off her glasses, stood up, and leaned across the desk to shake Steve's hand. "Sharon's the best interventionist we've got around here. I'm sure you'll benefit a lot from working with her."

"Thanks," replied Steve. "And could we get that prescription for Valium before we leave? It really helps with his crying at night. Without it, none of us gets any sleep."

"Sure," said Ann, sitting back down and pulling out a prescription pad. "There's no sense in adding the stress of lost sleep to your lives at this point. That problem should ease up over the next few months or so."

Valium? The idea of giving Valium to a 9-month-old didn't seem right to Sharon. Then again, maybe Ann had a point. As long as it didn't actually hurt the baby, maybe it was okay if it made daily living less stressful for the other members of the family. Still, it seemed a bit excessive.

A Life in the Country

Sharon called Emily the next morning, but she didn't manage to make her first home visit until a week and a half after meeting the family at Ann's office. The Turners lived a lot farther south in Garrett County than she had originally thought, only about 10 miles north of the state border. The drive through the rural countryside was picturesque, with acre upon acre of apple orchards lining the sides of the road. The sweet scent of newly opened blossoms drifted through the open windows of the car as Sharon drove along. She followed Emily's instructions, made the turn off the main road at an abandoned gas station, and soon found the dirt-and-gravel drive that led to the Turners' house.

The house was small and old, but the shady front porch and old-fashioned bench swing gave it a comforting, farmhouse appeal. Two tow-headed youngsters, a boy and a girl, appeared on the other side of the wooden screen door. Emily walked up behind the children and opened the door for Sharon. The inside of the house was as simple as the outside, with make-do furniture throughout and coiled braid rugs on the well-worn hardwood floors. Sharon talked with the youngsters while Emily went to get Robert out of his crib. They readily engaged in conversation, and Sharon quickly found out that Joey, the older of the two children, was 4 years old, and Sarah was 3 years old.

When Emily returned with the baby, she handed him to Sharon, then shooed the other two children out the back door to play in the yard. Robert lay limply in Sharon's arms, his hazel eyes wide open, not appearing to focus on anything in particular.

"Would you like a glass of iced tea?" asked Emily, returning to the living room.

"Thank you," said Sharon. "That would be nice."

Emily walked through the small dining room into the kitchen. Sharon followed her with Robert still in her arms and stopped in the doorway between the two rooms. "How have things been going?" she asked Emily.

"Oh, about the same, I suppose," said Emily, filling two glasses with ice cubes.

"It must be difficult, trying to take care of Robert and your other two little ones."

"Well, it's no picnic sometimes, but we're getting by."

"Do you have anyone to help out?" asked Sharon.

"Well, my mother and father live just up the road a ways. Sometimes Joey and Sarah go over to their place and stay with them for awhile."

"It's nice that they live so close, then."

"Yeah, it is. They're real good with the kids. But Daddy's been feeling right bad lately. His back's been hurting from an accident he had on the tractor about a year and a half ago." Having finished filling the glasses with iced tea, Emily carried them into the dining room and set them on the table. Sharon moved around to the other side of the table to make room for her. "I try not to leave the kids over there too long," continued Emily. "I think their constant noise might irritate him. He says it don't, but I'm not so sure he'd tell me if it did."

"How about Steve?" asked Sharon. "Does he help out much?"

"He helps some—playing with the older ones in the evenings and such. But, he works pretty hard, and he's tired when he gets home. And with me being home all the time, most of the taking care of the kids is my job."

"Does he have family nearby?"

"His parents live in that yellow house you passed coming up the drive. This is their land."

"Oh, I didn't realize."

"His family's lived here forever—apple orchards. 'Course, Steve's an only child, so most of the heavy work and harvesting has fallen to him as his daddy's gotten older. But it don't make the money that it once did—not with the bigger companies buying up the orchards. And the kids don't stay around to take over like they used to. They just sell out and leave."

"That's a shame," said Sharon. There was a pause in the conversation, and she looked down at Robert, who was still lying in her arms.

She noticed that he had turned his head toward the sun shining in through the lace curtains on the dining room windows. Was it an accident? She turned her body slightly, and, sure enough, the baby turned his head a little farther to face the bright sun.

"Wow, Emily! Do you see what Robert is doing? He seems to be turning his head toward the sun. Watch." This time she turned her body the other way around and, slowly but surely, Robert moved his head until he was facing the sun. "Did you ever notice him doing that before?"

"No. Not really," said Emily. "Dr. Harrington told us that he was probably what they call cortically blind. You know, where his eyes might be fine but he doesn't have the part of his brain that lets him know that he's seeing things."

"Well, that may be true, but I think he's at least orienting to the bright sun. Maybe he has a little more going for him than everyone thought he did."

"Maybe," said Emily.

Sharon was surprised that Emily wasn't more excited about the possibility that Robert could do something that no one thought he could. Maybe she just didn't want to get her hopes up for fear she might end up being disappointed. That was understandable.

They talked a little more about what Robert might be able to learn to do, and Sharon told her how they could set up some contingencies with various lights and sounds to see if he could demonstrate some simple learning. Again, Emily didn't seem all that excited, but she agreed that it might be worth a try.

Remembering the issue of nighttime crying that had been raised at Ann's office, Sharon asked whether it was still a problem. Emily said Robert still cried but that the medicine helped. Even so, Robert's crying irritated Steve because he had to get up early for work. Emily could occasionally catch a little extra sleep before the other children woke up or while they took their afternoon nap. Then Emily said something puzzling. "Steve doesn't handle the idea of having a child with disabilities very well—you know, being mentally retarded," she said. "It's just how his family is . . . how he was raised." But before Sharon could ask what she meant, Joey and Sarah came barreling back into the house.

Before Sharon left, she told Emily about some of the respite care services available in the county and asked if she was interested in using any of them. Emily said she would be very interested in out-of-home respite care for anywhere from a few days to a week. She thought a little break would be good for her and the rest of the family. Sharon said that she would check it out for her and see what she could come up with.

Renewed Hope

Sharon arranged a week of respite care for Robert at a state-run facility in a neighboring county. The Turners were pleased with the arrangement, and Emily thanked Sharon for working it out for them. This week of respite care occurred just a week and a half after Sharon's initial home visit. The following 2 weeks, Sharon was on vacation with her own family. All together, nearly a month had passed between Sharon's first home visit with the Turners and her second. After that, however, Sharon managed to visit the Turners nearly every week.

During home visits, Sharon and Emily worked together on positioning and feeding Robert. They had even begun to introduce some solid foods like baby cereal and strained fruits into his diet. They also worked to find things that Robert would respond to and to set up some simple contingencies. So far, the only thing he consistently responded to was bright light. Emily, however, felt that he might also be responsive to touch, in that he seemed comforted when she gently stroked the side of his head. During the last two home visits, they had tried setting up a contingency whereby they turned on a bright light when he turned his head to one side. Sharon was particularly proud of herself for thinking about including the Turners' other children in this activity. Joey and Sarah loved to be included in "teaching" their baby brother and fussed over who got to be in charge of turning on the light for him. They weren't very good about responding quickly to Robert's head turns, but Sharon felt that their involvement in teaching Robert might be more important than Robert's actual learning of the skill. So far, it was unclear whether Robert was actually making the connection between his actions and the consequences, but sometimes it seemed as though he was catching on.

In between home visits with the Turners, Sharon had been investigating the possibilities of learning for children who have anencephaly. In her search, she came across an old article about a child whose anencephaly sounded very much like Robert's, and, much to Sharon's amazement, the article told about numerous things that the child had learned to do with only a shell of a cortex. Maybe there was some hope for Robert after all.

Never once during a home visit had Emily mentioned residential placement for Robert. Sharon took this to mean that she had been correct in her initial assumption that institutionalization was Ann Harrington's idea. If by any chance it had been Emily and Steve's idea, perhaps early intervention services and the availability of occasional respite care had helped relieve some of the stresses they had been experiencing. At least, this is what Sharon had been thinking until Emily made her announcement through a Monday morning phone call.

A Birthday Surprise

"Hi, Sharon. This is Emily—Emily Turner."

"Hi, Emily. What's up?"

"I know we had arranged that you would come out to the house on Wednesday, but we've had some news."

"What's that?" asked Sharon cheerfully.

"Well, you know Robert's first birthday is this coming Friday, and—"

"That's right, it is. I nearly forgot. Big birthday plans?"

"I suppose you could say that," said Emily. "We're taking Robert out to Heaven's Glory on Friday morning."

"Heaven's Glory?"

"It's a residential facility," said Emily.

"Residential facility?" Sharon was shocked, and she couldn't help conveying her horror at the unexpected announcement. She immediately tried to soften her reaction: "I . . . I didn't know that you and Steve were—"

"Dr. Harrington found it for us. It's a small place in Sheffield, about 15 miles east of the city. It's run by a group of nuns."

Sharon didn't know what to say. She was still trying to take in the news. Why hadn't Emily told her that they were still looking into institutional placement? And why in the world hadn't Ann Harrington let her know what was going on? Surely this wasn't their final decision. It just couldn't be!

"They don't take children until they're at least a year old," continued Emily, "but they've been holding a spot for him for the last month or so."

So they've known all along, thought Sharon. *Why didn't they say so?* How foolish she felt, having worked so hard these past weeks with Emily and Robert and the other kids. And for what? To have him institutionalized? Maybe it was Steve. If only she had tried harder to talk to him and include him in working with Robert. . . . But even when Steve was home during her visits, he barely said two words to her. He was always busy working outside. Surely it wasn't Emily who wanted to put Robert in an institution. Was Steve forcing her to do this?

"Is this what you really want, Emily?" Sharon couldn't keep from asking. This was just too final a decision. She needed to know how Emily really felt.

"Yes. It's the best for everyone. We have to think about the other kids. And it's been hard on Steve and me, too."

But what about Robert? Sharon desperately wanted to plead his case. How could they possibly think that this was the best thing for Robert?

"It's going to be hard financially," said Emily. "We have to pay for the first month, and it's expensive. But since we'll be giving up parental rights, the state will take over after that. Medicaid will cover the costs."

Giving up parental rights! This couldn't possibly be happening. It went against everything Sharon believed in. How could Emily even *consider* giving up her parental rights? What kind of mother could do that? Maybe she had been wrong about Emily all along. How could she have been so blind?

"We were wondering," continued Emily, "if you would drive out to Heaven's Glory with us on Friday to take Robert there. I know how much you care about him. Could you go with us? Steve can drive the other kids and my parents in our car, and Robert and I could ride with you."

Did Emily see the trip to Heaven's Glory as just a pleasant little family outing? Shouldn't Ann Harrington be going instead of her? After all, if it wasn't for Ann, this probably wouldn't be happening. *No,* thought Sharon. *This was just asking too much of her. The whole idea behind early intervention is to keep children and families together, not to tear them apart.* Suddenly, Sharon felt as though she had failed . . . failed miserably.

Discussion Questions

1. Given the circumstances under which Sharon was first introduced to the Turner family, how well do you think she handled
   the initial contact? Was there anything in particular that you
   liked about the way she interacted with the Turners in the pediatrician's office? Would you have done anything differently?

2. Sharon is obviously frustrated by the way Ann Harrington operates, from the timing and manner in which she handled the referral to her failure to communicate with Sharon about the family's continued pursuit of institutional placement. Are Sharon's
   feelings about Dr. Harrington justified?

3. Is there anything that Sharon could have done to improve communication and coordination with Dr. Harrington in regard to
   the Turner family? Is there anything that Sharon or anyone else
   can do to alter Dr. Harrington's attitudes or actions in working
   with other "shared" families in the future?

4. While talking with the Turners in Dr. Harrington's office, Sharon
   desperately wants to say something that will "provide some measure of *hope*" for the family. Later, when Robert shows some responsiveness to simple contingencies, she again thinks in terms
   of whether there is any "*hope* for Robert." In general, how important is it for practitioners to provide families with a sense of
   hope about their children's development? Does your answer apply equally to all children—even children like Robert?

5. How do you feel about the way in which Sharon conducted her
   first home visit with Emily Turner? What did you like? What, if
   anything, would you have done differently?

6. During the brief time that Sharon worked with the Turner family, she appeared to have focused primarily on activities to facilitate Robert's contingency awareness, but she also arranged respite
   care for Robert. Do you feel these interventions were appropriate in this situation? Is there anything else that you would have
   done during home visits with the family?

7. Steve Turner does not appear to be very involved in Sharon's
   home visits, nor does he appear to be highly involved in Robert's
   daily care. Should Steve's apparent lack of involvement be of

concern to Sharon? What, if anything, should she do to try to foster his involvement?

8. Upon learning about Robert's placement at Heaven's Glory, Sharon asks herself "What kind of a mother would do such a thing?" She also thinks that Steve may have forced Emily into making this decision. Why might this family have been so persistent in their pursuit of institutional placement? Is it important for Sharon to understand why they have made this decision?

9. Is there anything that Sharon could have done differently that may have prevented or postponed the Turners' decision to institutionalize their son Robert? Should this have been one of Sharon's objectives in working with the family?

10. At the close of the story, Robert's institutionalization causes Sharon to feel as though she has failed. Should the fact that Robert is being institutionalized be considered a failure of early intervention? If so, is Sharon justified in claiming at least partial responsibility for this happening?

11. Is a program's mission *to prevent institutionalization* consistent with the principles of family-centered practice? Why or why not?

12. Should Sharon discuss the issue of institutionalization any further with the Turners or should she just move on? If you think Sharon should discuss the issue further, what would be the purpose of her doing so, and how should she go about it?

13. Supposing the Turners follow through with their plans, should Sharon honor their request that she accompany them on their trip to Heaven's Glory? And what role, if any, would Sharon have in working with Robert and his family after his placement?

14. Is institutional placement for young children available in your state? If so, what options are available, what procedures and eligibility criteria are used in obtaining placements, and what are the costs to families?

15. If a family is adamant about wanting institutional placement for their young child but none is available or their child isn't eligible, what alternative services or resources are available for the family in your community?

Recommended Readings

Adolescent Parenting

Helm, J., Comfort, M., & Bailey, D. (1990). Adolescent and adult mothers of handicapped children: Maternal involvement in play. *Family Relations, 39,* 432–437.

Hubbs-Tait, L., Osofsky, J., & Hann, D. (1994). Predicting behavior problems and social competence in children of adolescent mothers. *Family Relations, 43,* 439–446.

Moroz, K., & Allen-Meares, P. (1991). Addressing adolescent parents and their infants: Individualized family service planning. *Families in Society, 72,* 461–468.

Musick, J. (1994). Grandmothers and grandmothers-to-be: Effects on adolescent mothers and adolescent mothering. *Infants and Young Children, 6*(3), 1–9.

Pope, S., Whiteside, L., Brooks-Gunn, J., Kelleher, K., Rickert, V., Bradley, R., & Casey, P. (1993). Low birth-weight infants born to adolescent mothers: Effects of co-residency with grandmother on child development. *Journal of the American Medical Association, 269,* 1396–1400.

Richardson, R., Barbour, N., & Bubenzer, D. (1991). Bittersweet connections: Informal social networks as sources of support and interference for adolescent mothers. *Family Relations, 40,* 430–434.

Scott-Jones, D. (1991). Adolescent childbearing: Risks and resilience. *Education and Urban Society, 24,* 53–64.

Thompson, M., & Peebles-Wilkins, W. (1992). The impact of formal, informal and societal networks on the psychological well-being of black adolescent mothers. *Social Work, 37,* 322–328.

Child Abuse and Neglect

Barnett, D. (1997). The effects of early intervention on maltreating parents and their children. In M.J. Guralnick (Ed.), *The effectiveness of early intervention* (pp. 147–170). Baltimore: Paul H. Brookes Publishing Co.

Belsky, J. (1993). Etiology of child maltreatment: A developmental-ecological analysis. *Psychological Bulletin, 114,* 413–434.

Buchholz, E., & Korn-Bursztyn, C. (1993). Children of adolescent mothers: Are they at risk for abuse? *Adolescence, 28,* 361–382.

Feldman, M.A. (1998). Preventing child neglect: Child-care training for parents with intellectual disabilities. *Infants and Young Children, 11*(2), 1–11.

Ghuman, J.K. (1993). An integrated model for intervention with infants, preschool children, and their maltreating parents. *Infant Mental Health Journal, 14,* 147–165.

Huntington, G.S., Lima, L., & Zipper, I.N. (1994). Child abuse: A prevention agenda. In R.J. Simeonsson (Ed.), *Risk, resilience, and prevention: Promoting the well-being of all children* (pp. 169–182). Baltimore: Paul H. Brookes Publishing Co.

Child Assessment

Crais, E.R. (1996). Applying family-centered principles to child assessment. In P.J. McWilliam, P.J. Winton, & E.R. Crais, *Practical strategies for family-centered intervention* (pp. 69–96). San Diego: Singular Publishing Group.

Dinnebeil, L.A., & Rule, S. (1994). Congruence between parents' and professionals' judgments about the development of young children with disabilities: A review of the literature. *Topics in Early Childhood Special Education, 14*(1), 1–25.

Evans, W.H., Gable, R.A., & Evans, S.S. (1993). Making something out of everything: The promise of ecological assessment. *Diagnostique, 18,* 175–185.

Guidry, J., van den Pol, R., Keeley, E., & Neilsen, S. (1996). Augmenting traditional assessment and information: The videoshare model. *Topics in Early Childhood Special Education, 16*(1), 51–65.

Haney, M., & Cavallaro, C.C. (1996). Using ecological assessment in daily program planning for children with disabilities in typical preschool settings. *Topics in Early Childhood Special Education, 16*(1), 66–81.

Hundert, J., Morrison, L., Mahoney, W., Mundy, F., & Vernon, M.L. (1997). Parent and teacher assessments of the developmental status of children with severe, mild/moderate, or no disabilities. *Topics in Early Childhood Special Education, 17*(4), 419–434.

Linder, T.W. (1993). *Transdisciplinary play-based assessment: A functional approach to working with young children* (Rev. ed.). Baltimore: Paul H. Brookes Publishing Co.

McWilliam, P.J. (1996). Rethinking child assessment. In P.J. McWilliam, P.J. Winton, & E.R. Crais, *Practical strategies for family-centered intervention* (pp. 55–68). San Diego: Singular Publishing Group.

Myers, C.L., McBride, S.L., & Peterson, C.A. (1996). Transdisciplinary, play-based assessment in early childhood special education: An examination of social validity. *Topics in Early Childhood Special Education, 16*(1), 102–126.

Neisworth, J.T., & Bagnato, S.J. (1992). The case against intelligence testing in early intervention. *Topics in Early Childhood Special Education, 12*(1), 1–20.

Suen, H.K., Logan, C.R., Neisworth, J.T., & Bagnato, S. (1995). Parent–professional congruence: Is it necessary? *Journal of Early Intervention, 19*(3), 243–252.

Consultation

File, N., & Kontos, S. (1992). Indirect service delivery through consultation: Review and implications for early intervention. *Journal of Early Intervention, 16*(3), 221–233.

Hunt, F.M., Mayette, C., Feinberg, E., & Baglin, C.A. (1994). Integration of behavioral consultation in an intervention setting. *Infants and Young Children, 7*(2), 62–66.

McWilliam, P.J. (1996). Collaborative consultation across seven disciplines: Challenges and solutions. In R.A. McWilliam (Ed.), *Rethinking pull-out services in early intervention: A professional resource* (pp. 315–340). Baltimore: Paul H. Brookes Publishing Co.

McWilliam, R.A. (1995). Integration of therapy and consultative special education: A continuum in early intervention. *Infants and Young Children, 7*(4), 29–38.

McWilliam, R.A. (Ed.). (1996). *Rethinking pull-out services in early intervention: A professional resource*. Baltimore: Paul H. Brookes Publishing Co.

Wesley, P.W. (1994). Providing on-site consultation to promote quality in integrated child care programs. *Journal of Early Intervention, 18*(4), 391–402.

Cultural Diversity

Dennis, R.E., & Giangreco, M.F. (1996). Creating conversation: Reflections on cultural sensitivity in family interviewing. *Exceptional Children, 63*(1), 103–116.

Gonzalez-Mena, J. (1997). *Multicultural issues in child care* (2nd ed.). Mountain View, CA: Mayfield Publishing Co.

Harry, B. (1992). Restructuring the participation of African-American parents in special education. *Exceptional Children, 59*, 123–131.

Harry, B. (1997). Leaning forward or bending over backwards: Cultural reciprocity in working with families. *Journal of Early Intervention, 21*(1), 62–72.

Lynch, E.W., & Hanson, M.J. (Eds.). (1998). *Developing cross-cultural competence: A guide for working with children and their families* (2nd ed.). Baltimore: Paul H. Brookes Publishing Co.

Vincent, L.J. (1992). Families and early intervention: Diversity and competence. *Journal of Early Intervention, 16*(2), 166–172.

Family-Centered Practices

Bailey, D., McWilliam, R., Darkes, L., Hebbeler, K., Simeonsson, R., Spiker, D., & Wagner, M. (1998). Family outcomes in early intervention: A framework for program evaluation and efficacy research. *Exceptional Children, 64*(3), 313–328.

Baird, S., & Peterson, J. (1997). Seeking a comfortable fit between family-centered philosophy and infant–parent interaction in early intervention: Time for a paradigm shift? *Topics in Early Childhood Special Education, 17*(2), 139–164.

McWilliam, P.J., Winton, P.J., & Crais, E.R. (1996). *Practical strategies for family-centered intervention.* San Diego: Singular Publishing Group.

Powell, D.S., Batsche, C.J., Ferro, J., Fox, L., & Dunlap, G. (1997). A strength-based approach in support of multi-risk families: Principles and issues. *Topics in Early Childhood Special Education, 17*(1), 1–26.

Raab, M.M., Davis, M.S., & Trepanier, A.M. (1993). Resources versus services: Changing the focus of intervention for infants and young children. *Infants and Young Children, 5*(3), 1–11.

Sokoly, M., & Dokecki, P.R. (1992). Ethical perspectives on family-centered early intervention. *Infants and Young Children, 4*(4), 23–32.

Thompson, L., Lobb, C., Elling, R., Herman, S., Jurkiewicz, T., & Hulleza, C. (1997). Pathways to family empowerment: Effects of family-centered delivery of early intervention services. *Exceptional Children, 64*(1), 99–113.

Turbiville, V.P., Turnbull, A.P., & Turnbull, H.R. (1995). Fathers and family-centered early intervention. *Infants and Young Children, 7*(4), 12–19.

Inclusion

Bricker, D. (1995). The challenge of inclusion. *Journal of Early Intervention, 19*(3), 179–194.

Brown, W.H., Horn, E.M., Heiser, J.G., & Odom, S.L. (1996). Project BLEND: An inclusive model of early intervention services. *Journal of Early Intervention, 20*(4), 364–375.

Bruder, M.B., Staff, I., & McMurrer-Kaminer, E. (1997). Toddlers receiving early intervention in childcare centers: A description of a service delivery system. *Topics in Early Childhood Special Education, 17*(2), 185–208.

Buysse, V., Wesley, P., Keyes, L., & Bailey, D.B. (1996). Assessing the comfort zone of child care teachers in serving young children with disabilities. *Journal of Early Intervention, 20*(3), 189–203.

Eiserman, W.D., Shisler, L., & Healey, S. (1995). A community assessment of preschool providers' attitudes toward inclusion. *Journal of Early Intervention, 19*(2), 149–167.

English, K., Goldstein, H., Shafer, K., & Kaczmarek L.(1997). Promoting interactions among preschoolers with and without disabilities: Effects of a buddy skills-training program. *Exceptional Children, 63*(2), 229–243.

Guralnick, M.J. (1994). Mothers' perceptions of the benefits and drawbacks of early childhood mainstreaming. *Journal of Early Intervention, 18*(2), 168–183.

Guralnick, M.J. (1999). The nature and meaning of social integration for young children with mild developmental delays in inclusive settings. *Journal of Early Intervention, 22*(1), 70–86.

Haney, M., & Cavallaro, C.C. (1996). Using ecological assessment in daily program planning for children with disabilities in typical preschool settings. *Topics in Early Childhood Special Education, 16*(1), 66–81.

Janko, S., Schwartz, I., Sandall, S., Anderson, K., & Cottam, C. (1997). Beyond microsystems: Unanticipated lessons about the meaning of inclusion. *Topics in Early Childhood Special Education, 17*(3), 286–306.

Marchant, C. (1995). Teachers' views of integrated preschools. *Journal of Early Intervention, 19*(1), 61–73.

McCormick, L., Noonan, M.J., & Heck, R. (1998). Variables affecting engagement in inclusive preschool classrooms. *Journal of Early Intervention, 21*(2), 160–176.

McWilliam, R.A., & Bailey, D.B. (1995). Effects of classroom social structure and disability on engagement. *Topics in Early Childhood Special Education, 15*, 123–147.

Peck, C.A. (1995). Some further reflections on the difficulties and dilemmas of inclusion. *Journal of Early Intervention, 19*(3), 197–199.

Peck, C.A., Odom, S.L., & Bricker, D.D. (Eds.). (1993). *Integrating young children with disabilities into community programs: Ecological perspectives on research and implementation.* Baltimore: Paul H. Brookes Publishing Co.

Strain, P.S. (1995). The challenge of inclusion: Points well-taken and related challenges. *Journal of Early Intervention, 19*(3), 195–196.

Turnbull, A.P., & Turbiville, V.P. (1995). Why must inclusion be such a challenge? *Journal of Early Intervention, 19*(3), 200–202.

Intervention Planning

Beckman, P., & Bristol, M. (1991). Issues in developing the IFSP: A framework for establishing family outcomes. *Topics in Early Childhood Special Education, 11*(3), 19–31.

Bernheimer, L., Gallimore, R., & Weisner, T. (1990). Ecocultural theory as a context for the Individualized Family Service Plan. *Journal of Early Intervention, 14*(3), 219–233.

Bricker, D. (1998). *An activity-based approach to early intervention* (2nd ed.). Baltimore: Paul H. Brookes Publishing Co.

Haney, M., & Cavallaro, C.C. (1996). Using ecological assessment in daily program planning for children with disabilities in typical preschool settings. *Topics in Early Childhood Special Education, 16*(1), 66–81.

Linder, T.W. (1993). *Transdisciplinary play-based intervention: Guidelines for developing a meaningful curriculum for young children.* Baltimore: Paul H. Brookes Publishing Co.

McGonigel, M., Kaufmann, R., & Johnson, B. (1991). *Guidelines and recommended practices for the individualized family service plan.* Bethesda, MD: Association for the Care of Children's Health.

McWilliam, P.J. (1996). Family-centered intervention planning. In P.J. McWilliam, P.J. Winton, & E.R. Crais, *Practical strategies for family-centered intervention* (pp. 97–123). San Diego: Singular Publishing Group.

McWilliam, R.A. (1992). *Family-centered intervention planning: A routines-based approach.* Tucson, AZ: Communication Skill Builders/Psychological Corporation.

Schuck, L.A., & Bucy, J. (1997). Family rituals: Implications for early intervention. *Topics in Early Childhood Special Education, 17*(4), 477–493.

Slentz, K., & Bricker, D. (1992). Family-guided assessment for IFSP development: Jumping off the family assessment bandwagon. *Journal of Early Intervention, 16*(1), 11–19.

Winton, P.J. (1996). Understanding family concerns, priorities, and resources. In P.J. McWilliam, P.J. Winton, & E.R. Crais, *Practical strategies for family-centered intervention* (pp. 31–54). San Diego: Singular Publishing Group.

Parent–Professional Relationships

Dinnebeil, L.A., Hale, L.M., & Rule, S. (1996). A qualitative analysis of parents' and service coordinators' descriptions of variables that influence collaborative relationships. *Topics in Early Childhood Special Education, 16*(3), 322–347.

Dinnebeil, L.A., & Rule, S. (1994). Variables that influence collaboration between parents and service coordinators. *Journal of Early Intervention, 18*(4), 349–361.

Kalmanson, B., & Seligman, S. (1992). Family–provider relationships: The basis of all interventions. *Infants and Young Children, 4*(4), 46–52.

McWilliam, P.J. (1996). Day-to-day service provision. In P.J. McWilliam, P.J. Winton, & E.R. Crais, *Practical strategies for family-centered intervention* (pp. 125–154). San Diego: Singular Publishing Group.

McWilliam, R.A., Lang, L., Vandivere, P., Angell. R., Collins, L., & Underdown, G. (1995). Satisfaction and struggles: Family perceptions of early intervention services. *Journal of Early Intervention, 19*(1), 43–60.

Minke, K.M., & Scott, M.M. (1995). Parent–professional relationships in early intervention: A qualitative investigation. *Topics in Early Childhood Special Education, 15*(3), 335–352.

Pediatric HIV and AIDS

Barth, R.P., Pietrzak, J., & Ramler, M. (Eds.). (1993). *Families living with drugs and HIV: Intervention and treatment strategies.* New York: Guilford Press.

Beverly, C.L. (1995). Providing a safe environment for children infected with the human immunodeficiency virus. *Topics in Early Childhood Special Education, 15*(1), 100–110.

Bruder, M.B. (1995). The challenge of pediatric AIDS: A framework for early childhood special education. *Topics in Early Childhood Special Education, 15*(1), 83–99.

Crocker, A.C., Cohen, H.J., & Kastner, T.A. (Eds.). (1992). *HIV infection and developmental disabilities: A resource for service providers.* Baltimore: Paul H. Brookes Publishing Co.

Kelker, K., Hecimovic, A., & LeRoy, C.H. (1994). Designing a classroom and school environment for students with AIDS: A checklist for teachers. *Teaching Exceptional Children, 26*(4), 52–53.

LeRoy, C.H., Powell, T.H., & Kelker, P.H. (1994). Meeting our responsibilities in special education. *Teaching Exceptional Children, 26*(4), 37–44.

Lesar, S., Gerber, M.M., & Semmel, M.I. (1995). HIV infection in children: Family stress, social support, and adaptation. *Exceptional Children, 62*(3), 224–236.

Lesar, S., & Maldonado, Y.A. (1994). Infants and young children with HIV infection: Service delivery considerations for family support. *Infants and Young Children, 6*(4), 70–81.

Poverty and Environmental Risk

Bendersky, M., & Lewis, M. (1994). Environmental risk, biological risk, and developmental outcome. *Developmental Psychology, 30,* 484–494.

Bradley, R.H., Whiteside, L., Mundfrom, D.J., Casey, P.H., Kelleher, K.J., & Pope, S.K. (1994). Early indications of resilience and their relation to experiences in the home environments of low birthweight, premature children living in poverty. *Child Development, 65,* 346–360.

Bryant, D., & Maxwell, K. (1997). The effectiveness of early intervention for disadvantaged children. In M.J. Guralnick (Ed.), *The effectiveness of early intervention* (pp. 23–46). Baltimore: Paul H. Brookes Publishing Co.

Fewell, R.R. (1996). Expanding future directions in our second decade of services. *Journal of Early Intervention, 20*(4), 356–363.

Groves, B.M. (1997). Growing up in a violent world: The impact of family and community violence on young children and their families. *Topics in Early Childhood Special Education, 17*(1), 74–102.

Hanson, M.J., & Carta, J.J. (1995). Addressing the challenges of families with multiple risks. *Exceptional Children, 62*(3), 201–212.

Hart, B., & Risley, T.R. (1995). *Meaningful differences in the everyday experience of young American children.* Baltimore: Paul H. Brookes Publishing Co.

Hashima, P.Y., & Amato, P.R. (1994). Poverty, social support, and parental behavior. *Child Development, 65,* 394–403.

Ohlson, C. (1998). Welfare reform: Implications for young children with disabilities, their families, and service providers. *Journal of Early Intervention, 21*(3), 191–206.

Parker, S., Greer, S., & Zuckerman, B. (1988). Double jeopardy: The impact of poverty on early child development. *Pediatric Clinics of North America, 35*(6), 1227–1240.

Sontag, J.C., & Schacht, R. (1993). Family diversity and patterns of service utilization in early intervention. *Journal of Early Intervention, 17*(4), 431–444.

Vig, S. (1996). Young children's exposure to community violence. *Journal of Early Intervention, 20*(4), 319–328.

Service Coordination and Collaboration

Antoniadis, A., & Videlock, J.L. (1991). In search of teamwork: A transactional approach to team functioning. *Infant and Toddler Intervention, 1*(2), 157–167.

Briggs, M.H. (1993). Team talk: Communication skills for early intervention teams. *Journal of Childhood Communication Disorders, 15*(1), 33–40.

Bruder, M.B. (1996). Interdisciplinary collaboration in service delivery. In R.A. McWilliam (Ed.), *Rethinking pull-out services in early intervention: A professional resource* (pp. 27–48). Baltimore: Paul H. Brookes Publishing Co.

Garner, H.G., & Orelove, F.P. (Eds.). (1994). *Teamwork in human services: Models and applications across the lifespan.* Newton, MA: Butterworth-Heineman.

Guidry, J., van den Pol, R., Keeley, E., & Neilsen, S. (1996). Augmenting traditional assessment and information: The videoshare model. *Topics in Early Childhood Special Education, 65*(1), 51–65.

Hanson, M.J., & Widerstrom, A.H. (1993). Consultation and collaboration: Essentials of integration efforts for young children. In C.A. Peck, S.L. Odom, & D.D. Bricker (Eds.), *Integrating young children with disabilities into community programs: Ecological perspectives on research and implementation* (pp. 149–168). Baltimore: Paul H. Brookes Publishing Co.

McGonigel, M.J., Woodruff, G., & Roszmann-Millican, M. (1994). The transdisciplinary team: A model for family-centered early intervention. In L.J. Johnson, R.J. Gallagher, M.J. LaMontagne, J.B. Jordan, J.J. Gallagher, P.L. Hutinger, & M.B. Karnes (Eds.), *Meeting early intervention challenges: Issues from birth to three* (2nd ed., pp. 95–131). Baltimore: Paul H. Brookes Publishing Co.

Melaville, A.I., & Blank, M.J. (1991). *What it takes: Structuring interagency partnerships to connect children and families with comprehensive services.* Washington, DC: Education and Human Services Consortium.

Melaville, A.I., Blank, M.J., & Asayesh, G. (1993). *Together we can: A guide for crafting a profamily system of education and human services.* Washington, DC: U.S. Government Printing Office.

Phillips, S.L., & Elledge, R.L. (1989). *The team building source book.* San Diego: Pfieffer & Co.

Romer, E.F., & Umbreit, J. (1998). The effects of family-centered service coordination: A social validity study. *Journal of Early Intervention, 21*(2), 95–110.

Rosin, P., Whitehead, A.D., Tuchman, L.I., Jesien, G.S., Begun, A.L., & Irwin, L. (1996). *Partnerships in family-centered care: A guide to collaborative early intervention.* Baltimore: Paul H. Brookes Publishing Co.

Swan, W.W., & Morgan, J.L. (1993). *Collaborating for comprehensive services for young children and their families: The local interagency coordinating council.* Baltimore: Paul H. Brookes Publishing Co.

Substance Abuse and Prenatal Exposure

Arthur, C.R., & Gerken, K.C. (1998). Prenatal exposure and public policy: Implications for pregnant and parenting women and their families. *Infants and Young Children, 10*(4), 23–35.

Barth, R.P., Pietrzak, J., & Ramler, M. (Eds.). (1993). *Families living with drugs and HIV: Intervention and treatment strategies.* New York: Guilford Press.

Blythe, B.J., Giordano, M.J., & Kelly, S.A. (1991). Family preservation with substance-abusing families: Help that works. *Child, Youth, and Family Services Quarterly, 14*(3), 13–14.

Brooks, C.S., Zuckerman, B., Bamforth, A., Cole, J., & Kaplan-Sanoff, M. (1994). Clinical issues related to substance-involved mothers and their infants. *Infant Mental Health Journal, 15*(2), 202–217.

Carmichael-Olson, H. (1994). The effects of prenatal alcohol exposure on child development. *Infants and Young Children, 6*(3), 10–25.

Carmichael-Olson, H., & Burgess, D.M. (1997). Early intervention for children prenatally exposed to alcohol and other drugs. In M.J. Guralnick (Ed.), *The effectiveness of early intervention* (pp. 109–145). Baltimore: Paul H. Brookes Publishing Co.

Hanson, M.J. (Ed.). (1994). Substance abuse and early intervention [Entire issue]. *Topics in Early Childhood Special Education, 14*(2).

Kaplan-Sanoff, M., & Rice, K.F. (1992). Working with addicted women in recovery and their children: Lessons learned in Boston City Hospital's Women and Infants Clinic. *Zero to Three Bulletin, 13*(1), 17–22.

Poulsen, M.K. (1994). The development of policy recommendations to address individual and family needs of infants and young children affected by family substance abuse. *Topics in Early Childhood Special Education, 14*(2), 275–291.

Thurman, S.K., Brobeil, R.A., Ducette, J.P., & Hurt, W. (1994). Prenatally exposed to cocaine: Does the label really matter? *Journal of Early Intervention, 18*(2), 119–130.

Supervision

Arredondo, D.E., Brody, J.L., Zimmerman, D.P., & Moffett, C.A. (1995). Pushing the envelope in supervision. *Educational Leadership, 53*(3), 74–78.

Fenichel, E.S. (1991). Learning through supervision and mentorship to support the development of infants, toddlers, and their families. *Zero to Three Bulletin, 12*(2), 1–6.

Fenichel, E.S. (Ed.). (1992). *Learning through supervision and mentorship to support the development of infants, toddlers, and their families: A sourcebook.* Arlington, VA: ZERO TO THREE/National Center for Clinical Infant Programs.

Fenichel, E.S., & Eggbeer L. (1990). *Preparing practitioners to work with infants, toddlers, and their families: Issues and recommendations for educators and trainers.* Arlington, VA: ZERO TO THREE/National Center for Clinical Infant Programs.

Sergiovanni, T.J. (1991). *The principalship: A reflective practice perspective* (2nd ed.). Needham, MA: Allyn & Bacon.

Swarzman, J.B. (1993). Communication and coaching. In R.H. Anderson & K.J. Snyder (Eds.), *Clinical supervision: Coaching for higher performance* (pp. 113–134). Lancaster, PA: Technomic Publishing Co.

Transitions

Conn-Powers, M.C., Ross-Allen, J., & Holburn, S. (1990). Transition of young children into the elementary education mainstream. *Topics in Early Childhood Special Education, 9*(4), 91–105.

Hains, A.H., Rosenkoetter, S.E., & Fowler, S.A. (1991). Transition planning with families in early intervention settings. *Infants and Young Children, 3*(4), 38–47.

Hanline, M.F. (1993). Facilitating integrated preschool service delivery transitions for children, families, and professionals. In C.A. Peck, S.L. Odom, & D.D. Bricker (Eds.), *Integrating young children with disabilities into community programs: Ecological perspectives on research and implementation* (pp. 133–146). Baltimore: Paul H. Brookes Publishing Co.

Haymes, L.K., Fowler, S.A., & Cooper, A.Y. (1994). Assessing the transition and adjustment of preschoolers with special needs to an integrated program. *Journal of Early Intervention, 18*(2), 184–198.

Johnson, L.J., Gallagher, R.J., Cook, M., & Wong, P. (1995). Critical skills for kindergarten: Perceptions from kindergarten teachers. *Journal of Early Intervention, 19*(4), 315–349.

Rice, M.L., & O'Brien, M. (1990). Transitions: Times of change and accommodation. *Topics in Early Childhood Special Education, 9*(4), 1–14.

Rule, S., Fiechtl, B.J., & Innocenti, M.S. (1990). Preparation for transition to mainstreamed post-preschool environments: Development of a survival skills curriculum. *Topics in Early Childhood Special Education, 9*(4), 78–90.

Spiegel-McGill, P., Reed, D.J., Konig, C.S., & McGowan, P.A. (1990). Parent education: Easing the transition to preschool. *Topics in Early Childhood Special Education, 9*(4), 66–77.